TALES FROM THE
VICARAGE

A collection of writing inspired
by Watford Football Club

Volume I
Edited by Lionel Birnie

PELOTON PUBLISHING
www.pelotonpublishing.co.uk

First published in Great Britain in 2012
by Peloton Publishing

Typeset by Peloton Publishing
Printed and bound by SS Media

ISBN 978-0-9567814-2-0

Jacket illustration by Simon Scarsbrook

Peloton Publishing Ltd
2 Gaddesden Lane, Redbourn, St Albans, AL3 7NP
Registered company number: 7353619

www.lionelbirnie.com
www.pelotonpublishing.co.uk
info@lionelbirnie.com

TALES FROM THE VICARAGE

CONTENTS

INTRODUCTION

BY THE EDITOR

Welcome to the first edition of *Tales from the Vicarage*, a collection of original writing about Watford Football Club. This book features contributions from some of the best sportswriters in the country. You may have seen their work in newspapers or on television or heard them on the radio.

And they all have one thing in common – a deep affinity with the Hornets.

What makes *Tales from the Vicarage* special? Each writer was given the brief to propose the story they wanted to tell, so we have something for Hornets supporters of all ages. Our writers have covered a range of subjects and each individual's style comes shining to the fore. We have some excellent journalism as well as more personal pieces every fan will identify with.

David James started a goalkeeping career that spanned two decades at Watford. After two seasons he joined Liverpool. He went on to play for England at the World Cup and won the FA Cup with Portsmouth. And, as his column in *The Observer* demonstrates, he is one of the most perceptive and revealing commentators on the modern game. In this book he looks back at how his career began at Vicarage Road.

Simon Burnton of *The Guardian* looks at the football fan's fear of change through the prism of one of the most turbulent eras in the club's history. In the space of a couple of years at the end of the 1950s the club switched from blue to yellow shirts, redesigned their badge and adopted a new nickname. After years of stagnation on the pitch, all these changes heralded the most successful season the club had ever enjoyed. And yet, to this day, change remains something to guard against.

What if Graham Taylor wrote his autobiography? What would it be like? Well, that's what **Olly Wicken** has tried to imagine. In a manner of speaking. Olly's chapter is touched by genius and verges on fantasy. I can't possibly do it justice in a paragraph so you'll have to read Graham Taylor's incredible could-be-true story of the 1982-83 season for yourself.

John Anderson is a journalist, author and broadcaster. You may have read his hilarious book *A Great Face for Radio* or heard him on TalkSPORT. He's also a fan who has spent most of his adult life following Watford from afar. Does absence make the heart grow fonder? Let John tell you.

Adam Leventhal from *Sky Sports News* looks at the nature of loyalty in the modern game. His exclusive interviews with former managers Brendan Rodgers and Malky Mackay might – just might – make you regard them a little differently.

Andrew French was the club's press officer when the team reached the Premiership in 1999. His behind-the-scenes account of Watford's struggle to keep their heads above water is as eye-opening as it is heart-warming.

Tim Turner has written an evocative story of what it means to feel part of the Watford family, emphasising the importance of the football club in all our lives. Perhaps you have watched matches with the same group of friends for years? For Tim, the author of *First Time I Met the Blues*, watching Watford started as a solitary pursuit until he realised that at Vicarage Road you're never really alone.

For the best part of half a decade, **Oliver Phillips** chronicled the club's progress in the pages of the *Watford Observer*. For generations of fans, Oli's coverage each Friday was their link to the club. In an original piece written specially for the book, he charts six decades of the club's history and his own journey from schoolboy on the terraces to doyen of the press box.

Kevin Affleck was the journalist covering the Hornets for the *Watford Observer* during another, more recent, rollercoaster, era in the club's history. Most fans remember the joy of promotion which gave them a season in the Premiership, and rightly so. But, as Kevin's account reveals, there was much more to the story of boom and bust than the events on the pitch.

With the Pozzo family at the helm and Gianfranco Zola in charge of the team, Watford's fans embraced the latest Italian revolution with perhaps a little less fervour than they did last time. Gianluca Vialli oversaw the first Italian Job in 2001 and it didn't turn out too well. **Lionel Birnie** interviewed Filippo Galli, one of the few bright spots of Vialli's season, about how a 38-year-old European Cup winner came to Watford.

If you watched Watford's match against QPR on the BBC a couple of years ago, you probably marvelled at the half-time video montage set to Kate Bush's spine-tingling *Cloudbusting*. That was the work of **Stuart Hutchison**, a producer for BBC Sport. Stuart has travelled the world covering football but he's also spent hours trying to locate every bit of Hornets-related footage in the BBC archive. This is tale of how a profession became an obsession.

Thank you for reading this debut volume of *Tales from the Vicarage*. We hope you enjoy it and over the coming seasons, we aspire to build the series into a collection to cherish.

Along the way, we also aim to discover new writers and give them a platform to write about Watford.

So, if you want to contribute to a future edition, turn to the back of the book to find out how to get involved.

In the meantime, come on you Golden Boys.

The editor, September 2012

1

When **David James** started his football career, he did not dream of playing in the World Cup for England or lifting the FA Cup at Wembley.

He did both but he didn't plan it like that. Instead, he took his career one step at a time.

And some of the lessons he learned at Watford stood him in good stead when times were tough later on.

Here he looks back at how being part of Watford's youth team gave him a sense of belonging.

THE WATFORD FAMILY

BY DAVID JAMES

Watford has a reputation as The Family Club and for me, that description could not be more appropriate. When I was growing up, the club was like an extension of my family. Vicarage Road gave a teenage boy who didn't really have a place in life a home from home.

I didn't grow up dreaming of becoming a professional footballer. I didn't play the game because I wanted to one day pull on an England shirt or play at Wembley. I found myself gradually moving down a path that led to a career but I rarely looked further ahead than the step immediately in front of me.

I was born in 1970 and spent my childhood in Welwyn Garden City. We were a one-parent family, just me and mum.

For a while, I concentrated on athletics rather than football. High jump and javelin were my thing, because I was tall and I liked chucking the javelin. I went to a competition with the school when I was about 15 and an England athletics coach told my teacher that if I dedicated myself to the high jump for three years I might be good enough to represent England. He must have seen some raw talent but whatever it was must have been very raw. There wasn't anything refined about me. I looked as if I'd been dragged in off the street. I didn't have any spikes, instead I was wearing a pair of trainers with the front ripped off so my big toe was poking out.

I played football for Panshanger Yellow, a team in Welwyn Garden City. I was always the tallest and was pretty athletic but my touch with my feet wasn't the greatest so I went in goal when I was about 14. Jason Solomon was in the same team and we played Sunday football together then county football.

One day we were invited to go to Tottenham Hotspur, so Jason and I trained with Spurs for about a year. I played one youth team game for them, against Watford. We lost 6-3 and Rod Thomas scored five goals past me. If I'd had any dreams of being a professional footballer, I'd have assumed that was the end of them.

Despite the heavy defeat, Jason's dad got a call from the coach, Tom Walley, asking us to go down to Watford.

* * *

Pretty soon, Tom became like a father figure to me. He's an incredible man, Tom. Everyone who worked with him speaks fondly of him, even if he was terrifying at times. When I was about 15, he found out I smoked (I didn't give up until I was 30) and I didn't want to go to training because I thought he was going to kill me. He gave me a bollocking, alright, but he also put an arm round my shoulder when I needed it.

He went out of his way to help his boys. In the early days, he'd drive the club's minibus up to the Comet hotel in Hatfield to pick us up for matches and midweek training sessions. Other times my nan would take Jason and I down to Woodside in Garston. She'd sit in the car, going through her piano notes for Sunday school while we were off training. Mum didn't drive, so she wasn't really involved. I was off doing my own thing and it was keeping me out of trouble, so she was happy.

I trained and played at Watford for a while and was offered an apprenticeship when I was 15 but even then I wasn't thinking: 'I want to be playing football in ten years' time.' The only thing in my mind was: 'What's next?'

When I was in the youth team, I thought, so an apprentice contract is next? Let's go for that. What's after that? Try to turn pro. It was one step at a time. Other boys were looking further ahead, dreaming of playing for the first team. Most of them didn't make it. There were some very talented lads who didn't get that far. Maybe my approach helped me because I was never in a position where I was trying to run before I could walk. Things unfolded in front of me, I wasn't chasing anything.

Rod Thomas, for example, was going to be the next Pele. He had played for England schoolboys and he had tremendous talent, there's no doubt about that. He could dominate our youth team games. He could dribble and shoot and he had the full range of skills. You could see why people were calling him The Next John Barnes. The thing was, he was big for his age at 14 but he didn't get any bigger. Everyone else caught him up and the edge he had on other boys was lost.

He also didn't have the discipline and the way football was structured meant that once you were in the first team, you were a man, my son, you were on your own. As the saying goes, if you're good enough, you're old enough. But Rod was still just a 17-year-old kid. He was in the limelight, playing at Highbury and White Hart Lane and it takes a very strong-willed person to get through that on your own.

While Rod was playing for the reserves and on the fringe of the first team, I was still in the youth team, doing my apprenticeship. I worked in the club shop, in the kitchens and the admin office. I picked up the kit and cleaned the boots – John Barnes's boots were mine. The routine and the structure suited me. It was what I needed. I did my work then I'd head up to the Hornets Shop to hang out for the afternoon. There I'd chat with Tony Marks, who ran the shop, drink coffee, smoke fags and play darts in the back room. It was a good time and it stood me in good stead later on. I had that time as part of something that was serious without it being a high-pressure environment. The Watford Family made the difference.

* * *

I have never been a football perv. I don't pore over the league tables or study the fixture lists. I would watch a match if it was on television but I wasn't a student of the game – I was a Luton Town fan. You can add your own jokes here.

One of my fondest memories was going to see Luton play Watford in an FA Cup fifth round replay at Kenilworth Road in 1985. Luton won and Steve Sherwood, one of Watford's goalkeepers, spotted me in my Hatters scarf as they pulled away on the team coach afterwards. I remember wondering whether I'd get into trouble for that when I next went in for training, which is quite funny really.

I haven't seen Luton play for about 20 years. A few years back, I went to see them against Bournemouth and just as I took my seat in the stand the game was called off because of a frozen pitch.

I liked watching goalkeepers, Bruce Grobbelaar of Liverpool was a favourite, but it was always the game and the way it was played that interested me more than the statistics and tables.

My own career was developing well but I didn't get carried away or assume I was going to make it. In 1989, Watford won the FA Youth Cup, beating Manchester City in the two-legged final. We lost 1-0 up there but won 2-0 in extra-time at Vicarage Road. Of our team, six went on to have decent careers in the game – me, Jason Drysdale, Jason Solomon, Barry Ashby, Dominic Naylor and Rod Thomas. In the City side were Neil Lennon, Gerry Taggart, Ashley Ward, Michael Hughes and Mike Sheron.

If you assume that Watford and Manchester City were two

of the best youth teams in the country that year, you can see the percentage of players who have a chance of making it as a professional. The number that make it to the top is smaller still.

Up to that point, I'd always had a goal on the horizon that I could fix my sights on. When I graduated from the youth team, I felt lost. I was 19, too old for the youth team, miles away from the first team, third choice behind Tony Coton and Mel Rees. Suddenly, I had nothing to aim for. I'd signed a two-year contract as a professional but I only got to play for the reserves when Tony was injured or when Mel went out on loan.

During my second season in the reserves, I had a torrid time. I was awful. Basically, I had discovered nightclubs. I still wasn't looking at football as a ten or 15-year gig and without the routine of regular matches, I started to drift. I had a bit of money and a car, which gave me a sense of independence for the first time. I spent a lot of time in Cardiff because they had a great club scene and some of my friends from Welwyn Garden City were often down there. I didn't socialise with people from football (I still don't).

Free from the routine of boot-cleaning and office work that made up a young player's apprenticeship, I was now one of the big boys, finished with training by early afternoon and with days off. Suddenly I had a lot of time on my hands. How do you fill it?

I got heavily into music and started DJ-ing. I wouldn't think twice about driving to Cardiff, doing a gig and coming back in the early hours. Being slightly obsessive, as I am, I would sometimes go down there to a particular record shop, buy a load of records and drive straight back again.

But the football was going to pot. I was letting in a lot of goals and I wasn't taking it as seriously as I should have. One night Tom sent me down to Brighton to play for them against Spurs in a testimonial match for the goalie Graham Moseley.

I'm not sure why that happened, I think he was just helping them out and getting me a game. I played the second half and let in just about every shot. The nadir was when I let one in, picked the ball out of the net and half-volleyed it up towards the centre circle, only to hit Steve Foster straight in the back. If it hadn't been so embarrassing it would have been comical.

In a way, I was fortunate that my bad year came when I was playing for the reserves. Having a nightmare season in the reserves doesn't hurt a football club. I conceded more goals than I ever had before or since and if I had been honest with myself, I'd have recognised that my performances were poor. Friends were saying: 'You need to stop going out,' and I thought: 'What are you on about?' and headed to the nightclub.

At the end of the season, Tony Coton left for Manchester City. I thought Mel Rees was going to succeed him but I knew I would be number two and, at the very least, a regular for the reserves, so I made a change in my life. I started to concentrate on football instead of going out.

I had no idea I'd be first-choice goalie. We had a pre-season friendly at Reading. I played and conceded a goal from a corner, which I was not happy about. A couple of days before the first game of the 1990-91 season, against Millwall, the manager, Colin Lee, called me in and told me I was in the team. I was so nervous in the run up to that game but after about five minutes I came for a cross and punched the ball so hard it went into the stand. Then the nerves just seemed to disappear.

We lost 2-1 and the second goal should never have been given. Malcolm Allen, a former Watford player, headed it, I saved it, got up and spread myself as big as I could as Teddy Sheringham came in. Teddy put the ball the wrong side of the post but the referee gave it as a goal.

I thought that would be it – I'd be dropped for the next game – but the manager stuck with me. It wasn't until later that I found out Colin Lee had been trying to bring in another keeper – someone, anyone – before he decided to give me my debut. I think he approached quite a few players but no one fancied it.

Early on we played West Ham away and lost 1-0 to a Julian Dicks penalty. I was worried that if I saved it I'd be beaten up by West Ham fans on the way home. It's strange what goes through your head when you're young.

We didn't win a league game until mid-October and were bottom of the table until Boxing Day. Although we kept losing, I didn't feel under pressure. I didn't know what was normal. The only success I'd had at the club was in the FA Youth Cup. What constituted success for the first team? Were we supposed to go up? I didn't know. There were no goals set for us. We weren't told: 'Lads, we're expecting you to be at the top.' I didn't know the other teams either. All their players were new to me. Were we supposed to beat Barnsley or Oldham? I didn't know, I was just playing one game after another and trying to do my best.

Eventually, Colin Lee was sacked and Steve Perryman came in, bringing Peter Taylor with him. They were great because they gave me some specific targets and things to work on. For example, Steve and Pete asked me to aim in a particular place with my kicking.

But we were still going down. In March, we lost 3-0 at home to Blackburn and got booed off. We were well adrift at the bottom of the table and no one gave us any hope of getting out of trouble. All of a sudden, we had no fear. There was a lift around the place because we had nothing left to lose and we started to pick up some results.

The turning point was a win at Middlesbrough when David Byrne scored in the last minute. From then on, it was absolutely awesome. We'd spent so many weeks not achieving anything and now we had purpose and a target. We were winning games, giving ourselves a chance to survive, and we were buzzing.

Around that time, I got called up for the England under-21 squad. We had a game against Poland at White Hart Lane and I sat on the bench wondering what it was all about. For a start, getting personal recognition while Watford were bottom of the league didn't really make sense and secondly, going along, spending the best part of a week with the squad and not getting on the pitch seemed like a waste of my time.

Watford's season came down to a match against Oxford United at the Manor Ground. We knew a win would guarantee we avoided relegation. You know the story, we won 1-0 and stayed up. It was an amazing thing to be part of.

* * *

I worked with a number of goalkeeping coaches at Watford. In the early days it was Stuart Murdoch and Tommy Darling. Then I worked with Alan Hodgkinson, who was very old school. He observed a strict hierarchy. If it was me, Steve Sherwood and Tony Coton training together, Tony could do no wrong, because he was the first-choice keeper. If it was just me and Shirley, then Shirley was the top dog. If it was just me on my own, he'd tell me I was brilliant. I guess the theory was that the first-team goalie is preparing for the most important match.

Tony was a great keeper but he could get away with murder in training. I'd look at him sometimes and wonder why he wasn't trying but it wasn't until I was older that I realised how frustrating it must've been for him to work in training with a 17-year-old who couldn't kick straight.

I always trained the way I played. If I was between the posts, I wanted to stop goals. I used to hate shooting sessions when it was geared towards the strikers scoring. I didn't think they should have it easy, so I tried to stop everything.

Later on, Peter Bonetti, the former Chelsea goalkeeper, came in as a coach and he said: 'I can't teach you how to keep goal because you are a completely different shape to me and a completely different style, but if I can give you something that will improve you and you can get bits and pieces from other people too, you'll get better.'

I immediately liked that approach. Bob Wilson was another one who tried to improve me as the goalkeeper I was instead of trying to make me into a version of himself.

As a team, we improved a lot in my second season, 1991-92, but it wasn't until after Christmas that we hauled ourselves away from the bottom of the table to finish tenth.

I'd only been in the team two years, I was still only 21, and there was quite a lot of speculation that other teams were looking at me, which felt strange. Aston Vila and Chelsea put in bids for me and I heard Liverpool and Everton were interested too. It was all very surreal. I'd played less than 100 first team games and here I was travelling to meet Ron Atkinson, the Villa manager, to talk about a move.

It might sound ridiculous but I wasn't excited at all. I had such a good rapport with Steve and Pete that I thought: 'What is going on here? Why don't Watford want me? Why don't my family want me?'

One day, I was walking off the training pitch and Steve said: 'We've had a bid of a million pounds and we've accepted it.'

I didn't say anything. I just felt a sense of rejection.

Leaving Watford felt like leaving home. And arriving at Liverpool was bewildering.

You have to remember that this was August 1992. Liverpool had been league champions just two years earlier. The days when they dominated at home and in Europe were still very recent.

I made my Liverpool debut in the first televised match in

the new Premier League. We lost 1-0 to Nottingham Forest at the City Ground. After that, my performances dipped week by week. Five weeks later we lost 4-2 at Aston Villa and drew 4-4 at home with Chesterfield in the League Cup and I was dropped. I hadn't drunk alcohol during my two seasons at Watford but being in a big city, I had discovered nightclubs again.

When I was out of the side, I felt isolated, but being in the team and making mistakes was an even more lonely feeling. I'd gone from a club that was like a family to a place of business.

There wasn't a goalkeeping coach at Liverpool. We were the cream of English football and were expected to know what we were doing. And the expectation from the supporters was something I had never experienced before.

I say this fondly but the expectations at Watford were very different. If I conceded a bad goal, I won't say no one cared, but the impact on the football world was low. When things weren't going right at Liverpool it felt like the whole world cared. The newspapers were on your back. During those first couple of years I got absolutely battered.

At one point I asked someone on the coaching staff for some advice. How do I cope with all this? The answer was not the one I wanted to hear. I was told: 'You'll get through it.'

The lengths that the supporters went to in order to follow the team was incredible but it could weigh you down. We had a cleaner at Liverpool who took out a bank loan so she could buy her son a season ticket. When you're playing and that's on your mind, wow, it can be overwhelming.

A very famous Liverpool manager once said: 'Some people believe football is a matter of life and death. I can assure you it's much, much more important than that.'

It's not. It's a game, but keeping it in perspective when things are going badly can be hard.

I gave an interview to the evening paper in Liverpool in

which I said: 'I walked into Tesco and thought "everyone in here thinks I'm a dodgy goalie".' One day, a woman turned round and said to my wife: 'We still think he's great.'

That was such a nice thing to hear.

* * *

When I was about 15, I played a game for one of Watford's youth teams at Woodside in Garston. I came off the pitch and a man came up to me and told me I'd had a good game.

'Tell me,' he said. 'You've got a very good throw but can you do it with your left hand?'

'Not as well, no,' I replied.

'Well practice throwing left-handed until you can. Secondly, have you got any superstitions?'

'One or two,' I said.

'Break them before every game.'

I didn't know who he was. I just thought it was some old bloke watching a game of football on a Saturday morning but someone told me it was Bertie Mee, the legendary manager who led Arsenal to the double in 1971 and was then a director at Watford.

I could have done with listening to the second piece of advice, in particular. Being an obsessive character, when things started to go wrong at Liverpool and I felt lost and alone, I sought solace in routine and structure. I could easily get drawn into a pattern of repeated behaviour thinking that these patterns would lead to a positive result. They don't, of course.

I got stuck in a rut. I could have told you everything I had to do in the 48 hours leading up to a match. I had a series of things I had to do, meticulously and in order, and if any of them broke down I could tell you that was the reason for letting in a goal. At its worst, I felt paralysed by this routine.

Eventually, a sports psychologist came to my house and we had a chat for a couple of hours and things began to make more sense. Slowly I dismantled the routine I'd constructed and my form improved.

* * *

Watford fans may remember me for my two years in the first team but to me, the time I remember best was being in the youth team with Jason Drysdale, Jason Solomon, Rob Wignall and Rod Thomas. In the first team, I played with 'Mad Dog' Andy Kennedy, who was a fruit loop, Barry Ashby, Nigel Gibbs and David Holdsworth, who were all good lads.

I don't keep in touch with any of them these days. I am anti-social, not the best at keeping in touch, hence my decision to live in Devon and choosing not to work near home. It's a deliberate choice. I'm not the best at staying friends with people, which is fine. I don't mean I fall out with people, I just carry on with life. It goes back to my childhood. The nomadic style of a goalkeeper's career didn't make me but it suited me. But I look back at my time with the Watford Family and feel like I belonged.

David James was voted Watford's player of the season after his debut season in the first team. He moved to Liverpool for £1m in 1992, won the FA Cup with Portsmouth in 2008 and played for England in the World Cup. He also writes a column for *The Observer*. The David James Foundation helps Malawian communities move towards long-term food security. www.djf.org.uk

2

COMIC BOOK SUPER HEROES

BY LIONEL BIRNIE

In the 1980s, two weekly football magazines competed for every young football fan's attention. You read *Match* or you read *Shoot!* Or if you were very lucky, you got both.

For less then 50p you got news about wantaway strikers and midfield maestros, colour posters and question and answer interviews in which players revealed their favourite food (always steak), the car they drove (usually a Ford Capri) and their advice to youngsters (work hard and don't smoke).

In the early 1980s, Watford featured regularly in the pages of both magazines. I still remember a terrifying poster of Steve Terry without his headband and a heart-breaking interview with Mo Johnston on why he 'had to leave the Hornets'.

Some time around 1983, *Match* took a clear lead over *Shoot!* in the battle for my affections when it introduced a brilliant cartoon strip called *Cannon*.

Cannon charted the fortunes of a fictional Fourth Division club (that's League Two to anyone under 20) called Stanton Town. They were managed by Harry Cannon, a moustachioed, sheepskin coat-wearing Tom Selleck look-a-like and although the cartoon was in black and white it was so vivid, I imagined Stanton wore red shirts with white sleeves, just like Arsenal.

Cannon steered Stanton through all sorts of soap opera style dramas. Their best player was injured in a car crash, the manager's son (Nick Cannon) fell out with one of the high-profile new signings and the council threatened to repossess the stadium and turn it into a supermarket. So far, so realistic.

Then, in 1984, with Cannon engaged in a power struggle with a shadowy new chairman called Dave Dawkins – who imagined a chairman could act in anything other than the best interests of his club? – something magical happened.

I can still feel the frisson of excitement when, in late July, *Match* magazine dropped through the letterbox. I flicked through to the latest installment of *Cannon* and saw a familiar face pop up at the end of that week's cartoon.

It was Graham Taylor. There he was, on the phone, arranging a pre-season friendly between Stanton Town and Watford as if it were the most normal thing in the world.

The memory can play tricks and at times over the next 25 years, I doubted whether this clash been fictional minnows and real-life greats had happened, until the power of Google proved that it did. At great expense, I bought half a dozen copies of *Match* on eBay and then wallowed in a fuzzy, nostalgic glow.

Thinking the cartoon would make a neat addition to this book, I set about tracking down Steve McGarry, the artist who devised *Cannon,* and found that he now works in Los Angeles as a successful graphic artist. He did not draw these particular strips but he confirmed he owned the copyright and very kindly gave permission to reproduce them here. After a courtesy call to *Match* magazine, I scanned the artwork.

Looking at *Cannon* now, it seems quaint that a black and white cartoon could capture the imagination so completely but the beauty was in the storytelling. The plot may have seemed out-landish at times and yet there was more truth in it than perhaps I realised.

I was only nine so, back then, it was just thrilling to see Mo Johnston and John Barnes depicted in a cartoon. I hope you agree. But it also dawned on me that perhaps football clubs could be places of conflict and intrigue.

THE STORY SO FAR

Harry Cannon, the Stanton Town manager, has been bolstering his squad before the team begin their debut season in the Third Division. To get them ready for the campaign, he lines up a friendly with a top flight side.

Back in his office, Harry finalises the details of a friendly match the following week with Watford manager Graham Taylor.

FINE, HARRY, WE'LL SEE YOU AT ABBEY ROAD ON SATURDAY. I'LL BE BRINGING A FULL—STRENGTH SIDE.

I WOULDN'T HAVE IT ANY OTHER WAY. THE LADS HAVE GOT TO FIND OUT WHAT IT'S LIKE AT THE TOP—BECAUSE THAT'S WHERE I INTEND TAKING THEM.

NEXT: Can Stanton handle last season's FA Cup finalists?
Turn to page 39 to find out

3

In the space of 18 months at the end of the 1950s, Watford underwent more change than ever before or since.

They swapped their blue shirts for yellow, changed the club's badge and adopted a new nickname, which was not embraced by all.

Simon Burnton tells the story of the 1959-60 season which saw Watford's first ever promotion in the Football League, and studies the typical fan's trepidation when change is afoot.

ALL CHANGE AT VICARAGE ROAD

BY SIMON BURNTON

The names of many of the people who have played a significant role in shaping the club are familiar to us all, and will feature elsewhere in this book and even in this chapter. But inevitably, along the way, many more have played small but significant parts, and of those among the most significant, and almost certainly the most obscure, is a man now in his sixties and living in the tiny village of Gooderstone in Norfolk.

This man earned a place in the club's history despite the fact he made it into the Vicarage Road dressing rooms only once, and that as a nine-year-old child, thrust through the door on a matchday, whose primary reaction was astonishment at the quantity of naked adult flesh to which he was exposed. His name is Iain Walker, and it was his idea to call the team The Hornets. His reward was a cheque for £5, brief access to a roomful of naked footballers and an immediate return to obscurity.

'Every time anyone in my family sees something about Watford they think there will be something about me, but there never is,' Walker says. 'There's been several books about the history of Watford and I've never got so much as a mention. I remember when we got to the FA Cup final in 1984 I wrote to Graham Taylor. I said, "You must have heard of me. I nicknamed the club. You could take me to the match." I never got a response. I just can't believe it has lasted so long, but I suppose once you get a nickname that's it, for ever and a day.'

More than half a century since Walker's role in the club's

rechristening, that is how it seems. The club was involved in more change in 18 months leading up to their adoption of the new nickname than in all the years since, and for many fans this is how they like it. For a lot of us, the club we support is one of few constants in life. Friends come and go, we move from house to house and fall in and out of love, and still it's there, lurking about, ruining our weekends on a regular basis.

But this is a confusing kind of constancy, in that few football clubs fall into any rational definition of the word: they are always there, but what they are doing there and how well they are doing it can change quite a bit. Stonehenge could be used as a shining example of what clubs should be aiming for. It's never less than convincingly constant – always in the same place, doing the same thing in the same way. Not a very exciting thing, it must be said, but at that one thing that it does – sitting in a field, looking stoney – it has few peers, and absolutely never lets anyone down.

Though it often lets people down, and certainly has some peers, Watford's supporters have been blessed over recent years with a surprisingly stable club. Sixteen of the 20 years to 2012 have been spent in the same division, with an average final league position of 12th in what is currently referred to as the Championship. Two seasons have been spent in the division above, and two seasons in the division below. Along the way the club has never been lavishly rich nor unbearably poor, though it has come close once or twice.

Few fans born after the mid 1970s will have any memory of Watford being anything other than they are now – a club that bumbles along in the second tier, occasionally getting worryingly close to the bottom or encouragingly close to the top and very occasionally getting an opportunity to be rubbish in the top flight or pretty good in the third.

That, for most fans under the age of 40, is what Watford is, and what it always has been. And whatever our age, it is what we have become comfortable with. This is important. Humans like comfort. That is why we invented slippers, cuddles and sofas, why Americans spend $11bn each year on massages, and why we normally choose to live in temperate regions, avoiding anywhere that is bone-janglingly cold or flesh-simmeringly hot, unless we're scientists or there's a lot of oil in it for us.

So we don't just fear disruption to whatever is familiar, we fear the very possibility of disruption. We might oppose the building of a nearby power plant, or our neighbour's rear extension. Our votes are biased towards the party in power, even when they've already proved themselves irredeemably hopeless. And we will certainly experience some anxiety when our bumbling, lovably mediocre club gets bought by a family of Italians who not only install another Italian as manager and bring in a numerous posse of unfamiliar players but have a history of taking bumbling mediocre clubs into the Champions League.

But it's not as if this club has never experienced rapid transformational change, and change on a scale that the club's current owners – short of forcing the team to play in blue and renaming them the *Azzurri* – could scarcely come close to matching. And when we write our history, it is those who have wrought the greatest change who are most celebrated. So how did we get to a point where fans resent and resist change so much that when in 2005 an attempt was made to replace something as insignificant as the old, random and frankly rather irritating music the team has run out to for a while, it was abandoned under an avalanche of hate mail?

A leaf through the history books will prove that change, however discomforting, can be inspirational, and never have its profound effects been more evident than at the very end of the 1950s. At the heart of this massive transformation was a group of people whose backgrounds could scarcely have been more different: in addition to the cameo role played by a nine-year-old boy from Orchard Drive, Watford, the most significant contributions came from a businessman from Preston, a former coalminer from Wales, and a part-time engineer from Oxford.

So rewind to the summer of 1958. Watford had just lost their last three games to topple unexpectedly out of the Third Division South and into the newly-formed Fourth Division, dropping at the last minute into a relegation zone that due to the league's structural changes had a bloated intake of 12 teams.

This blow was so hard to take that the club's chairman, T Rigby-Taylor, declared himself 'depressed and disillusioned', and 'tired and disappointed' to boot, and resigned. 'My enthusiasm has been damped by 20 years of failure to achieve success for the club,' he said. Jim Bonser, the Preston-born businessman, replaced him. By the time Bonser was booted out of the boardroom nearly two decades later he cut a decrepit and rather detested figure, but his initial impact could scarcely have been greater nor brought more success.

In little over a year, the club had adopted yellow shirts, redesigned their badge, switched nicknames from Blues to Hornets, built a new stand, appointed a new manager and made the highest-profile signing in their history. They then enjoyed success on a scale never witnessed at a ground known at the time as Vicarage-road: one of the club's greatest FA Cup runs, its first ever promotion, and a triple-headed glut of goal-scoring that has never been and will surely never be bettered.

That first year, though, was a bit of a disaster. The name of Cliff Holton, who chose to exchange First Division football at Arsenal for the Fourth Division and Watford in exchange for more time to spend on his engineering business, remains prominent in Watford's folklore, but upon his arrival in October 1958 he appeared more damp squib than shooting star. So disappointing was he that the manager at the time (if not for very much longer), Neil McBain, called the signing 'a tragedy', particularly given that it came at a time when the Blues 'were showing signs of settling down into a successful combination'.

A 2-1 defeat to Torquay in January 1959 – Watford's fifth home game without a win – left the club stuck in the bottom half of the table. A depressing report in the *West Herts & Watford Observer* concluded: 'It is now beginning to look unhappily clear that the tremendous enthusiasm which greeted the Holton signing two months ago was over-optimistic. Cliff, we thought then, was the man to supply the finishing punch that was all Watford needed to make sure of promotion. But it has not worked out that way.'

When McBain was sacked in February, he admitted that he had tried to leave Holton out of the team altogether, only for the board to overrule him. His replacement, the caretaker manager Ron Burgess, played Holton at centre half. In February the Blues went 2-0 up at home to York and still lost 3-2. 'Never were Watford more baffling!' exclaimed the *Observer*.

The season limped disconsolately to a close, and to make matters worse at the time the club's local rivals were in the First Division and heading for the FA Cup final. 'The team's lack of success, coinciding with the glamorous feats of not-too-far-away Luton, have sapped interest in activities at Vicarage-road to a dangerous degree,' reported the *Observer*, with a handful of games remaining. 'In fact, Watford's 1958-59 season bids fair to develop into one of their most disastrous, for not only is an early escape from the Fourth Division now out of the question, but it is doubtful whether the Blues can even make the top half of the table. On top of that, the reserve team, which should be a reservoir of talent for the league side, is rooted to the foot of the Football Combination. It is a gloomy picture. The big need now, when Watford supporters of long, loyal standing are pinning on Luton's colours on a Saturday, is for a sign that the club mean business and are hell-bent on ending a depressing chapter which has included the departure of a manager and the playing of a costly attacking spearhead in a defensive role.'

The season ended with one final humiliation, as Shrewsbury arrived – late, having been held up by a broken-down bus that blocked the road ahead of them and only got moving when the Shrews donated some of their own petrol – hoping to seal promotion. As night fell and the floodlights remained resolutely dim it was discovered that someone had stolen the fuses from a locked room, forcing the referee – Denis, later Baron Howell, an MP who officiated football matches in his spare time – to abandon the match with 14 minutes to go and the away side 5-2 up. The Shrews won the replay 4-1 and got their promotion; Watford remained rooted in the bottom half and were considered so unattractive a prospect that despite the promise of 'a salary comparable to a First Division club' for the 'right man', most of the 23 applicants for the vacant managerial role were inexperienced local chancers and in the end it went to the caretaker.

It was a time for desperate measures. After a period of sustained under performance 32 years earlier the club had binned their black and white stripes in favour of blue in order 'to leave off semi-mourning'. 'Today Watford are switching colours for a similar psychological reason,' reported the *Observer* that May. 'After a series of disappointing seasons there is a feeling that a change to more cheerful colours may bring a brighter outlook and end what has been very much an "attack of the blues".'

It is not hard to imagine what the reaction would be should a new chairman decide unilaterally to totally change the traditional colour of a team's kit today. Not that there is any need to imagine, Cardiff City's Malaysian investors having imposed a red rebranding on the team in the summer of 2012. A large group of the Welsh club's fans wrote an open letter describing the move as 'an insult' that turned the club into 'a laughing stock'. Half a century earlier, Watford's Supporters' Club offered to foot the bill for the new yellow shirts.

Perhaps they were not shocked, the club had surveyed fans a little under a decade earlier about what alternative colour they might want to see their team wear. Tangerine had been among the favourite answers then, and the chosen shade was just a little bit brighter. As it happened the manager when that survey was undertaken, Len Goulden, had just been invited back to the club as coach, and led the team on an innovative pre-season footballing assault course. But the most telling new arrival that close season came courtesy of the director Doug Broad, the man who had first proposed the signing of Holton. This time Broad reported that he had identified the perfect foil for the misfiring former Arsenal man, in the shape of Mansfield Town's Dennis Uphill.

But a fan would have needed a crystal ball and a healthy amount of optimism to get truly excited about the arrival of Uphill, a 28-year-old who had been far from prolific the previous season, and the take-up of season tickets was miserably slow despite the attempts of all at the club to talk up their chances. 'For some years past the Watford FC playing record has been a pretty dismal one,' wrote Bonser. 'While I would be foolish to pretend that all our troubles are over, I am hopeful that a much better future is in store for us.' Burgess insisted that 'football is a funny game – you are up one year and down the next' and that he was aiming at promotion – 'We are doing all we can to pull it off.' The *Observer*'s season preview concluded: 'It is important that Watford – the Wasps, the Golden Boys or what have you – should at least make a good enough start to pull back the crowds driven away by last season's bitter disappointments. Another season like that last could put an ominous question mark over League football at Vicarage-road.'

And so the season began, a year in which local headlines

were made when the first stretch of the M1 opened, connect-
ing Watford and Rugby, when the town centre played host to its
last cattle market, and when the unfortunate Watford resident
Doris Morgan, 53, choked to death on some custard.

But the great transformation was not instant. The season
started with a dismal 0-0 draw at home to Stockport. 'As they
left Vicarage-road, some of the more critical fans were already
writing Watford off as "the same old Blues in new shirts",'
wrote the *Observer*. Then came a 1-1 draw at Bradford, and a
2-0 defeat at Exeter City, by which time Uphill had already lost
his place in the team. After five games Watford sat 20th in the
table, having enjoyed a single win.

And that is when it happened.

In those first five games Watford had scored twice. In
desperation, Burgess rejigged his forward line once again, shift-
ing Holton from centre forward to inside right (a more creative
role playing off the striker), with Uphill leading the line. In their
next two games they scored nine.

And Watford continued to play well, even when hammered
8-1 at Selhurst Park. 'Incredible! Simply incredible! There is no
other way of describing the fantastic game at Crystal Palace,'
enthused the *Observer*. 'To anyone not in Selhurst Park the score
indicates the most one-sided game in Division Four this season, but the facts are that Palace were handed six of their goals
on a plate and Watford had the lion's share of the play.'

Given that Watford had scored only twice in their first five
games, and Holton just once, it is a measure of how spectacular
his and their turnaround in fortunes was that by mid-October
he had scored 17 goals in 16 games and the club record single
-season goal tally, the 35 managed by Frank McPherson in
1928-29 and Billy Lane in 1934-35 already looked at risk.

From the start of November until the second day of
January Watford played seven matches in the league and won

six, ushering in the new year with a 5-2 routing of Exeter City.

The reserves were no less prolific. John Fairbrother, a first-year professional, was emulating Holton's goalscoring feats with the second string, whose outstanding result came in late November when they came back from a 4-1 half-time deficit against Shrewsbury to win 5-4. At the end of 1959, Holton had 25 goals, Uphill 22 and Fairbrother 21.

By then the FA Cup run had started, in understated fashion, with a replay needed to dispose of non-league Cheltenham Town in the first round. Another non-league side, Wycombe Wanderers, visited in round two, attracting 23,907 people into Vicarage-road to see a 5-1 victory, and the third round draw paired Watford with Birmingham City, their first top-flight opponents since Manchester United's visit ten years earlier.

The game drew so much attention that when the club announced that fans who saw the reserves play Mansfield would be entitled to buy tickets, 6,399 people turned up. To cope with the crowds Watford hired 36 people who normally worked at Arsenal as 'expert packers', to ensure that every possible spot on the terraces was occupied. Watford won 2-1, Uphill and Holton inevitably with the goals, even though an injury to the defender Sammy Chung with 20 minutes played effectively reduced the home side to ten men.

'This was not a case of Fourth Division brawn beating First Division skill,' insisted the *Observer*, 'but a triumph of real football.' The *Birmingham Post* did not disagree. 'If a Rip Van Winkle, suddenly returned to the world of men in time for this third-round tie, had been asked which was the club used to playing in the higher grade of football, he would undoubtedly have picked Watford,' they wrote. 'The contrast was as marked as that.' Inevitably, the following week the Golden Boys lost 2-1 at home to third-bottom Doncaster.

But the cup adventure was not over yet. In round four

Watford faced free-scoring Second Division high-flyers Southampton away, where they drew 2-2 thanks to 'probably the
finest display by a Watford defence in living memory'.

Oli Phillips describes Burgess, a player of some repute who
had been working as a miner when Tottenham spotted him
playing for Cwm Villa and went on to win 32 caps for Wales,
as a limited manager, 'unable to transfer into words what he
knew, nor able to man-motivate'. But that was not the impression Watford gave in the cup run, with his team changing their
shape against Birmingham, where the fleet-footed Bobby Bell
replaced John Price at full-back to stifle Blues' Harry Hooper,
and again at Southampton to counter the threat of their wingers, Terry Paine – who Burgess felt was uncomfortable when
he couldn't come inside – and John Sydenham, who Burgess
decided was uncomfortable when he couldn't go outside.

Cup fever gripped the town when the Saints arrived for the
replay three days later, and the turnstiles were closed with 6,000
people still locked outside, at least a third of whom managed
to squeeze over gates and through broken fencing to watch the
game anyway. Watford again frustrated Southampton's attack,
and won 1-0 to reach the last 16 for the first time in 28 years.

There were more bespoke tactics for the fifth round visit to
Sheffield United, and although Freddie Bunce twisted his ankle
in the 15th minute they seemed to be working as the Hornets
took a 2-1 lead into half-time (Holton, of course, with both).
Shortly afterwards Chung was injured again and nine versus 11
was a handicap too far, the Blades eventually winning 3-2. 'What
a tragedy it was that such a display, so brilliantly planned and
so skilfully put into operation, should have gone unrewarded,'
lamented the *Observer*.

And that left just two things to be decided: promotion, and
that nickname. 'Now that the name of Watford is really on the
lips of all football followers, the committee of the Watford

Football Supporters' Club feel that a suitable nickname should be found,' it was announced. 'During the FA Cup run some very amusing and clever phrases were used on banners carried by supporters. With so much originality, it should not be difficult to decide upon a name for our teams. Go to it, and all the best for your entries.'

The subject had inevitably been keenly discussed since the change in colours. Over the season fans had suggested various possibilities – The Wasps, The Comets, even The Goldilocks. The Supporters' Club first tried to encourage more creative suggestions with an appeal in the matchday programme towards the end of September, which in the first fortnight prompted just a single response – The Tigers. This time they add further encouragement by promising £5 (not far off £100 in modern money) to the person who submitted the chosen name. The club also got involved, with Bonser and Broad both sitting on the four-man selection panel. In all, 187 suggestions were received.

'The competition produced some highly original suggestions,' the *Observer* wrote. 'One supporter, for instance, took the initials of Watford's leading print firms and arrived at the name Oscars; another suggested The Hoboes, obviously recalling the nearness of the old workhouse [which had been built on Vicarage Road, though it was called Hagden Lane then, in 1837 and later became Watford General Hospital].

'Many suggestions had to be discarded because the names were already being used by other clubs. It was felt that the Hornets was easy enough to shout, as well as having an association with the club's new colours.' Walker was one of four people to propose the chosen name, and scooped the £5 jackpot when his name was drawn from a hat. 'I think I bought a watch,' he says. 'I don't still have it.'

The choice wasn't unanimously popular. 'Phonetically and otherwise, "Up the Hornets" lacks the common touch,' said one fan. 'May I suggest that "Up the Stingers" is much more full-blooded.' 'I for one am not at all inspired with such a poor name for such a good team,' moaned another. 'I should have thought The Grasshoppers more appropriate than The Hornets.'

As we now know, the name stuck. The good form, however, did not – a 3-1 home defeat to Aldershot at the start of April was a fifth defeat in ten league games, of which only two had been won. The run prompted the *Observer* to speculate that the team had 'shot their bolt in the bid for promotion', although they were only three points behind Millwall, in the fourth and final promotion place, with two games in hand.

Just as the combination of Holton and Uphill had been the product of a desperate bid to halt the team's previous dodgy run, Burgess again struck gold when changing his line-up. This time he concentrated his efforts on the defence, and discovered that the lanky young Scottish forward Andy Porter made a decent right half. The team didn't lose another game, winning five and drawing two in the run-in, which included three victories over the four-day Easter weekend and two Holton hat-tricks in 24 hours.

On the final Saturday Watford beat Workington 1-0, Northampton lost at Stockport, and promotion was secured. Three days later 21,000 turned up at Vicarage Road as Walsall provided the opposition at the promotion party. Watford came back from 2-0 down to draw 2-2. 'We promised you good football and I think we have kept our promise,' Burgess told the crowd.

Uphill finished the season with 36 goals, enough to have broken the club goalscoring record had Holton not been around; the Big Man's penalty against Walsall was his 48th goal of the season. Watford won 24 games, beating their previous record of 21. The reserves won the Combination, with Fairbrother scoring 40. The first team and the reserve team both scored precisely 107 goals, in all competitions. Before the season started the first team coach Pat Molloy had been asked what he hoped for from the season. 'Promotion for the first team, the championship for the reserves, and a good cup run,' he replied, presumably while stroking a rabbit's foot and munching on a four-leaf clover.

It was a season as remarkable as any in Watford's history. It may have felt at the time as if the club would never be the same again, an impression reinforced when Ken Furphy took the club into the Second Division in 1969 and Bonser was carried shoulder-high around Watford town hall. But that was when the good times ended; by 1975 the Hornets were back in the Fourth Division, the chairman had got the blame and the town was desperate, once again, for change.

Unlike Bonser's ultimately botched revolution, what happened next has never been undone. In May 1976 Elton John bought control of the club from Bonser, and the following year he appointed Graham Taylor as manager.

The pair never hid their desire to reinvent Watford. 'I have been brought in to change the club,' the new manager said on his appointment. 'I'm not so much interested in creating a good team but a good club,' he said in 1978. 'I want something solid so that at some time in the future I can say to myself, "Well, I built something at Watford." I want to leave something behind.' John backed him to the hilt. 'Already Graham is changing things. It is a different club from last year,' he said.

The rest is very well-known history. But perhaps more credit for this second revolution should be given to the creators of the first. John and Taylor took Watford into the top flight and to the FA Cup final and created two generations of fans – and counting – who have never seen the club compete in the Fourth Division, or its current equivalent. A couple of years before his takeover John had told an interviewer that the two main reasons why he would not move permanently to America were 'my family and Watford Football Club, which means as much to me as my family'. But this love had not been born in a vacuum – it was the product of a young Reg Dwight watching Holton and Uphill ransack Fourth Division defences from the Vicarage Road terraces nearly 20 years earlier.

Not all change is good, of course – Watford fans have witnessed enough bad ideas to know that, from pre-recorded crowd noise to the shortlived marriage between Harry and Harriet Hornet (though to be fair, they were quite a good match). Perhaps the most comic illustration came in the shape of the young Zimbabwean goalkeeper Peter Gibbs, who in 1976 was plucked from non-league obscurity and thrust into the first team. At the end of his fourth game, a 4-0 defeat at Cambridge, Gibbs raised two fingers at the away support, ripped up his contract and was never heard of again. 'I enjoy football as a hobby,' he explained. 'I enjoy a beer and a few late nights as much as the next 20-year-old. I cannot treat football seriously enough. I'm just not that dedicated.'

Not all change is good, and the avalanche of loan signings with which the Pozzo family announced their arrival was surely enough to make most fans wonder how kindly history will come to judge their tenure. But perhaps they, and the change they have brought, should be nervously embraced, just as we should embrace the memory of the club's previous revolutionaries. For whatever it is that we love about a somewhat ramshackle ground and its occasional inhabitants, there's a good chance that Bonser, Burgess, Holton and, in some small part, Iain Walker, once of Orchard Lane, Watford, had something to do with it.

Simon Burnton has been writing about sport for *The Guardian* and *The Observer* since 1998. He has also written for *FourFourTwo*, *FHM*, the sadly now-defunct *Arena* and anyone else who has asked nicely and paid reasonably. He once co-wrote a semi-humorous football book called *Balls!* but tries not to mention it these days.

STANTON TOWN v WATFORD
Pre-season friendly: August 4, 1984

Tough-talking coach 'Mad' Mike Burnham has really
been putting the Stanton players through their paces in
pre-season training as newly-promoted Town prepare for
life in Division Three.

Manager Harry Cannon is keen to see they go
through an equally testing time on the pitch by pitting his
team against top opposition.

The visit of Watford, the FA Cup runners-up, to
Abbey Road for a friendly gives him an ideal chance to
see how his players are shaping up – particularly the new
lads Roy Randall and Miguel Santina.

However, the club's chairman Dave Dawkins is up to
no good behind Harry's back...

cannon

IT'LL BE INTERESTING TO SEE HOW SOME OF THESE NEW FACES SHAPE UP.

YEH, IT'S CERTAINLY A DIFFERENT-LOOKING SIDE TO THE ONE THAT FINISHED LAST SEASON

STANTON TOWN

Kooney
Baranski
Cannon J
Paterson
Saunders

Tarrant
Cannon N
Santina
Randall
Taggart
Strider

Subs:
Steele
Howlett
Barnes
McEwa

Before the players go out...

THIS MAY BE A FRIENDLY, BUT IT'S A CHANCE TO SEE HOW FAR WE'VE COME SINCE LAST SEASON. ONE OR TWO FACES ARE NEW TO THE TEAM, BUT YOU ALL KNOW WHAT I WANT FROM YOU. YOU'LL ALL BE GIVEN A CHANCE BUT REMEMBER, THERE ARE GOOD PLAYERS ON THE BENCH WAITING TO COME INTO THE SIDE. WATFORD ARE A CLASS OUTFIT: LET'S TRY TO PLAY FOOTBALL AT ALL TIMES AND DO THE THINGS WE WORKED ON IN TRAINING.

NEXT: The game gets underway at Abbey Road stadium.

Turn to page 119

4

Graham Taylor's autobiography is surely the most eagerly-awaited sports book of the century.

Olly Wicken has made a startling discovery. GT is indeed writing the story of his career.

So, we offer this exclusive, unofficial extract, which reveals the astonishing secret behind Watford's rise through the divisions and the role played by an Oxford University student called Benjamin.

At times it defies belief but this is the story of a parable that has become known as The Watford Way.

GRAHAM TAYLOR
THE UNOFFICAL AUTOBIOGRAPHY

AS TOLD TO OLLY WICKEN

1977-1982 THE BIG I AM

Wherever I was manager, I always made people call me 'Boss' or 'Gaffer'. It was a hard and fast rule: if players used any other name, they were in trouble. But part and parcel of being a football manager is that you have no control over what the fans call you. And in September 1980 I came across a name that really bothered me.

I saw it scrawled on a boy's text book when I was visiting a local Watford school after the 7-1 League Cup win over Southampton. Well, I didn't like it one bit. So I gave the lad a piece of my mind for defacing school property and sent him to the headmaster. Now, as you may know, I'm a great believer in nipping bad behaviour in the bud – like that time I dropped Cally a few minutes before kick-off because he was getting too big for his boots – so people at the school probably thought I was being my usual disciplinarian self. But, on this occasion, that wasn't the whole picture. You see, when I spotted that graffiti on the boy's book, I was absolutely terrified. I'm not kidding you: I thought my cover was blown. GT IS GOD, it said, in stark black ink. Well, I thought to myself, if one of them has worked it out, they'll all work it out.

Luckily, the lad was only trying to be funny. He didn't know he'd stumbled on the truth. No one knew the truth. And it was vital to my master plan to keep it that way. Making little old

Watford the most successful team on the planet wouldn't have had nearly the same impact if everyone knew the team's Gaffer was in reality the universe's Supreme Being. So I had to move in mysterious ways.

Back in 1977-78, of course, when I arrived at Watford, no one had reason to suspect anything. I'd set a new Fourth Division points record with Lincoln City, but it wasn't as if I'd made them win every game 40-0 – which, in fairness, I could have done. Even when I made Watford run away with the Division Four title, no one smelt a rat. After our first game of that first season – when we won away at Stockport – a few people said it was 'a bloody miracle', but that was as close as anyone got.

The next year, in 1978-79, to divert suspicion after a good start, I sent us on a run of one win in nine games after Christmas to make sure no one suspected me of divine intervention. And when we thumped Hull City 4-0 to win promotion in the very last match of the season, I made sure Roger Joslyn got much of the credit. There was never anything heavenly about Roger Joslyn.

After that, just to cover my tracks, I made sure we had a grim first couple of years in Division Two. I thought I handled it rather well. No one who's omniscient would have signed Mick Henderson.

In those days, a lot of what I did on a day-to-day basis involved putting people off the scent. When I insisted on being called 'Boss' or 'Gaffer', for instance, I was just pretending to be an insecure mortal giving it the Big I Am. In reality, I could have made people call me 'Almighty One, Master Of The Heavens And Of The Earth' – quite justifiably – but that wouldn't have gone down well with the gnarled old pros I had to deal with on the training ground. Dennis Booth would definitely have put a little extra into his tackles on me.

It wasn't until May 1982, when I sent Watford into Division

One for the first time in the club's history, that 'God' began to catch on among Watford fans as a kind of nickname for me. But it was all in jest: no one actually meant it or believed it. So I didn't mind. As nicknames go, it was definitely a lot better than Turnip.

By the time the 1982-83 season began, I was well on the way to making us the most successful team in the world for the rest of all time. They were heady days. But perhaps I became a little too pleased with how things were going – maybe I took my all-seeing eye off the ball. I say this because, early that season, something unexpected happened.

A fan discovered my secret.

It would change the course of history.

SEPTEMBER 26 1982: DIY

The trouble starts on September 26th 1982.

These are halcyon days. It's less than a month since we battered Southampton 4-1 at The Dell – when their England midfielder David Armstrong said it was a 'revelation' that we played with two wingers. Since then, I've used up near enough another whole book of revelations: two weeks ago we went top of Division One with a 3-0 win over West Brom, and yesterday I made us beat Sunderland 8-0. Watford's true place in the universe is already starting to take shape.

Watford fans are happy. After yesterday's record win, I looked around town and saw an elderly gentleman tottering down Wiggenhall Road with tears in his eyes, hugging strangers. I saw a father run home, burst into his garden, and leap into his kids' paddling pool. I saw a husband, in a daze, agree to a new sofa in a bold floral print. Religious scholars would probably call this kind of thing 'mass ecstasy'. All I know is that we spanked Sunderland's bottoms.

Pleased with my week's work, I give myself the Sunday off. At this point in space and time, my earthly form is living in Mandeville Close, just off Nascot Wood Road, and I often enjoy a nice bit of DIY to help me relax. But this particular afternoon, while I'm stripping paint from the exterior window sills of the lounge, I have a small accident.

Mistakes happen. Obviously, we all know about human imperfection. (It's a little known fact that I actually invented the substitute's bench with Gerry Armstrong in mind.) But Gods can make mistakes too. Anyone remember Gary Plumley?

Anyway, my little accident this Sunday afternoon is with a blowtorch – which sets my privet hedge on fire. When I peer over the top to check there's no danger to anyone on the other side, I see a teenaged lad walking along the pavement. He sees me between the flames, and his jaw drops. But, unlike someone in a similar incident thousands of years earlier, he doesn't stop to chat to me over the burning bush. He sprints off, terrified.

While my earthly form douses the privet, I take a celestial look at the teenager – whose name is Benjamin. He's 19 – a long-haired skinny lad – and I watch him rush home to his bedroom. His room is full of maths books, posters of heavy metal rock groups, and pictures of Watford players – including a photo of the 1981-82 team squad. He shuts the door and goes over to the photo.

Now, the thing about Benjamin, it turns out, is that he's a little unusual because he regularly talks to the people in this photo. He speaks to individual players, assessing their performances, and he speaks to me about tactics and potential new signings. In fact, no subject seems to be off-limits – whether it's comparing Cally's hairstyle to a drowning mongoose, or observing how Eric Steele looks strangely like the missing Lord Lucan. Worst of all, late at night, he keeps asking Kenny Jackett for certain details about his Page Three girlfriend that I would expect to remain private. Anyway, I'm in the middle row in this photo, between Tom Walley and Billy Hails, and right now this lad Benjamin is bowing to me with his arms raised in homage. I've seen fans do this in jest, but never in private – so he must mean it. His long black hair is flopping down over his face and his voice is all over the place.

'I bow to you, GT!' he says. 'You are MIGHTY! You are OMNIPOTENT!'

He's right, of course, but he needs to keep his voice down.

He lights a couple of candles in front of the team photo. Then he tears out more photos of me from old programmes, and sticks them on the wall. It's unmistakably a shrine. Then, in some kind of God-fearing faint, he swoons back onto his bed in a way that reminds me of Glenn Hoddle after he's been tackled. After a while, he sits up. He stares at me in shock.

'I've never been religious,' he mumbles. 'I'm a mathematician. I deal in stuff that can be proved.'

He goes to a shelf and pulls down a box file of newspaper cuttings. He starts to go through it and pulls out a report of the 2-1 cup upset at Old Trafford in October 1978, several accounts of the 7-1 Southampton game, and a report of the 3-0 win over West Brom that sent us top two weeks ago. Then he puts these reports into a new box file, adds a match report from today's *Sunday Telegraph*, and scribbles a title on the side: PROOF THAT GRAHAM TAYLOR IS GOD.

This doesn't bode well.

SEPTEMBER 26 1982: THE WATFORD WAY

Why do human beings become football fans?

This is a rhetorical question, by the way – in my position, I do actually know the answer. But, on the Sunday evening, I take a look at Benjamin's particular history. His parents split up when he was three. He regularly finished last in egg-and-spoon races at junior school sports day. His attempts to ride a bicycle would make Norman Wisdom proud. He has a crush on Linda Potter – a girl at Pembroke College, Oxford, where he's studying maths – but he's never spoken to her. And he made only one friend in his entire first year at university – a bearded postgrad called Stuart who once didn't see sunlight for six weeks due to an unhealthy fascination with Dungeons And Dragons.

You don't need to be omniscient to suspect that these aspects of his character might somehow be connected to the fact that Benjamin prides himself on having been a Watford ever-present last season. (A terrace version of Ian Bolton, if you like, but without the porn star moustache.) Being a full-on Watford fan makes him feel good about himself – especially now we've arrived at football's top table.

But if humans become football fans because of deep-seated egotistical needs, why, you might ask, would God attach himself to a particular football club – when, as everyone knows, God is as unselfish as Luther Blissett's off-the-ball running.

Well, in my case, it's all to do with kind of God I've chosen to be. You see, some people like their God vengeful – but I'm not really that type. (I realise I may be looking a little bit pitiless now that I've banished Luton to non-League football for all eternity, but I hope everyone can see it was thoroughly merited.) Other people like their God wrathful, but that's never really been my style either. (I've always kept a bit of brimstone in the garden shed in case I feel the urge after playing a Terry Venables team, but I'm fairly sure Rita wouldn't stand for that kind of behaviour around the house.) Instead, I've always seen my role as teacher.

In September 1982, teaching is the whole idea behind my master plan with Watford: I want to show mankind the right and proper way to approach life. It's the Parable of the Good

Football Team, if you like. And all parables need to be easy to understand, so I have been keeping my message simple. I don't come out with incomprehensible gobbledegook like 'I am the Way, the Truth and the Life'. I only ever talk about The Watford Way.

The Watford Way. I've never spelt it out directly, but fans of the club know exactly what it is. They've seen us rise from the bottom division through dedication, effort, spirit and belief. They've seen us take our place in the higher echelons without any of the big clubs' airs and graces. They've seen us be positive – always attacking. And yesterday, at home to Sunderland, they've witnessed what some people might call a gospel statement – when 90 minutes of hard-working, skilful, relentless attack resulted in an 8-0 victory.

And now the world is taking notice. Today, the newspapers are saying we taught Sunderland a footballing lesson. But that's just the start. It's my mission to teach the entire global population that The Watford Way is the right and true path to future human happiness.

Frankly, however, on this particular Sunday night, the whole thing's looking shot to pieces. Thanks to a blowtorch, Benjamin, and a bloody box file.

I need to adjust my plans.

OCTOBER 1982: FAMINE

Watford fans of a certain age probably remember Terry Challis's 1977 painting of Elton John astride a giant hornet, pointing the way towards the Liver Bird and the Eiffel Tower – symbolising Liverpool and Europe. Those fans were probably amazed when it predicted the events of the next few years so accurately. But they shouldn't have been. In 1977, I was standing over Terry Challis's shoulder telling him exactly what to paint.

But that painting was an overview. In practice, my master plan has always had room for flexibility from game to game. So, directly after the Sunderland game, I decide we'll go a calendar month without a league win – to make Benjamin doubt the perfectly correct conclusion to which he's just jumped. A football fan's faith in a manager rarely survives three points from a possible fifteen.

At the same time, as a precaution, in case Benjamin tries to spread word, I get cracking with a plan to make myself seem anything but divine. I do this by drawing the media's attention to my team's direct style. The newspapers immediately take the bait and denounce our style as 'kick and rush', painting me as the enemy of sophisticated modern football – a footballing anti-Christ. Job done.

I also attempt to distract Benjamin from his obsession with football. I do this by trying to intervene on his behalf at the college disco on October 16th. I'm quite pleased with the plan: I arrange matters so that, at 9.37pm, Linda Potter will spill her drink on her blouse near a back wall where, I suspect, Benjamin will be inclined to lurk awkwardly. Unfortunately, however, at the appointed hour, Benjamin is still on his way back from our 0-3 defeat at Aston Villa thanks to a broken down train I hadn't foreseen. As a result, Linda is now going out with a geographer called Dave who has hair exactly like Ray Train's. (So Benjamin would definitely have had a chance.)

Back at the day job, over the course of the month, I'm quite creative with how I make us fail. I gift Birmingham a late equaliser at St Andrews, and I craftily let slip a two-goal lead to lose 2-3 at Notts County.

I worry that I might be taking things too far when I inflict a 324-minute goal famine on the team – but luckily it doesn't strike Benjamin as being too biblical. By the end of the month, I've taken us down to eighth in the table and he's disgruntled.

He seems to have forgotten the whole burning bush incident.

'I was wrong about you,' he says to me in the team photo after the defeat at Notts County. 'The only thing out of the Old Testament I've seen this month is Brian Kilcline's beard.'

He removes the candles and takes down the extra photos. The shrine is no more.

Again, job done.

NOVEMBER 6 1982: SUCKERED

But all my hard work is undone as soon as I try to get my master plan back on track.

On November 6th, I make Watford beat Spurs 1-0 at White Hart Lane. It's a result with a real story to it: scruffy, down-at-heel Watford put one over aristocratic Tottenham. On Sunday and Monday the newspapers will scream in outrage, and the *Daily Mail* will even describe it as a *lèse majesté*. (Benjamin, as a mathematician, will have to look this up in a dictionary.) But, on Saturday night, ordinary football fans around the country are rather amused and not a little impressed.

Benjamin returns to college that night, still wearing his Watford scarf and clutching a copy of the *Evening Post-Echo* Sports Final with a front page headline that reads HORNETS GRAB LATE VICTORY. By the porter's lodge he passes Linda Potter and her new boyfriend Dave – who's wearing a red and white scarf with a Liverpool crest.

'Watford fan, eh?' Dave says, seeing Benjamin's scarf. 'D'you go today?'

Benjamin glances at Linda, and fails to find words in his voice box. He nods.

'Impressive,' Dave says.

At first, Benjamin isn't quite sure whether Dave is referring to the result or to him – Benjamin – for attending the match.

Then he assumes it must be the latter – because Linda smiles at him. Suddenly he feels breathless. His insides are numb and his heart is racing. He turns and hurries away to his bedsit.

In his room, he slams the door and leans back against it.

'Linda Potter thinks I'm impressive! There is a God!' he gasps.

'It's you!' he adds, pointing at me in the 1981-82 team photo.

He finds the box file he started after the Sunderland game. He puts tonight's *Post-Echo* inside and scrawls an extra word on the side: DEFINITE PROOF THAT GRAHAM TAYLOR IS GOD.

He comes over to the team photo and moves in close to my face on the photo. At first I think he's going to kiss me – which would be unsavoury – but he stops just short.

'I started to doubt you,' he whispers. 'But we've just beaten Spurs. At White Hart Lane. You are God. It's the only way to explain all the utter improbability. Old Trafford in 1978-79... reaching Division One... Pat Rice scoring...'

This distracts me for a moment. I must admit I am proud of that goal.

He leans in even closer to my face: 'The burning privet hedge. I know the truth.'

Unfortunately, at this moment, I'm still remembering how I got Neville Southall to carry Pat Rice's cross over the goal line. 'Nonsense,' I reply distractedly. 'Absolute nonsense.'

My voice booms and echoes around Benjamin's bedroom like thunder. He's horror-struck.

So am I. I've just given myself away.

Understandably, the lad starts to panic. He backs away, trips over a bed leg and ends up on his bottom – like a defender in John Barnes's wake.

Looking back, of course, I realise I should have kept my mouth shut at that point. Why didn't I? Well, Rita always tells me I talk too much, but actually it was what he said next that suckered me in. Sat on the floor, trembling, Benjamin says: 'Graham, I need to know... Albert McClenaghan's throw-in...'

My disembodied chuckle resounds off the walls. 'Yep – my doing. Funny, wasn't it?'

The lad sits on the carpet, nodding to himself, taking in his new-found knowledge of the world. And I realise I have no idea what he's going to do with that knowledge.

I've just made an almighty cock-up.

NOVEMBER 6 1982: HEAVY METAL

After Benjamin has pulled himself together a little, I ask him if he'd mind strolling down to the banks of the river Isis to continue our chat in a quiet spot where my voice won't reverberate so much. He agrees.

'So can you make anything happen? Anything at all?' he asks.

At some length, I explain the full extent of my powers.

'And are you behind absolutely everything that happens?'

'Do you mean,' I ask, 'everything in all aspects of time and space across this and other universes?'

'Actually,' he says, 'I was thinking of the time Andy Rankin broke his collarbone fetching coal. Was that because you wanted to give another keeper a run in the side?'

I answer him honestly.

'And how do you make things happen? Is it magic?'

I explain how making Watford successful has involved no magic or trickery of any kind – how it's largely a matter of influencing people's Free Will. He kindly replies that this makes me an even better man-manager than he thought I was. When he asks if I'm always successful, I mention that I wish one of our wingers was better at keeping his trousers on around town.

Benjamin laughs. He's more relaxed now. He's standing by the water's edge, casually tossing stones into the flow.

What Benjamin doesn't know, though, is that, while he and I have been talking, my earthly form has jumped into the Jag and driven to Oxford. I now arrive, silently, on the river bank behind him.

It's dark, and there's no one around. I know I could solve my problem here and now – I could use the heavy car tool I've brought with me from the Jag, for example. But I've never been that kind of God, and I don't want to be now. I'm undecided what's for the best. It's unlike me, but I don't have a plan.

Benjamin hasn't seen me yet. He's looking for more stones to throw into the water, but can't see any. In a pocket, he finds a few copper coins.

'How you decide what to make happen?' he asks. 'I mean, do you listen to people's prayers or wishes?'

If I speak, it'll give away that I'm right behind him. I weigh the cold and heavy car tool in my right hand.

'I mean, I don't need to ask you to make Watford win the league. As our Manager/God, or God/Manager, or whatever the technical term is, that's bound to be your plan, next year if not this. I'm talking about smaller, more specific stuff.'

He throws a coin into the water.

'I wish we win at Arsenal. With lots of goals. I don't know, 4-2 or something.'

The thought of that makes me smile. He throws another coin into the river.

'And I love last-ditch winners. How about beating the European Champions – Villa – in injury time. In the mud. With a long-distance strike from – ooh, I know, Wilf Rostron.'

Again, I smile.

'And as for when we play Luton...'

He throws the remaining handful of coins into the Isis.

'...I've got quite a few wishes there.'

I've made up my mind. I hide the car tool beneath my coat and leave the riverbank. I'm warming to the lad. I think we could have some fun together.

NOVEMBER 1982: A DECENT TEAM

After that, for the next few weeks, Benjamin and I get on really rather well. He continues to talk to me using the medium of his 1981-82 team photo. And when he's worried that the League Cup might be a distraction to our league campaign, and suggests we bow out with a bang, I make us lose 3-7 at Nottingham Forest. Benjamin thinks it's a hilarious scoreline, and I'm inclined to agree – until Brian Clough comes into our dressing room and kisses me and all my players. Do I not like that.

Then, when Ross Jenkins is injured for the home game against Stoke City, Benjamin suggests I give a full league debut to young Jimmy Gilligan. He says it'll help convince people that The Watford Way has a strong future. So I start Jimmy up front, but I make him hit the woodwork twice without scoring – just to keep his feet on the ground. Afterwards, Benjamin says that's very me. We have a good laugh about that.

A couple of weeks later, after I've lifted Watford into second place in the league with a 4-1 win over Brighton, I take the team to Highbury and make us win 4-2. Benjamin is jubilant – like all Watford fans. But he's also touched that I've granted his wish.

'Thanks,' he says to me through the photo – slightly wet-eyed it seems to me. 'That means a lot.'

Then he reaches up to his box files and says: 'I love that this is all our little secret.'

Next, he scratches out the words DEFINITE PROOF THAT GRAHAM TAYLOR IS GOD, and empties the newspaper cuttings back into their original file. He's a good lad, I think to myself, is Benjamin.

DECEMBER 1982 – MARCH 1983
A MIGHTY SMITING

In early December, Benjamin is terribly disappointed when I allow back-to-back defeats against Manchester United and Liverpool. After our recent all-conquering run, he wants us to spank the bottoms of the two biggest clubs in the country. So I take time out to explain to him that this isn't realistic – we can't be too successful too soon.

I need to play the long game, I explain, if I'm to convert the whole of humanity to The Watford Way. But I'm not sure Benjamin's really listening. He mutters that my best conversion will always be Wilf Rostron to left back.

After that, across the winter and spring of 1982-83, I start seeing signs of improvement in Benjamin's approach to life at Oxford. He's definitely developing more social confidence.

The way confidence works in human beings still amazes me – even though I invented the stuff. For instance, in December, when I arrange for Luther Blissett to score a hat-trick on his England debut, Benjamin feels brave enough to venture down to the college bar for the first time ever to mark the occasion. Unfortunately, he's still not brave enough to say anything when Linda Potter smiles at him again, but at least he doesn't actually scarper as if he's part of our 'exploding wall' free-kick routine. Then, in mid-March, a run of six consecutive home wins and a 5-3 thrashing of Notts County gives him the self-assurance to speak to Linda at last. He discovers she's sweet, funny, and intelligent and has a copy of Motörhead's debut album on white vinyl. (He'd been worried she might like the kind of nonsense Cally plays at discos.) Unfortunately, she's still going out with

Dave, the Liverpool fan, but that doesn't stop Benjamin from being totally smitten.

So Luther's England hat-trick is the nudge that eventually sends Benjamin tumbling head-over-heels in love as if he were Wilf Rostron going over the advertising hoardings at St Andrews a year later. That's how confidence operates. It's a mad old world.

Soon after, when he goes home for the Easter vacation, Benjamin feels the urge to write Linda a letter. He's never written to a girl before, so he's unsure quite what to say. So he writes about Luther.

In due course Linda receives several scented pages about the honesty, effort and bravery of a man she's never heard of. She's a bit bemused. But, as an English student, she's good at spotting subtext. When Benjamin describes how Luther is prepared to miss goals in order to score them, and how he keeps going even when something looks like a lost cause, Linda interprets this as Benjamin expressing his intentions towards her while she's going out with Liverpool Dave. This time she really is impressed by Benjamin – by his subtlety and his use of metaphor. So she writes back.

And that, unfortunately, changes everything.

APRIL 4 & 5 1983: THE TURNAROUND

I rather enjoy the home game against Luton Town on Easter Monday. It's the culmination of several years' work.

Over the previous three years, I've deliberately made us lose 0-1 to the filthy Hatters five times – each one a narrow, unjust, and agonising defeat. Testing your followers is the worst part of a God's job, so it's hugely satisfying to be able to reward believers in spectacular fashion.

At first, I let Luton go into a 2-1 lead – then I turn it all

around. I start with an equaliser just before half-time, just to
raise the spirits a little. Then I make Barnes and Blissett score
in quick succession early in the second half. But the real devil,
so to speak, is in the detail. Luther's goal is – finally, against
Luton – at last! – a penalty. The next – exquisitely agonising
for Luton, this – is a Paul Elliott back pass that Barnes stretches
to deflect, looping, into the net. Later on, as icing on the cake,
I see to it that Luton's Raddy Antic is sent off, and that Cally
scores a fifth.

A five-goal destruction of Luton. One of the perks of my
job is making people happy. But that day, after all those 0-1
injustices, I'm making people insanely, impossibly happy.

Take Benjamin, for example. A four-fold wish he'd made at
the riverside has come true – a penalty, a sending-off, a back-
pass mix-up and going nap. He's delirious with joy.

'Thank you!' he whispers to me in the team photo that night,
tears of gratitude in his eyes. 'Thank you, God!'

Next morning, though, he's in a different mood. A letter
from Linda has arrived.

In his room, he's turned up his stereo and is leaping around
manically – as if he's Steve Sherwood coming for a cross. He's
listening to a song called *I Know A Girl*, by a band called The
Undertones. I'm pretty certain I've never heard Vera Lynn sing it.

When the music stops, he comes over to the team photo.
His eyes are shining like Luther's thighs under floodlights.

'Change of plan required,' he says, out of breath. 'We need
to win the league. This season.'

I'm not sure I like where this could be going. I wonder
whether I'm going to have to take him somewhere quiet like
the riverside again.

'I need us to overhaul Liverpool. We can still do it, I've
worked it out. They're 16 points clear at the top, but we've got
seven games left – so we can get 21 points. It's possible. You

just have to make Liverpool collapse. Astonishingly.'

This isn't on. The pace at which I establish The Watford Way is critical to my master plan. In the photo, I shake my head from side to side – as vehemently as if Pat Rice was asking to go up for a corner.

That freaks him. He's not seen me do that. He recovers quickly, though. 'We're playing them in the last match of the season. Imagine it: a final day showdown. Winner takes all.'

There's no doubt the boy's got imagination, and for a brief moment I'm tempted. But I shake my head.

'I could take Linda. She could bring her boyfriend too. He's a Liverpool fan, after all.'

Now I understand Benjamin's motivation: he thinks that if his team beats Dave's it'll prove he's the alpha-male round these parts. It's a common delusion among football fans. Benjamin's alpha-maleness would be much better measured by a 50-50 tackle with Jan Lohman.

'You have to do it,' he pleads. 'You have to.'

My photo shakes its head again. Benjamin thinks. Then he changes his tone.

'You have to. I saw the deflection for Barnes's goal.'

I raise an eyebrow in the photo.

'I was right behind the Vicarage Road goal,' he says, 'so I saw exactly what happened. When the ball looped up, it was missing the goal by a mile. The bounce it took defied physics.'

It's true. The ball hadn't been sailing straight into the net, so I'd had to make a late adjustment. It was the only time I'd ever interfered with time or space to help Watford. But my tiny refinement is looking a huge mistake – because Benjamin is swallowing hard and setting himself to say something of great magnitude.

'If you don't make us win the league this season,' he says. 'I'll tell the world who you are.'

APRIL 9–12 1983: MY WAY

Just to recap. I'm God, and a spotty and socially inept mathematician is trying to blackmail me. Well, I'm not going to stand for that, am I?

The following Saturday, I prove who's Boss. Sure, I make Watford win 3-1 at West Brom – but I also make Liverpool win 3-0 over Swansea. Then, in a re-arranged game on the Tuesday night, I give the Reds another point at Coventry. Watford's maximum is now only 82 points, and Liverpool already have 81.

I am God and Benjamin is Benjamin. I'm going to establish The Watford Way my way.

1PM, APRIL 16 1983: MIDFIELD BATTLE

On Saturday, April 16th, Benjamin arrives early at Vicarage Road for the home game against Nottingham Forest. He's waiting when my earthly form arrives at the Players' And Match Officials' Entrance – the hole in the wall on Occupation Road.

'We need to talk,' he growls through gritted teeth.

Several other youngsters are crowding round me with autograph books, so I take Benjamin through into the stadium to avoid a scene. At the bottom of the steps, Oliver Phillips from the *Watford Observer* distracts me with a question – and when I turn around Benjamin has mysteriously disappeared, like a goalkeeper beneath a John Barnes cross.

Twenty minutes later, Benjamin re-appears. I decide to take him down onto the pitch where we can chat quietly in private. On seeing us, Les Simmons takes a break from his last-minute work preparing the pitch and heads back down the tunnel, leaving Benjamin and myself alone in the centre-circle.

'So. We meet at last in person,' he says.

'You're making this sound like a showdown. Or a play-off, if you like,' I joke.

Benjamin looks at me quizzically.

'Ah. Yes. I'm not introducing those for another four years,' I say. 'Carry on.'

Benjamin begins. He demands that we win the league this season. Given that my plan is to make Watford the best team in the world, he says, he can't see why I can't just do it straightaway. What's to be gained from waiting?

I explain that the narrative of the Parable Of The Good Football Team needs to be established slowly – so that people can live with it and absorb the lessons fully. I tell him I'm not prepared to jeopardise everything I've been working towards for the last five years.

Benjamin is unmoved. He re-iterates his ultimatum: unless I make us win the league, now, this season, he'll expose me.

I try a different tack. 'Benjamin,' I say. 'What I'm trying to achieve here will benefit every single human being on the planet. You're taking a very selfish position.'

'Nothing wrong with that,' he says. 'I bet you've told Ross or Luther to be more selfish in front of goal.'

'Only for the greater good,' I reply.

This seems to get through to him a little. But he still won't back down.

I start to get a tiny bit impatient. 'Look, Benjamin, I'm God. It really would be the work of an instant to crush any attempt by you to expose me.'

'Is that meant to be a threat?' he asks. Then he laughs. 'You're Graham Taylor. Behind that whole Gaffer act, you're the wisest, most generous, most warm-hearted man anyone could wish to meet. Every Watford fan knows that.'

I feel the need to demonstrate my powers. To intimidate Benjamin, I point to the Rookery end of the pitch and make the ground fall away in spectacular biblical fashion – rending it in twain, I think people call it.

'There's always been subsidence there,' he says, unimpressed. 'I've seen a photo from the match against Grimsby in 1961 when a hole opened up during the game.'

To save Les Simmons too much work, I re-fill the hole instantly. Then I try something else. I point at the Vicarage Road end of the pitch and make the earth rise up. We're now standing on a dramatic incline.

'So Terry Venables was right about the slope all along,' Benjamin says mockingly, in reference to the excuse Venables gave after we'd thumped QPR here the previous year.

I can see the boy's not scaring easily. I put the ground back to normal.

'Look,' Benjamin says. 'Here's the bottom line. I have Free Will. And I've got evidence I want to show the world.'

Benjamin lifts the bright yellow Hornet Shop carrier bag he's carrying and pulls out a VHS cassette. 'This is the master copy of the Luton match. I've liberated it from the AV Suite in the public interest.'

So that's where he went for those 20 minutes. Now I realise how serious he is.

'I know four billion people who'll be very interested in Digger's deflection,' he says.

'OK. Give that to me,' I snap, and I hold out my hand for the cassette.

Benjamin puts the VHS back in the bag, gripping it tightly.

'Listen, son,' I say. 'You need to think of the consequences. If everyone finds out I'm God, they'll view Watford's success as a fix – a cheat. It hasn't been, but that's what people will think. Is that what you want?'

Benjamin doesn't waver. So I get personal.

'What will Linda think? Do you suppose she'll be impressed

by someone who supports a team that seems to have an unfair advantage?'

'Dave's team have got Rush and Dalglish,' he says. 'So, yeah. Obviously.'

The argument continues.

'Expose me and everyone loses,' I say.

'Do what I say and everyone wins,' he replies.

I'm becoming exasperated.

'That's enough,' I say. 'Put the VHS down,'

He refuses. 'I'm taking it to the newspapers,' he says. 'Jeff Powell would love to get hold of this.'

At the mention of this name I'm genuinely spooked: Jeff Powell is my nemesis. I defeated him at the battle of Armageddon a while back – many legends refer to him as Beelzebub – and I punished him by putting him to work as a *Daily Mail* journalist for a thousand years.

He doesn't know I've disguised myself as Graham Taylor, but in recent months, quite coincidentally, he's been spreading poison about me and The Watford Way in that disgusting rag. He's the last person on earth I want receiving the evidence that reveals my secret.

I look around the empty stadium and rub my chin in thought. Benjamin has raised the stakes more than he realises.

'OK,' I say. 'I'll see to it that Liverpool lose 2-3 at Southampton today. Then 0-2 at home to Norwich next week, 0-2 again at Spurs the week after, and 0-1 at Forest on the Bank Holiday Monday.'

'Good,' Benjamin says, smiling. 'Is that a promise?'

I make him a solemn promise.

'OK,' he says. 'But I'm keeping this, just in case...'

He waves the Hornet Shop bag at me and walks off the pitch.

'Champions!' he chants. 'Champions!'

2.30PM, APRIL 16 1983
A DEMONSTRATION OF BELIEF

I've always believed that football should benefit the wider community. (This was a new idea to people in 1977. When I first started sending my players to visit geriatric centres, people assumed we were looking for a home for Denis Bond.) But my master plan is designed to benefit the whole world. And at this point it's in serious danger.

As my earthly form trudges off the pitch, I bump into Brian Clough.

'I love you lot,' he says to me. 'Are you playing with ten men up front again?'

Cloughie's a wonderful character. Five years earlier, I'd re-arranged the grand scheme of things so that Nottingham Forest went up into Division One, immediately won the league and League Cup, and then won the European Cup twice in a row. It was a sort of reconnaissance exercise before I began the real thing with Watford.

I was happy to let Cloughie take all the credit, of course – especially when he announced to the press that he could walk on the River Trent if he wanted to. It meant no one guessed I was the true divinity behind the whole thing. I suppose I was lucky the world believed that the occasional one-liner team talk could result in so much silverware.

Anyway, Cloughie and I have a good old laugh together for a few moments. When he heads off to the bar, I feel a little sad that, over the next few years, he'll have to survive on just a couple of League Cup wins. I hope he copes.

While my earthly form enters the home dressing room, I start wondering what to do about Benjamin and his threat to tell Jeff Powell about me. Today's team are already getting changed: Sherwood, Rice, Rostron, Terry, Jackett, Taylor, Lohman,

Jobson, Callaghan, Blissett, Barnes and Armstrong. They're psyching themselves up. Music is blaring.

Suddenly I have an idea. I take Tom Walley aside and send him away with a little task. I stay with the lads, briefing them individually on their jobs for the afternoon. A few minutes later, after a Tannoy announcement to the crowd, Tom Walley returns with Benjamin in tow. I step into the corridor for a brief word with the lad.

'Benjamin,' I say, 'I am not going to comply with your ultimatum.'

'Well, that's your funeral,' Benjamin replies contemptuously.

I look at him askance. He doesn't see fit to correct himself. His mind is made up.

'I won't back down,' I say. 'Luther is going to put us 1-0 up from the penalty spot this afternoon, but we're going to lose 1-3.'

'That would be a mistake,' he says coldly. 'That would mean we can't catch Liverpool, even when you make them lose. You don't want to do that.'

'I'm doing it,' I say. 'And this is the point where you have a choice. It's your Free Will to take the course of action you see fit. But whatever you decide, I don't want there to be any hard feelings. So I thought you might like to take a quick look inside the dressing room. Not many fans get to do this.'

I open the door. He wants to resist my offer, but can't. He follows me.

Inside, the players are going through their warm-up routines – hammering the walls and roaring. Benjamin – who's never been in a professional football dressing room before – is almost physically knocked back by the aggression in the air.

I whisper in his ear: 'None of these players know I control their destiny. Look at them, they believe they're the ones who can make anything happen.'

Benjamin gazes around the room.

'Look how confident they are in their own abilities,' I whisper, as John Barnes juggles a rolled-up sock – effortlessly, astonishingly – from foot to shoulders to foot.

'Look how committed they are,' I whisper, as Jan Lohman headbutts a wall until he's cross-eyed.

Benjamin is awestruck.

'Luther! Come here!' I shout, and Luther saunters over, shining his huge white torch of a smile at Benjamin. Benjamin's knees buckle a little in the great man's presence.

'Luther, this is Benjamin – a young student. Tell us what you're going to do out there this afternoon.'

'I'm going to run for 90 minutes, Boss. Drag defenders around, close them down, create space, chase everything. Shoot when I get the chance.'

'Are you going to score?'

'Yes, Boss.'

'You missed a penalty up at Forest. If we get one today, are you going to take it?'

'Yes, Boss. And score it.'

I squeeze Luther's shoulder and take Benjamin back out into the corridor. I walk him towards the tunnel.

'See that, Benjamin? How Luther absolutely and totally believes in himself?"

Benjamin nods, still awestruck.

'Well, here's your choice. You can opt to keep him that way – sure in the belief he can forge the future – or you can wipe that smile off his face forever by letting mankind know that everything in the world is actually down to me. Do you want to do that to Luther and all the lads in there?'

Benjamin lowers his eyes to the floor.

I hold the door open for him to exit into the tunnel.

'Take one for the team, Benjamin. It's The Watford Way.'

7.30PM, APRIL 17 1983
SAVING GRACE

The next day, with Watford now unable to catch Liverpool, Benjamin returns to Oxford for the new term. He sits in his room all afternoon, feeling bad that he's been so selfish in trying to blackmail me. Having met Luther, he can see the bigger picture now.

As I watch him, I feel sorry for him. He's a likeable lad, but you couldn't call him a social success. His problem, I now realise, is that he hasn't approached his time at university in The Watford Way – he hasn't attacked it with gusto.

He ought to have joined societies; attended all those free lectures on art, history and philosophy; tried new sports; met new people, and gone to stay in their 23-bedroom stately homes. But he hasn't. Instead, he's spent his time listening to heavy metal music in his bedsit, popping spots, and trekking off to Watford matches.

It's amazing, really. He and Watford have been in identical situations – new to the top tier of their respective fields, football and education – but he still hasn't twigged that The Watford Way is exactly how he needs to approach life at this higher level. He hasn't put the parable into practice.

This thought troubles me. Even though Benjamin has been part of events at the heart of the parable, he hasn't applied its lesson to his own life. Which presumably means no one else is likely to, either.

And now I think harder about it, parables aren't really very effective, are they? How many people around the world actually behave like Good Samaritans? I don't like this train of thought. Is my whole master plan flawed?

Troubled by doubt, I keep watching Benjamin. By the evening, he's feeling more positive: Watford are still second

in the league after all. And this gives him the confidence to
venture back into the college bar. Liverpool Dave is there with
a couple of other Liverpool fans, celebrating their team's sixth
league title in eight years. Benjamin sits quietly in the corner
watching. He knows he just has to wait a year or two, then it'll
be his turn.

But his turn for what? This is what Benjamin starts to
wonder as he watches Dave chanting derisively from the
bottom of his lungs.

Will it be his turn to become just another boorish football
fan bigging himself up and belittling others? Is that his future?
Is that where The Watford Way is leading him?

His thoughts are interrupted when he sees Linda enter the
bar. His heart leaps like Ross Jenkins at the back stick. It nearly
stops beating when she waves sweetly at him.

Linda makes her way towards her Dave, but she stops when
she sees him shouting in the face of a girl who's politely asked
him to quieten down.

'I'm Liverpool, so I'll do what I want!' he swears drunkenly,
spraying the girl with beery spittle. Linda changes her mind
about joining her boyfriend, and goes over to sit with Benjamin
instead.

'I'm glad you're a Watford fan,' she says. 'It means you'll
never be like that. Fancy another drink?'

Benjamin nods. As she buys him a pint, he thinks about
what she's just said – what it means to be a Watford fan. And
he thinks back to the way he's behaved with me – at odds
with the moral code he's seen me trying to establish with The
Watford Way.

As Linda returns with the drinks, Benjamin looks over at
Liverpool Dave – who's frothing at the lips and lurching in his
seat. Benjamin says quietly to himself: 'There, but for the grace
of Graham Taylor, go I.'

10.30PM, APRIL 17 1983: THE OTHER WAY

Benjamin enters his bedsit later that night. He walks straight over to the team photo.

'Graham, we need to talk,' he says earnestly.

In the photo, I cup a hand behind my ear to show I'm ready to listen.

'Later,' he whispers – as his bedsit door opens and Linda walks in.

Respectfully, I and everyone in the photo turn and face the other way.

1PM, MAY 14 1983: THE FINAL REVELATION

Over the next month, suffering doubt about my master plan, I let our results slip. Benjamin's obsession subsides a little too. He has another interest in his life now, and he's very committed to her. It's all new to him, of course, but he's properly throwing himself into the new world of emotional openness and intimacy in which he's found himself. He's attacking it with gusto, I'm pleased to say – The Watford Way.

But he does come down to Vicarage Road on May 14th for the final game of the season – against Liverpool. He makes a point of not bringing Linda. He arrives early and waits for my earthly form on Occupation Road again.

'We still need to talk,' he says – not through gritted teeth this time, but with a kind of earnest urgency. I take him through onto the bright sunlit pitch and we stand in the centre circle again.

This time, he gazes around the ramshackle stadium: the brick and concrete of the Vicarage Road end; the old main stand; the old 'new' stand; the *Watford Observer* clock on the shabby Rookery roof; the 'Bend'; the dilapidated Shrodells.

'You've got it wrong,' he says quietly.

'Great. Here we go again,' I say. I'm not really in the mood.

'No, I don't mean it like that. I just mean... Your master plan to make us the best football team on the planet – it doesn't feel right.'

Given my own doubts, I'm feeling a bit sensitive to criticism, but I let him go on.

'Winning won't establish The Watford Way. If anything, it'll kill it. I worked it all out when I saw Linda's old boyfriend celebrating Liverpool's title. The Watford Way isn't about winning. It's about being your best. It's about respect for yourself and others. If you do things The Watford Way, it doesn't actually matter whether you win or not. It just means you've done things the right way.'

I nod. I see what he's saying.

'I don't want to win all the time,' he continues. 'I don't think it'll be good for me. I'll turn into someone I don't want to be – someone who demands success because he feels entitled to it. I've met people who win all the time, and they think they're above The Watford Way.'

'So what do you suggest I do?' I ask.

'I think you shouldn't make us the best team in the world. It'll only corrupt us.'

Benjamin's words hit me like an Ian Bolton free-kick. He's just identified the real fatal flaw in my master plan.

'Man's innate corruptibility,' I murmur.

Benjamin nods. 'Absolute success corrupts absolutely.'

'But...,' I burble. 'Not Luther.. Surely he wouldn't...'

'No, not Luther,' Benjamin says. 'But the fans. Future players. Glory hunters. As soon as they taste success, they'll forget The Watford Way. Your disciples will deny you.'

Realising my master plan is definitely in tatters, I get a sinking feeling in my stomach. Not just my earthly stomach, but all over the universe. The sun disappears behind a cloud.

'But if I don't make us the best team in the cosmos, how else can I demonstrate that The Watford Way is the way all people should live their lives?' I ask Benjamin.

'Leave it to Luther,' he replies. 'To Wilf, to Kenny. Players who play The Watford Way won't always win, but they'll never stop trying. Take the Forest game, for example. You'd decided we'd lose 1-3, but the players never gave up. They hit the bar three times. We lost, but it was brilliant. For people who can see it, surely that's enough to instill The Watford Way for life.'

I smile ruefully. The boy saying this is the boy who couldn't apply the lesson of the parable to his own life.

'And as for people who can't see it,' he continues. 'Well, will human beings ever really change?'

My rueful smile remains on my face. Maybe he doesn't realise how much he has changed in the last month – thanks to another human being, though, not an allegory.

Shattered, I gaze around the ramshackle stadium – this patch of grass up the hill from the allotments – and I have yet another revelation. The Watford Way is to earn success through honest toil and effort – but I'm using supernatural ordainment. I've had it all wrong on this front too.

For two or three minutes, I can't think of anything to say – which Rita later tells me is a record. Feeling stressed, I start thinking about some of the other things around the universe that I need to be paying attention to. Things like the Cold War, now that Brezhnev has died. Things like climate change – which I'm just starting to bring to the attention of a couple of scientists in the USA. I've got a lot on my plate.

But right now I need to formulate a new plan for Watford.

'You know what, Benjamin?' I say. 'I'm going to give your way a go. Today, I'm going to sit back and see how we get on against Liverpool on our own merits. We could lose and finish

sixth, or win and finish second. I'm leaving it to the lads. Maybe
we'll get into Europe, maybe we won't.'

Benjamin nods. 'OK.'

'And next year – well, I'd planned that we'd win the FA Cup,
but – who knows? – maybe we won't. We'll see. I'm going to
leave it to footballers playing The Watford Way – honest, hard-
working players who never know they're beaten.'

Which makes me think of someone in particular. I start
heading back towards the dressing rooms.

'Where are you going?' Benjamin calls out.

'To find Martin Patching and tell him he's playing today.'

4.40PM, MAY 14 1983: WONDERFUL

That afternoon, in glorious sunshine, my players defeat the
champions Liverpool – with no divine assistance of any kind.

It's a wonderful afternoon – not least because Martin Patching, who had decided to retire from football because of a knee
injury, agrees to one final game and scores our first goal. At
the end of the afternoon we've finished runners-up in Division
One and earned a place in the UEFA Cup. What's almost more
satisfying is that Martin Patching decides not to give up the
game after all. That's definitely The Watford Way.

Thereafter I coach and manage the team the same way any
mortal Gaffer would – with no divine nudges of any kind. So
my own expectations of the team are lower. What's more, when
Luther, Ross and Gerry leave, and my only signing to replace
them up front is Cambridge United's centre-half, the fans'
expectations plummet too. But it turns out that 1983-84 is
full of totally wonderful moments from start to finish. In the
league, we win at Spurs again and beat Arsenal as usual. And we
have fun away from home by scoring four goals at Stoke and
West Ham, and five goals at Wolves and Notts County. In the

UEFA Cup, we beat Kaiserslautern 3-0 at home, then go on to beat Levski Spartak with an away win in Sofia. In the FA Cup, we start by knocking out Luton and finish by reaching the club's first ever FA Cup Final.

It's an even more wonderful and extraordinary season than 1982-83. Without my divine influence, the outcomes are much more unpredictable – reinforcing The Watford Way by proving that the unlikely is always possible. We don't win any trophies but, as Benjamin taught me, that isn't the point. The majority of Watford's players and fans have the best footballing year of their lives bar none.

Benjamin especially.

And that pleases me more than anything.

APRIL 2012: JUST FOR FUN

Thirty years on, I'm finally getting around to writing my autobiography. It's 2012. (Since you're probably wondering – no, I don't have The End Of The World planned for December 21st. I might arrange a cataclysmic defeat for Luton that day, but there's nothing globally apocalyptic in my diary.)

I've stayed in touch with Benjamin over the years. He and Linda drifted apart after college, but he's happily married with a family now. Not many people know he was once a socially inept football obsessive. Even fewer know he changed the course of history.

We talk a lot. It was actually Benjamin who suggested I come back to Watford in 1996. His kids hadn't been born during my first spell at the club, and he wanted them to understand what The Watford Way was all about. He called it 'the second coming' and insisted that I return to drive out the infidel Kerry Dixon. In the end I did rather more than that, with the help of some more natural disciples of The Watford

Way in the shape of Steve Palmer and Tommy Mooney. As a result, Benjamin's two sons witnessed the late-season run-in of 1998-99 – and it's no coincidence they've grown up to be fine young men. They know the power of teamwork, self-belief and commitment. They've also lived through – and seen through – the empty sheen of the Premier League, and they're not interested. Like I say, fine young men.

Having said that, Benjamin and I do often wonder whether I did the right thing in stepping back from my original master plan. Maybe we're getting old (he's 49, I'm almost 13.8 billion), but when we go for a quiet pint together we always find ourselves moaning about the lack of moral substance in football these days. Some of the top British clubs are run by men who behave as if they're omnipotent, but no one ever talks about The Chelsea Way or The Manchester City Way. There's no underlying philosophy. The power in football lies with money – and the world is poorer for it.

We're still agreed, though, that I was right to put distance between The Watford Way and success. Man needs to understand that life is not about winning. It's about honour, honesty and effort. It's about doing things the right way, as well as you can, and accepting the outcome with good grace. It's about having Les Taylor and Kenny Jackett in your midfield.

At the moment, I still believe that Watford being known as the 'Family Club' brings more value to humanity than being known as the 'Utterly Globally Dominant Club'. The question remains, of course, whether the two could ever be combined. In fact, I'm thinking of running a controlled experiment in one of my parallel universes one day, just so I can find out for sure. But in the meantime I'd advise people just to keep watching and learning from The Watford Way's latest incorruptible disciple. He wears the number 12 shirt in case you hadn't noticed.

So what does the future hold? Benjamin sometimes jokes

that he's still got the VHS cassette of the Luton game safely tucked away somewhere – in case he changes his mind and fancies blackmailing me to bring Watford a league title just once before he dies, just for fun. And when I think about it, I must admit the idea quite appeals.

Hmm.

Watch this space.

Olly Wicken has written for *FHM* and *When Saturday Comes,* and wrote about his season as a Watford ballboy in Nick Hornby's anthology *My Favourite Year.* He still owns a pair of Graham Taylor's old boxer shorts – and still treats them as a religious totem.

5

Absence makes the heart grow fonder, they say.

John Anderson has spent his whole life following Watford from afar.

His radio career has meant he has spent some of the club's greatest days behind the microphone somewhere else, stifling cheers or holding back tears as the team's fortunes hang in the balance.

As he explains, you can take the boy out of Watford and even take him as far as Guildford but you can never take Watford out of the boy.

ON THE OUTSIDE LOOKING IN

BY JOHN ANDERSON

I sometimes feel like a bit of a fraud. When I consider the people who travel to watch the Golden Boys home and away, season after season, it almost seems indecent that I have been invited to join this wonderful project and write about my love for Watford Football Club. Compared to you, I am the type of fan who can be described as a Commodore; as in 'once, twice, three times a season'. This, I hasten to add, has been dictated by circumstances rather than a lack of enthusiasm; being a football reporter makes it difficult to maintain a close relationship with your own club, as you invariably spend most match days working at the homes of others.

To make matters worse, I have spent less than two per cent of my worldy existence actually living in Watford, but my first breath, burp, fart and smile took place in the town. I have a birthright.

Sadly there isn't a blue plaque to commemorate the event, but I was born in November 1960 at Watford Maternity Hospital. I had long believed this to be part of what is now Watford General Hospital behind the Rous Stand at Vicarage Road, but subsequent research has, rather depressingly, uncovered that the site may in fact have been in King Street about half a mile from the ground.

Notwithstanding that (and with a journalistic obligation to never let the facts get in the way of a good story), I will continue to stick to the romantic notion, as related to me by my mother, that the first sound I ever heard was the roar of the crowd emanating from the stadium and drifting zephyr like over my cot. One of those voices would doubtless have belonged to a 13-year-old then known as Reg Dwight.

What can be verifiably confirmed is that, four days after I was born, Watford played out a 2-2 draw with Brentford in an FA Cup first round tie at The Vic. My late father attended that match, popping in to check on his first born before heading up to the ground. Although he had grown up in Berkhamsted, my Dad was not a true Watford supporter. He was one of those pioneering southern Manchester United fans who supported the club from afar and had never made the trip up from the Home Counties to Old Trafford.

Instead he adopted the far less glamorous but far more conveniently situated Watford as his second team and was a regular at Vicarage Road in the 1950s. Fate, however, was to decree that I would rarely have the chance to accompany him on such typical father and son outings. Before I had taken my first step, the family moved to Guildford in Surrey which, despite my birth certificate, I consider to be my home town. It was to be the start of a lifetime spent not quite within touching distance of the club.

Granted we hadn't relocated to Singapore or Colombia, but we were sufficiently distant to make trips to Watford far from frequent affairs and the arrivals of my sister and brother further complicated matters. When I grew up the M25 was not even a twinkle in a Department of Transport planner's eye and the route from Surrey to West Herts felt like the Paris-Dakar rally. Even now I can recall the names of the places we puttered through in our bright red Austin A40: Weybridge, Chertsey, Staines, Slough, Uxbridge, Chalfont St Peter, Rickmansworth, it was hardly an odyssey of Route 66 romanticism.

'Get your kicks, on the A412.'

Nonetheless, these rare treats were to be savoured as I would buy a copy of the *Hornet Express*, find a place as close to the halfway line as possible, shove a hot dog down my gob and cheer on the likes of Stewart Scullion, Barry Endean, Keith Eddy, Tom Walley and Terry Garbett. Not that my support seemed to have a great effect on any of them, as none of my first dozen or so visits culminated in a home win.

Unfortunately I didn't get to see any of the matches in the 1970 FA Cup run and had to make do with infrequent updates on the BBC's *Grandstand* programme, in between coverage of racing from Haydock Park and rugby league matches between Featherstone Rovers and Wakefield Trinity. At least we had seen highlights of the fourth round win over Stoke City on *Match Of The Day*, in which Colin Franks somehow beat Gordon Banks from about 100 yards for the winning goal. With its grainy black and white images and wobbly graphics, football coverage in those day bore about as much resemblance to today's epic outside broadcasts as a Charlie Chaplin silent film does to *Avatar*. Had the match been played out with the benefit of today's dazzling TV technology, Sky Sports would no doubt have trotted out a sponsored caption telling us that the possession count was Watford 2% and Stoke 98%.

A shocking editorial decision on the part of the BBC meant that the fifth round win at Gillingham wasn't deemed worthy of a *Match of the Day* highlights slot, so my Dad and I had to endure the Saturday afternoon ritual of waiting for the result to come through on the archaic *Grandstand* teleprinter.

This, I imagine now, was operated with the two chubby index fingers of a soporific clerical worker in between puffs on a B&H Special Filter and slurps from a large mug of tea. Mistakes and misspellings were commonplace and the printer itself had an annoying habit of jamming for what seemed like an eternity, leaving the viewer in a ghastly limbo before the final

digit was typed out. This nerve shredding experience reached
its agonising apex on the day of the quarter-final against
Liverpool. We knew Watford had gone in front early in the
second half and sat through a further half an hour of mud,
sweat and Eddie Waring, hoping (or perhaps fearing) that an
update would appear on the screen. The rugby league ended
without further enlightenment and so we sat transfixed as the
cack handed stenographer began to trap his keys.

Since the teleprinter was merely a visual representation of
the Press Association sports wire, all manner of information
flashed before our eyes; Rosslyn Park had beaten Metropolitan
Police at Imber Court, Tulse Hill and Southgate fought out a
draw in hockey and in amongst all this the occasional FA Cup
score would flash up. After QRP 2 CHESLEA 4, suddenly a W
appeared on the screen like the Oracle at Delphi. We held our
breath as our result finally came through with greater than average torpor WATFORD 1 LIVERPOOL (inevitably the printer
paused to increase the agony) and then with one tap of the
keyboard, the figure 0 sent us into paroxysms of delight and
unthinkable dreams of a possible day out at Wembley.

Later that evening in front of *Match of the Day* we cheered
belatedly as Endean's diving header beat Tommy Lawrence on a
morass of a pitch, through which the odd blade of grass poked
out rather sheepishly. Of course the Wembley dream remained
unfulfilled as Chelsea won the semi-final comfortably, but to be
watching Watford on TV three times in the space of a couple
of months seemed as improbable as watching Neil Armstrong
take his first step onto a surface every bit as barren and inhos-
pitable as the Vicarage Road pitch less than a year before.

As a schoolboy in Guildford in the 1970s, my friends all supported Chelsea, Arsenal, Spurs, Manchester United or Leeds, so
I was a lone dissenting voice in yellow, and my isolation was to
be compounded by my parents' split up early in that decade.

This drove a rent through more than just my family life since my Mum, who couldn't drive and had no interest in football, was hardly in a position to start chauffeuring me to Vicarage Road and back. With no other Watford mates, no real connection with the town, no money and no transport I was unable to go to matches and in danger of upgrading my Commodore status to 'once, twice, three times a decade'. My sole consolation was the occasional pilgrimage to nearby Aldershot whenever the two clubs were in the same division and, even then, every visit culminated in an away defeat.

Inevitably, faced with the dual heartbreak of unrequited love and diminishing returns, a young man's head starts to turn. Because of my Dad's allegiance to them and my fond memories of Best, Law and Charlton and the 1968 European Cup final, Manchester United were, and still are, my second team. I cheered on Tommy Docherty's exciting side, with contrasting emotions, in successive FA Cup finals in 1976 and 1977 and there was a real danger that I was about to spurn my first love and fall inexorably into the arms of a glamorous new mistress.

What I needed was someone who could convince me that my heart should remain loyal to the club which had nurtured my nascent love for the game and had been a constant companion through thick and largely thin. Step forward Luther Blissett.

In 1978 with signs that Watford's fortunes were finally on an upturn under the aegis of Graham Taylor and a 31-year-old now answering to the name of Elton John, a promising League Cup run had led us to Old Trafford and the showdown which would test my loyalty and affection to the limit. It was a no brainer in the end. After Joe Jordan had put United ahead, Luther's deadly double had me levitating off the sofa face contorted, fists clenched in that bizarre mixture of euphoria and disbelief which only football can serve up. And so United were the bridesmaids as Watford and I walked up the aisle from that day forward, for better for worse, for richer for poorer, in sickness and in health, to love and to cherish, till death us do part.

Okay so United have gone on to win titles, doubles, trebles and everything else on offer while playing some of the most exciting football ever seen in this country and I'm delighted for them every time, but the heart rules the head and it's a decision I have never regretted. To draw an analogy from a popular television sitcom of the time, United were Penelope Keith but I had Felicity Kendal.

However, like a man condemned to a lengthy stretch inside, life itself conspired to restrict my conjugal visits. By the early 1980s I was an impoverished aspiring broadcaster at college in Portsmouth, further away from The Vic and spending what little money I had following the likes of Echo and the Bunnymen, Teardrop Explodes and The Smiths rather than eleven men in yellow. It's a little strange to recall now that the lure of post punk miserablism was greater than that of the most exciting period in Watford's history but, at the time, attending gigs in Pompey and Guildford was the cheaper and less complicated option. I did manage the odd excursion to Watford in that period which included a top flight encounter between the Horns and Swansea which had been a Fourth Division fixture only four years previously.

Largely though I was relying on radio and TV to follow the promotion to Division One, an amazing first season in the top flight and the subsequent European adventure which had been secured by that second place finish. While some lucky Watford fans were flying out to Kaiserslautern, Sofia and Prague in the early part of the *annus mirabilis* that was the 1983-84 season, I was entombed in a depressingly soulless Pompey semi with a lumpy landlady and her curry eating dog, neither of whom were particularly impressed with having their lounge taken over on weekday nights by a spotty, streak of piss with a yellow and red scarf and six pack of Harp lager. I did once manage to escape this suburban straitjacket and was on hand to witness one of the best goals ever scored at The Vic. Sadly, this came from an opposing player, as Glenn Hoddle's sublime chip helped Spurs to a 3-2 win that autumn.

For me, George Orwell comes a very distant second whenever anyone mentions 1984. It began inauspiciously enough for me, marooned on the Hampshire coast following the club's fortunes via Radio 2. One Saturday in January I recall tuning in to the car radio and being informed by the presenter that Watford had scored at Coventry through Steve Sherwood. In the age old tradition of smart-arse students who consider themselves to be world experts on subjects with which they have only the faintest grasp, I greeted this revelation with howls of derision.

'He doesn't know what he's bloody talking about, Sherwood's the goalkeeper. What kind of idiot would make a basic mistake like that.'

A subsequent visit to the reporter at Highfield Road confirmed two things. Firstly, that the Watford keeper had indeed scored with a mighty clearance and secondly that I was the idiot.

It was another inopportune time to be miles away from the action, as the seeds of another Watford cup run had begun that month with an astonishing and immensely pleasing third round replay success over Luton.

This was followed by victories over Charlton, Brighton and Birmingham, as we enjoyed the kind of generous cup draws which suggested our name might just be on the trophy. This reached its zenith with the news that, rather than Everton or Southampton, our semi-final opponents would be Third Division Plymouth Argyle.

On the day of the semi-final I found myself in the some-

what surreal situation of sitting in the Institute for Contemporary Arts in The Mall. This was not for an exhibition of 20th
century Peruvian tribal sculpture or a screening of films from
Federico Fellini's neorealist period, but a talk by TV producer
Gerry Anderson (no relation, sadly) who created Thunderbirds,
Stingray and Captain Scarlet, the wonderful action based puppet shows which had lit up my childhood.

Even in the presence of such a giant of post war culture, I
found it difficult to concentrate and enjoy the presentation; my
mind was racing elsewhere especially as the clock ticked round
to 3pm and they were kicking off at Villa Park. My friend Ed
lightened the feelings of tension a little during the concluding
question and answer session, when he enquired whether Stingray's Troy Tempest had ended up marrying Marina or Atlanta
once he had hung up whatever submarine captains hang up.
Gerry Anderson, an understated and soft spoken man, main-
tained a straight face and a serious eye as he replied.

'I'm afraid it is our policy not to discuss the private lives of
the puppets.'

When the final applause had subsided I ran out of the ICA
and found the nearest television shop, so as to catch up with
events in the FA Cup.

Upon learning that big George Reilly had given us an early
lead, I leapt around like a demented punk fan, only to be ordered out of the store by an irate assistant who had somehow
worked out that I wasn't there to discuss the HP terms on the
latest Rediffusion set.

For the whole of the second half I stood outside in the
rain, peering through the window at the seemingly endless
rugby league and racing coverage, desperate for any update that
might appear on the screen. None were forthcoming, and so
this became another agonising wait for the teleprinter to deliver
its verdict and I was transported back 14 years to the Liverpool

game. Happily the outcome and the emotions were the same and I resolved to get myself to the final at Wembley if it was the last thing I ever did.

In the midst of all this euphoria was the rather more mundane reality of trying to gain a qualification which would help me achieve my longer term ambition of working as a broadcaster. To this end, I was sent on a student attachment to BBC Radio Bristol to gain some first-hand experience of life in a newsroom. This placement was due to end the day before the cup final, so I was relieved that, as long as I could get a ticket, I would be back in time for the game.

Half my mind was set on trying to do a good job and curry favour with the radio station while the other half was fixated on the increasingly fruitless search for a Wembley ticket as every avenue turned quickly into a cul-de-sac. I had almost given up hope when my Dad called out of the blue on the Wednesday before the game to say that he had finally tracked down a couple via the dodgy mate of some business colleague, although they would cost the then staggering sum of £35 apiece. I solemnly promised to pay him back when I got some cash and returned to my apprenticeship with renewed vigour. I have to confess he never did get his money, but I was able to repay him in kind years later, by sneaking him into the press box for a Manchester United game for what was to be his first and only ever visit to Old Trafford.

News that I would be going to the final must have inspired me because, on the last day of my stint at BBC Radio Bristol, the lugubrious news editor declared himself sufficiently impressed by my efforts to offer me a further opportunity to show what I could do.

'I'm delighted to announce that we'd like to extend your stay by a couple of days so that you can work as a runner on this weekend's breakfast programme. I'm afraid there's no money in it but it'll be a great experience and you can help out with the sport if you like.'

My response took him rather by surprise.

'Thanks very much, it's a wonderful offer but I can't do it, I simply can't.'

He looked up, no doubt expecting me to announce sombrely that a dearly beloved, aged relative had suddenly passed away and that I had to dash back for the funeral.

'It's the FA Cup final tomorrow, my team Watford are playing Everton. I've waited all my life for this and my Dad's got a couple of tickets. I have to be at Wembley to cheer the boys on as it's probably the only time they'll ever get there. Sorry.'

It was a decision which threatened to derail my journalistic career, since news eventually filtered back to my lecturers in Portsmouth that I had snubbed this golden opportunity and they were less than impressed.

However, nothing could have been further from my mind as my father and I drove to Harrow On The Hill station for the short tube journey to Wembley Park. The radio stations had been playing *I'm Still Standing* and *I Guess That's Why They Call It The Blues* all morning, and you really did get the impression that every fan in the country, barring Evertonians, were behind us. Years later I learned that a mate of mine who supports Liverpool had spent the whole day dressed from head to foot in yellow just to wind up the blue half of Merseyside. When you stop to consider it, this was no mean feat; I mean how many people can lay their hands on a pair of yellow trousers at the drop of a hat?

When we walked out onto the platform, every shirt was of that hue as we were engulfed by a joyous tide of Hornets fans. At the next stop this mighty yellow sea was interrupted by two tiny specks of blue as a couple of startled Everton fans boarded the train. One wag couldn't resist the temptation to have a go.

'Is that all you've brought down with you?' he jeered, to mountainous applause.

To be at the tunnel end of Wembley on that day made up for all my years of non attendance at Watford matches. I was scarcely able to believe that, less than a decade after suffering mediocre Fourth Division tosh at Aldershot's Recreation Ground, I was at the FA Cup final watching Watford among 40,000 others trying to suck the ball into the net during the hugely promising opening 20 minutes. The real fairy story, of course, didn't transpire as Everton won thanks to a first half goal by Graeme Sharp and a second half foul by Andy Gray. I've since encountered Gray several times in my travels as a reporter but, thus far resisted the temptation to verbally harangue him about his dreadful assault on Steve Sherwood.

My strongest image of the day was the players applauding the crowd at the end clutching their losers' medals to a rousing chorus of 'we'll support you evermore'. For those of us who follow clubs outside the ever decreasing elite, these moments are almost as infrequent as Halley's Comet, but light up our footballing stratosphere just as brightly.

The other reason I have for looking back on 1984 so fondly is that it was the year that I became a fully fledged sports broadcaster. Initially this appeared to be an unlikely outcome, since my cup final decision almost came back to haunt me. I failed the course and was told by my lecturers in no uncertain terms that I was not deemed employment material. Happily my local radio station County Sound Radio in Guildford, with whom I had also had an attachment, had rather more faith in me and I covered my first games for them in the autumn, ironically at Aldershot's Recreation Ground.

In April of the following year I landed a full time job as the sports editor at Signal Radio in Stoke-On-Trent, having turned down a place at Chiltern in Dunstable; this, of course, had the tantalising prospect of having Watford on its patch, but it was a news reporter's job and I wanted to concentrate on sport.

The downside to being lucky enough to earn a living watching football is that you can virtually kiss goodbye to any notion of following your chosen club, since you will be working every Saturday and most midweeks too. So once again I was in Hornets exile as I threw myself into my new role as the presenter of Signal's Saturday afternoon sports show, but my allegiance to the club was to bear wonderful and unexpected fruit during my first year in the Potteries. One of the lads who used to help me out on the programme casually announced one day that he'd been to college with a girl who was a Watford supporter and that she was coming to visit him that weekend.

It was fate that Carolyn and I would end up together, since her background bore uncanny similarities to my own. She had been born in Bushey but moved away at an early age while still remaining loyal to her native town club.

Like me she had had scant opportunities to watch them, but had won an FA Cup final ticket in a raffle and travelled down from Manchester on her own to watch the game. She may even have been one of the yellow army in the same carriage as me on the tube from Harrow On The Hill. We were married in 1993 and have two daughters.

Shortly after we met, Carolyn won a place at Watford College which started her successful career in theatre marketing and she became a regular at The Vic while I remained in exile, although at least I could now justifiably claim that a piece of my heart was there. Every now and then when I wasn't working I would drive south in my Fiat Panda and join her for a game. The most notable of these was the 1-0 victory over Manchester United when the winner was scored by 18-year-old Iwan Roberts, who I later got to know via his role as a TV and radio pundit and is a prime contender for the 'nicest man in football' award.

Although radio was a new medium for me in terms of my career, it remained the primary source of Watford info in the days when there were still very few games shown live on TV. I recall Carolyn and I spending a particularly miserable night in a pub car park in Stoke listening to commentary of the 1986 FA Cup quarter-final against Liverpool when we were three minutes from glory only to lose out to Ian Rush's extra time winner.

Worse was to befall me the next season when another cup run did take us to the semi-final and a showdown with Spurs at the scene of our 1984 triumph, Villa Park. I wasn't there of course, I was 40 miles up the M6 in the main studio at Signal presenting a four-hour sports show and linking to our reporters covering the local clubs Stoke, Port Vale, Crewe and Stafford Rangers while keeping an eye on scores elsewhere via the BBC's Ceefax service. After taking an early update from Stoke's match at Derby I glanced at the screen to be greeted with the horrifying caption under Tottenham's name.

Hodge 11

I picked up in a cheerily upbeat fashion as befitted my supposedly impartial status.

'FA Cup news from Villa Park. Spurs have taken an 11th minute lead in the semi-final against Watford through Steve Hodge. The Hornets have Gary Plumley, a wine bar owner, in goal after an injury crisis and he's been beaten early on.'

All the time I was suppressing the urge to say: 'Bollocks, bollocks, bollocks.'

A mere ad break later it got worse.

C. Allen 13

'Spurs go two up at Villa Park through their top scorer Clive Allen. It already looks like Spurs are on their way to Wembley.'

'Bugger, bugger, shit, shit, bugger.'

And then...

P. Allen 35

By this time I had lost the will to live, but still had to valiantly attempt to maintain a professional interest in Crewe's home game against Lincoln. The fact Watford's consolation goal in the eventual 4-1 defeat was scored by another Allen (Malcolm) seemed merely to add insult to injury.

Unfortunately Sod's Law dictated that, as my broadcasting career took off, my opportunities to watch Watford remained slim. I'd landed a fantastic job at the national agency Independent Radio News in London but my arrival coincided with the 1988 relegation season, and, while it was great on a personal note to be covering matches at places like Old Trafford, Anfield and Highbury, there was little demand for Division Two football so I couldn't even watch my own club professionally.

Fortunately I found an ally in a new workmate called Tony Darkins, a lifelong Hornets fan who lived in Northwood and had been a contemporary of Elton John at school in Pinner. When my schedule allowed, we would dash off to catch the Metropolitan Line to a midweek game and I would crash at his place afterwards. I remember we once got stuck on a tube somewhere between Wembley Park and Watford, and arrived a minute or so late for a cup game against Newcastle. Literally the first thing we saw as we got into the ground was the ball flying past Dave Beasant and into the net and joined the celebrations even though we didn't have a clue how it got there. We later discovered it had been a Neil Redfearn free kick which, I think I'm right in saying, went in before a single Newcastle player had touched the ball in the game.

The same season I persuaded my editor at IRN to allow me to cover the play-off ties against Blackburn, travelling to Ewood Park for a grim but gritty goalless draw, but then despairing as Watford lost on away goals in the return at The Vic. After the second game I had to remain impartial but it was difficult to enthuse about Rovers' success while nursing a heavy heart. I do recall speaking to their striker Simon Garner, which was notable for being the one and only time I have ever interviewed a footballer while he was smoking a fag.

To be honest I've never really enjoyed mixing business and 'pleasure' in this way, since your professional duties must always take precedence over your emotional feelings. I once had to tell BBC Radio 5Live listeners how thoroughly well deserved a Luton equaliser was at Vicarage Road; what they didn't know was that I had my fingers crossed behind my back as I delivered the words. I was also behind the microphone when we lost to Southampton in the 2003 FA Cup semi-final at Villa Park; fortunately the Saints players I interviewed afterwards were unaware that I was wearing a Watford top under my shirt.

The one occasion when I could really enjoy the dual role of reporter and supporter was against Liverpool at Anfield in our first Premier League season in 1999, when Tommy Mooney scored the winner. As well as match updates I was providing off-air commentary on the match which stations could use later in their programmes and when the goal went in the commentary sounded something like this:

'Kennedy plays in the free kick... Liverpool can't clear it... falls for Moooneeeeeeyyyyy!!! Sensation at Anfield... Watford have the lead against Liverpool in front of the Kop... and Tommy Mooney is engulfed in a seas of yellow shirts.'

On this occasion, the one-sided hyperbole was completely justifiable, since the goal would have been greeted rapturously by most neutrals and Watford's victory was to be the big story of the day. During that season I was also on hand to describe Allan Smart's winner against Chelsea as well as less auspicious visits to Spurs and Bradford which contributed to the eventual bottom place and relegation.

The very fact that Watford were back in the big time had

at least allowed me the chance to cast a professional eye over them and I always find it odd when people suggest it would be better for the smaller clubs not to reach the Premier League, since they are bound to go straight back down. To paraphrase Humphrey Bogart in the closing scene of Casablanca:

'We'll always have Anfield.'

Happily I was not in the Wembley press box during the play-off final against Bolton earlier that year, having decided that maintaining impartiality would be akin to attempting to remain dispassionate on your own wedding day. Besides, I was mindful that if Watford won, radio listeners needed to be spared the sound of a grown man blubbing on air.

It was of course a highly emotional experience for everyone involved but I had special reasons for walking up Wembley Way with a strange sense of destiny. My father had died in March of that year at his home on the Spanish island of Gran Canaria. He was 63. My sister, brother and I flew out for the funeral; it was a secular affair in which I read a light hearted poem he had written years earlier about his dreams and aspirations, which included a line about how one day he hoped to see Watford win the FA Cup. We also played some of his favourite music, including the ever cheerful Leonard Cohen, and were all then invited to write a personal tribute on a piece of paper which would be dropped into the coffin and cremated with him be-fore his ashes were scattered over the Atlantic.

Although my Dad had taken me to my first football match and engendered a love of the sport which was to shape my future career, he had not played an enormous part in my life since my parents split up when I was 12. At that time, especially in stockbroker Surrey, there was still a social stigma attached to divorce and I think I was one of only two or three kids out of 90 in my year at secondary school from a broken home. The situation wasn't helped by the fact that he remarried soon afterwards and, although he looked after us financially and visited at weekends, a gaping chasm had begun to develop between his life and ours. In 1986 he emigrated to the Canary Island and so, for the final 13 years of his life I only saw him once, maybe twice, a year.

Of course I was sad to lose him, but I never had that 'empty chair in the corner of the room' heartache which makes bereavement so unbearably tough for most people. And so when it came to choosing my parting words, I wasn't feeling particularly inspired. The fact that the funeral fell on April Fool's Day and was largely attended by people who I had never met, seemed to add to the awkward nature of the situation and, for one of the few occasions in my life, I was actually lost for words. He was more like a close mate to me than a father really, so in the end, I scribbled this rather prosaic epitaph:

'Don't worry Dad, I'll get them into the Premiership.'

At the time it seemed an absurdly fanciful notion since Watford had won only one of their previous eight games but, although I am the least religious or superstitious person you will ever meet, I have to admit something rather magical started to happen from the moment I arrived home. Tommy Mooney somehow transformed himself from a man hopelessly chasing bovine livestock with a four stringed instrument into a yellow shirted, tubbier, older Michael Owen; scoring seven goals in an extraordinary end of season run-in which yielded 22 points from a possible 24 along with fifth place in the table and a tilt at the promised land.

Meanwhile, in that very El Dorado that we were hoping to reach, Manchester United were sweeping all before them on the road to the treble. I was working at Old Trafford on the day they clinched the league title against Spurs, and so missed Watford's slender 1-0 win over Birmingham in the first leg of the play-off semi-finals.

Four days later for the return at St Andrews, Carolyn was away on business so I couldn't even go to the pub to watch the game since I was housebound looking after our two-year-old daughter Becky. Alas, my babysitting efforts that evening will not be found among the pages in any of Penelope Leach's estimable baby and childcare guides.

My friend Nod (don't ask), an Arsenal fan, came round to offer moral support and we settled down in front of the telly with a seemingly inexhaustible supply of beer, as Becky occupied herself with her toys in a corner of the room.

Although Watford held a one-goal lead from the first leg we were very much underdogs and, as the whistle blew for the start of the game, I said to Nod: 'If we can just prevent an early goal and start to frustrate them, we've got a chance.'

About 120 seconds later I was on the floor, head in hands, as Dele Adebola's goal levelled up the tie on aggregate. What followed was the most gut wrenching, nerve wracking, stomach churning two hours I have ever spent watching a game of football. It's on nights such as these that what starts out as entertainment slowly metamorphoses into the kind of mental torture that would have been deemed unduly harsh in the days of the Spanish Inquisition.

Every time Becky would doze off on her play mat, the latest heroic Alec Chamberlain save would see me leap six feet into the air with a guttural cry of such ear piercing intensity that she would awake screaming as if in the grip of some apocalyptic nightmare. This only served to further shred my nerves and my patience. I would pick her up and try to rock her back to sleep in my arms, but yet another agonising close call from Birmingham would send my body arcing into spasms and hers flying upward in the air landing back into my lap or onto the sofa amid more hysterical shrieking.

Unwilling to move her into her own cot for fear of missing

a second of the action, her yo-yo like momentum continued through the, thankfully goalless, extra time period.

The ensuing penalty shoot out merely increased the Torquemadan torture to previously unimaginable levels, until the final, glorious moment when Chambo scrambled away Chris Holland's spot kick.

In one of those other worldly, psychosomatic responses over which your body has no adequate control, I found myself standing on the coffee table my arms outstretched in a messianic pose, screaming 'yyyyesssssssssssssssssssssssssssssss' with a seismic ferocity of Krakatoan proportions which drowned out even the terrified cries of the toddler in the corner.

The next day Nod called to ask if I wanted to join him for lunch at a local cafe and clearly the events of the previous night had addled my brain to a greater degree than I had imagined.

'Sorry, I can't mate,' I said, following it up with the finest Freudian slip I have ever uttered, 'I've got to pick up Watford from nursery.'

I had to sober up quickly though because two days after that momentous night I was at Wembley covering United's FA Cup triumph, before flying to Barcelona to report on their astonishing last-minute Champions League final victory over Bayern Munich. When the interviews had been done and I had packed away my broadcasting kit, I stood in the media tribune at the Nou Camp and took a few moments to think about what this would have meant to my Dad, as the team he had supported all his life completed an unprecedented treble. I'm sure he would have been pleased and proud that I was there to witness it for him.

I was delighted for United too of course, but I spent the whole journey back thinking about the far more important matter of Watford's forthcoming play-off final against Bolton at Wembley and I swear that I have never been more relaxed ahead of a match of such magnitude. The events of the past few weeks had convinced me that there could only be one conceivable outcome and I never doubted for a moment that Watford would win.

My old mate Tony Darkins came to the game with Carolyn and me, and as we walked up Wembley Way I spotted someone I knew from Sky Sports who was conducting interviews with fans. He pointed the camera at me and I launched into an enthusiastic speech outlining how confident I was about the outcome.

Nicky Wright's breath-taking execution of the greatest goal ever scored at Wembley drove my optimism into undreamt of heights, and the moment when Allan Smart sealed it at the end is so indelibly etched on my memory that I can still feel the wave of ecstasy now. By the time the trophy was hoisted, the Bolton contingent had long gone and Wembley was a joyous semi-circle of red and yellow as the team embarked on a 200 metres rather than full lap of honour.

Five days earlier I had been at the Champions League final, and was lucky enough to have enjoyed a career which had taken me to World Cups, European Championships, Olympic Games, Rugby World Cups and world title fights, but as Graham Taylor led the players across to milk our applause, I remember thinking that I would gladly swap the lot for the sheer enjoyment of those 90 minutes of football. Once again I thought of my Dad and couldn't suppress the wryest of smiles; the silly old sod had managed to time his death so carelessly that, in the two months that followed it, he had missed United winning the treble, Watford reaching the Premier League at Wembley and even his favourite Scottish club Hibs running away with the First Division title. I realise that always being in the wrong place at the wrong time had become a family trait, but this was taking things too far.

But I was there when it mattered on that last day of May 1999 and after the team had finally disappeared back down the tunnel, Carolyn and I clambered our way across the emptying seats to the opposite side of the stadium and jumped into the press box. Luckily I knew the steward on the media room door from my frequent visits to the stadium, and she let us in to the complimentary bar to partake of a few celebratory beers, which tasted as good as any I've ever had before or since.

Carolyn eventually dragged me away from my fellow hacks at the bar, and as we drove home along the elevated section of the North Circular at Brent Cross, we caught up and pulled alongside the Watford team bus as it headed home. I leant drunkenly out of the passenger side window waving my scarf as Carolyn tooted the horn and some of the players waved back. Rarely had I had the chance to experience such boyish joys and so I make no excuse at all for how ridiculous I must have looked to my fellow motorists.

Seventeen years after guiding us into the top flight for the first time, Graham Taylor had done it again and I can still picture his smiling face at the front of the coach as we drove past. Like so many other Watford fans of my age, Graham had been the pivotal figure in all our finest footballing hours and it has been my privilege to get to know him a little during trips abroad with England when he was working for BBC Radio 5Live. He's always charming, intelligent and amusing company and while we were in Vienna in 2004 5Live's chief football correspondent Mike Ingham kindly invited me to an impromptu dinner in honour of Graham's 60th birthday which was a wonderful evening. I also had the bizarre experience of sharing a fondue with him, Terry Butcher and a few others after a game on a particularly freezing night in the Azerbaijan capital Baku.

My first encounter with Graham hadn't suggested that we would end up convivially spearing pieces of steak on the shores of the Caspian Sea. When he was manager at Aston Villa, I covered the climax of the 1989-90 season in which they lost out in a title battle with Liverpool and was at Highfield Road when Villa had played very poorly in a 2-0 defeat at Coventry which put a huge dent in their title aspirations. Graham was never one to shirk his media responsibilities and came out to give his reaction to the assembled radio reporters and, as was the protocol, the local radio guys would get the first crack of the whip after which time we could ask a few questions of our own.

I was becoming increasingly weary of the sycophantic line of questioning from the Midlands based reporters who seemed to be acting as apologists and so, when I got my chance, I waded in with both barrels.

'Graham, what would you say to people who now believe Villa's title hopes are over?'

His response was swift, concise and emphatic.

'Bollocks,' he said before bringing the interview to an abrupt end by storming off

This got picked up by the press, and the papers ran stories about Graham's 'eight letter response' amid suggestions that the pressure was beginning to get to him. The following day he appeared on a Granada football programme hosted by Clive Tyldesley who asked him to explain what had happened.

Graham claimed I had shoved a microphone under his nose and said something like: 'Well that's it, you've lost the title, what do you think of that?' and his terse reaction had been a reaction to my rude intrusion.

I was a little annoyed as this wasn't a fair representation of what had occurred and I wrote to him to clarify the position. Graham, to his eternal credit sent me a wonderful letter back insisting he was not having a go at me personally and that he perhaps should handle certain interview situations differently.

His final line was a classic.

'I could have given you a five-letter response meaning the same thing but as usual I tend to go on a bit.'

Later that year of course he became England manager and I covered virtually every game, home and away, in the ultimately fruitless bid to reach the 1994 World Cup. It was hard not to feel sorry for him the way things turned out and I certainly didn't enjoy, as some journalists clearly did, having to file highly critical reports of his international failures.

He never lost his sense of humour though, even in those dark days. On the eve of a crucial qualifier I interviewed him about the team's prospects, although I had clearly lost my bearings: 'Finally Graham, what sort of problems do you think the Swedish strikers will pose tomorrow night?' I enquired.

'None whatsoever, we're playing Norway,' he chuckled and walked off, leaving the howls of derision from my fellow reporters ringing in my ears.

Another example of Graham's good humour was when I interviewed him at Watford near the end of his second spell as manager at a time when things weren't going too well. My rare appearances at The Vic as a fan in that period had, more often than not, culminated in defeats and I mentioned to him afterwards that I felt a bit like an unlucky charm for the club.

'I don't get here that often which is probably just as well, because they never win when I come,' I told him.

His response came as quick as a flash.

'They never bloody win when I come either.'

As I was writing this chapter, Graham announced he was to stand down as non-executive chairman of the club, signalling the end of an era. The sooner a sculptor is contracted to start work on a permanent tribute to the great man, the better.

By the time Watford found themselves in the play-offs again, I had left IRN and was freelancing for Sky Sports, talkSPORT and the BBC among others and, on the day of the semi-final first leg at Crystal Palace I found myself at the Memorial Ground for a none too exotic end-of-season League Two encounter between Bristol Rovers and Macclesfield. It was one of those games where only an unlikely sequence of events could render it remotely newsworthy; ie Macclesfield would go down if they lost, seven other teams won, Jupiter was in conjunction with Saturn and the bonus ball number was 17.

Unfortunately, as a freelancer it is neither professional nor profitable to turn down work on the grounds that you would much rather be somewhere else, and so I arrived at Rovers' ground about three hours before kick off, hoping that I could at least catch the Crystal Palace v Watford game, which started at lunchtime and was live on Sky. Unfortunately the ground, which is primarily a rugby arena, was near deserted when I got there and had none of the normal press facilities where you could pull up a chair, have a cup of tea and watch the early game on TV.

Eventually I persuaded a steward to let me into the empty Rovers supporters club bar which had a small telly in the corner and I was able to take in the goalless first half. The room slowly began to fill as the fans headed for the bar, largely ignoring the twitchy figure hunched over the TV. There were around a dozen enjoying a drink when Marlon King's opener had me leaping upwards and screaming with joy. When I'd recovered I looked round to see a group of less than approving Rovers fans who clearly felt I had taken leave of my senses.

'Ahh... erm...er...sorry lads...Watford fan...one up at Palace,' I mumbled apologetically as they returned to their beers.

By the time Ashley Young's sumptuous free kick raged into the Palace net there were probably 30 stunned faces looking on at my latest bout of gymnastics and when Matthew Spring applied the *coup de grace* I was lying on my back in the middle of the floor punching the air, prompting a ripple of applause from the Bristolians. Only when I finally got up did I realise that I had but minutes left before my match preview was due to go out live on air, and I ran out of the bar, into the stadium and leapt into my press seat to deliver a minute or so of high octane drivel which, between the puffing and panting, can't have made an awful lot of sense given my hyperactive demeanour. I can imagine the listeners' reaction. 'That bloke sounds pretty excited about the Bristol Rovers v Macclesfield game and it hasn't even kicked off yet.'

Once again my wife's high-flying career got in the way of my ambitions to go to Cardiff for the final against Leeds. She was away on business in America that weekend and so I had to endure a further bout of neglectful single parenting with Becky having now been joined by my second daughter Katie who was four. Once again I celebrated another joyous afternoon, thankfully without attracting the attention of the social services.

This second stab at life in the Premier League gave me the chance to commentate on Watford games for Sky Sports' *Football First* programme for which I had been working for a couple of years and I was behind the mic for the goalless draw at home to Spurs, a 2-0 defeat at Aston Villa and a 4-1 reverse at Middlesbrough. The highlight though was the home game against Wigan for which I was on the commentary gantry alongside former Nottingham Forest striker Garry Birtles, while Carolyn, Becky and Katie all tagged along to watch from the front row of the Rous Stand.

About ten minutes before kick-off it started to rain and the heavens remained defiantly open for the next hour, quickly rendering the pitch more suited to cultivating rice than playing football, although Emile Heskey for the visitors and Watford's Tamas Priskin both managed to score in the game of water polo that ensued.

At half-time the two managers walked out onto the sodden

pitch to assess the situation with Aidy Boothroyd delighting the crowd by plopping the ball down into a puddle and then firing it into the empty net.

Eleven minutes into the second half the referee took the sensible decision to abandon the game but, because our commentary was being played out live to foreign stations, Garry and I had to carry on talking until we were told by the director that the feed had ended. And so, basically, we spent the next ten minutes or so commentating on the falling rain, a task which was helped by the Vicarage Road DJ who started playing records which reflected the weather such as *Sunshine On A Rainy Day* by Zoe and REM's *Nightswimming*. Like me, Garry's a big music fan and we started making our own suggestions in the commentary, like *I Can't Stand The Rain* by Anne Peebles, *It's Raining Again* by Supertramp and Bob Dylan's *Buckets Of Rain*. At one stage Garry brilliantly requested anything by Wet Wet Wet. Fortunately we got the call to down our microphones before it all got too absurd.

I then had to conduct post-match interviews with Aidy and Paul Jewell and by the time I was reunited with my family, the kids were cursing me for forcing them to endure a monsoon of such biblical proportions. They had got absolutely drenched throughout the game and then had to sit in the car in their soaking clothes for an hour as I finished working.

Our second attempt to transmit the love of the club to our offspring was nearly as unsuccessful. Although the weather was fine when we took them along to a Championship game against Stoke in 2008 the match was anything but. John Eustace was sent off in the first half of a very physical encounter which finished goalless thanks to Darius Henderson's penalty miss. Despite their glee at the barrage of abuse being directed at referee Rob Styles, there was little here to spark the passions of two girls aged six and 11.

You can talk all you like about a gritty display and a hard fought point against high-flying opposition in difficult circumstances, but for them a soft seat in front of the telly would have represented a better way to spend an afternoon.

Scarred by these twin experiences, Becky has little interest in football although, bless her heart, if push came to shove, she would declare herself to be a Hornets fan out of blind loyalty. Katie supports Arsenal which is fair enough given that she was born within the Highbury catchment area and the fact that her first visit to the Emirates resulted in a thrilling 6-2 win for the Gunners over Blackburn. Sadly these days the likes of Watford can no longer compete for a child's imagination in the same way as they had when I shunned Manchester United in the 1970s.

My life since then has dictated that I will always be touching from a distance as a Hornets fan, but one thing's for certain; I will never let go.

John Anderson is a freelance sports broadcaster and commentator who works for Sky Sports, talkSPORT and the BBC among many others. He has covered six Olympic Games, three World Cups and five European Championships in a 30-year career. He is also the author of the humorous memoir *A Great Face for Radio*. You can follow him on Twitter @GreatFaceRadio

6

Like the break-up of any relationship, when a football manager leaves a club the split can be harmonious or bitter.

Adam Leventhal talks to Brendan Rodgers and Malky Mackay, two young managers who coped with extraordinary turmoil during their spells at Watford.

Many fans have been slow to forgive them for leaving. Some still haven't.

These interviews explain some of the conditions they were working under, why they left and offer an insight into the fickle nature of football.

For the fans, a club is for life but for managers things can change in the blink of an eye.

A QUESTION OF LOYALTY

BY ADAM LEVENTHAL

The loyalty is only one way.
The loyalty is with the supporters.
Brendan Rodgers, 2012

O nce again in the summer of 2012, Brendan Rodgers was
on the move. This time swapping Swansea, who exceeded
expectations in their debut season in the Premier League, for
one of the most successful clubs in the world, Liverpool.

It was a transition widely accepted and understood; it made
sense for a highly-regarded manager to move up the Premier
League pecking order to an historic club in need of a lift.

However, that relatively smooth repotting can trace its roots
back to a seed that had been sewn in a bed of controversy in
2009 when the issue of loyalty in football had been laid bare.

Three years earlier, the upgrade was less economy to first
class, more window to aisle seat, when Rodgers swapped
Watford for Reading despite having been at Vicarage Road for
only five-and-a-half months.

Rodgers calls that first summer of movement 'the defining
moment' of his professional life. He confesses that a managerial career that had only just started almost ended then.

'In all my time at Watford I was never left to walk alone,'
says the Northern Irishman. 'The disappointment is how that
ended and I can never take that back and that is certainly a

regret. I made a mistake, I shouldn't have left but it's been a great learning curve.'

This chapter features two exclusive interviews, one with Rodgers as he looks back at his short time at the club and the departure that upset so many Watford supporters; the second with his successor Malky Mackay, who reviews his time in charge and gives an insight into the financial uncertainty that affected not only his tenure but also led ultimately to his exit.

* * *

Watford Football Club and Jose Mourinho have two things in common. Both can be considered special, and both gave Brendan Rodgers an opportunity to advance his career. On November 28, 2008, Watford appointed the former Chelsea youth and reserve team coach, who had been promoted by Mourinho at Stamford Bridge, to succeed Aidy Boothroyd.

The initiation of his career at Watford is a link that Rodgers is prepared to talk about not only with warmth but also with an olive branch to hand so he can counter the stinging criticism that followed his departure after less than six months.

At the time of his appointment, being described as a Mourinho-moulded disciple didn't sit as comfortably as perhaps the public was lead to believe.

He says: 'My actual methods were born before I met Jose, my philosophy was already formed. What he gave me was an opportunity, he believed in my way of working. At the beginning I was a little frustrated that people wanted to speak about Jose, but I understood why they did.'

He succeeded Boothroyd, who had enjoyed comparisons with Mourinho too. He was a young, positive, scarf-wearing maverick who had originally identified Rodgers as someone who was worth snapping up.

'It started back a year earlier,' says Rodgers. 'I was a good friend of Aidy's and he wanted to try to change the style [at Watford]. He spoke to me about becoming the number two to try to take the team in a different direction.'

Rodgers says he thought 'long and hard' before turning down the opportunity to assist Boothroyd. It proved to be a key moment in his relationship with the Watford hierarchy.

'The board started to understand who I was, but after some thinking time I decided to stay at Chelsea. So I suppose my name was born to the board at that time. They had a good amount of information about me before contacting Peter Kenyon when they wanted to speak again.'

Meanwhile, after Boothroyd was sacked following a 4-3 home defeat against Blackpool, Malky Mackay was promoted from first team coach to caretaker manager.

As the Tangerines returned to the Riviera of the North, Watford's former centre half was about to take his first spin of the managerial roulette wheel.

'I was at the cinema watching *James Bond: Casino Royale* with the family,' recalls Mackay of the day he was asked to step up. 'When I came out and turned my phone on I had 38 missed calls from people at the club telling me to come into the office. I was thinking, "My God, what have I done?" When I got in, I was told I was going to be taking over.'

Mackay was in charge for five matches including two wins, one at Swansea in the Carling Cup, the other a 3-0 victory at Vicarage Road against QPR. Having been interviewed for the vacant position, he was told after the win over QPR that he wouldn't be keeping the job on a permanent basis but would be holding the reigns for Rodgers when Watford travelled to Bristol City.

'I was delighted I had that month,' he says. 'It gave me a look at what it was like managing a football club. It was like

opening Pandora's box to see if I liked it and I got the chance
to do the things you don't need to do as an assistant. I enjoyed
it and it meant that after Brendan left I was ready.'

Although he'd been competing for the job, Rodgers decided
to keep Mackay on his staff after doing some work James Bond
would have been proud of. Behind-the-scenes reconnaissance
was necessary to check that Mackay would be worth keeping on
having been loyal to Boothroyd as a player and coach.

'Brendan took advice and didn't move me on, he got my
loyalty and I'll be forever grateful,' explains Mackay. 'We
became good friends and had similar ideas and I kept him
informed about the lie of the land.'

Rodgers did have to negotiate a sensitive situation, as he
puts it, with Boothroyd once he'd taken over. They didn't speak
at the time but did get an opportunity to resolve any lingering
differences at close quarters in the summer of 2011.

The two managers went on an expedition to Kilimanjaro to
raise money for the Marie Curie cancer charity. There's something quite symbolic about a man and his successor scaling
great heights together. As Rodgers says: 'Aidy knows I'm an
honest guy and we shared a tent going up Kilimanjaro. We were
close enough to be in a two-man tent and that wouldn't have
happened if you've not got a friendship.'

When Rodgers took over Watford, they were at ground level.
Survival was the aim, with the club on the precipice, just above
the relegation zone in 21st position in the Championship.

Before he could even begin to look upwards, Rodgers had
to prevent the fall. He'd been rubbing shoulders with Chelsea's
millionaires, now he needed to sprinkle some of that stardust
on his new squad.

'The first talk with the players was exciting and I made it
clear the first thing I wanted to ensure was communication,'
Rodgers says. 'I'd polished up a philosophy that they would

enjoy and I promised I would be open and speak to them as men.'

His philosophy was to dominate with the ball, but with regular penetration, a model that would later see Swansea rise from the Championship to Premier League. Rodgers believed it would work, even among the muck and nettles of a relegation scrap in the Championship, but patience would be needed.

'It would be difficult for me to get them to train one way and then play a different way on a Saturday, so there was only going to be one football philosophy that would be drip fed on a daily basis,' he says.

The first time Watford's fans saw Rodgers' new model was against Doncaster Rovers. He recalls that replacing the straight line approach of previous years with the aim of joining the dots more regularly raised a few eyebrows.

'I remember a real poignant moment. The goalkeeper rolled it out and then there were four passes and I could sense the feeling amongst the crowd growing a little uncertain and the trepidation.'

One of the challenges was to instill confidence in both the crowd and the players. One of the methods Rodgers revealed he used was imagining that a person had the words 'MAKE ME FEEL IMPORTANT' tattooed on their forehead.

Rodgers wanted to put his own indelible mark on a beleaguered squad, creating a high-performance environment with motivation as a key building block.

'If you look at the top of the pyramid, what is success?' asks Rodgers. 'Success comes from confidence, which comes from consistency. An open, honest relationship can make them get better and feel good about themselves. I've never seen anyone in the world not perform well when they're feeling good, it's simple human needs. They're not just footballers, they're people.'

Changing personnel was on the manager's agenda but above him departures weren't far away either. A week into the job chairman Graham Simpson resigned following an extraordinary general meeting on December 1. It proved to be an early blow at an unexpected time for a fledgling manager, who thought highly of the man who had appointed him.

'Graham Taylor had told me when you're a young manager it's important not only to pick the right club but the right chairman, and that stuck with me,' Rodgers recalls. 'Graham Simpson had shown that he believed in young managers, having brought in Aidy and then me.

'In the middle of a training session the chief executive Mark Ashton interrupted and said "I don't want you to panic, everything will be okay, the chairman has just resigned," so of course you panic. So that was the only period where I thought, "has this been the right move and the right club to come to?"'

The impact of that uncertainty was reflected on the field with only three league wins from Rodgers's opening ten matches and a slip into the relegation zone by the end of January. But there would soon be an upturn in fortunes.

From February distance grew between the relegation zone and Watford. Although a Valentine's day meeting with Chelsea ended in a 3-1 defeat to his former employers and ended the season's FA Cup run at the fifth round stage, it started what would prove to be Rodgers's best run at the club. Watford won five of their next six matches including wins over Swansea, Blackpool, Crystal Palace, Charlton and Nottingham Forest.

'From then on, what was great for me was the confidence that was building within the players that the possession game could be effective with enough penetration,' Rodgers says, 'so I could see the players were going into games with real confidence that they could beat anyone.'

Promotion was always going to be out of reach that season,

however Rodgers was keen for promotion of another kind. For years the television cameras at Vicarage Road had been housed in the Rous Stand facing the now largely condemned East Stand. Rodgers saw no sense in that. 'It wasn't an image that the club stood for. It was a great club, a good community club. What was being projected was of an empty stand and an old run-down stadium. So I got the cameras to go over to the empty stand so at least when we were promoting the club and we had live games the cameras were focussing on the great parts of the club and great supporters.'

Watford finished the season with victory over Derby, leaving them 12 points away from the drop in a comfortable mid-table position. All seemed bright for the future.

'I remember walking around Vicarage Road with my kids, we finished 13th, had become one as a club, Graham Taylor was back involved,' says Rodgers. 'I had a great relationship with Elton John, who was an iconic figure at the club and whom I spoke regularly to once or twice a week, the supporters had an identity with the team. We grew together.'

That growth under his stewardship was soon to stop. The link with his former club Reading had been growing stronger as Steve Coppell departed at the end of the season. Nevertheless, Rodgers dismissed the speculation with these now infamous words in an interview with the *Watford Observer*: 'When I am asked about other clubs, people are questioning my integrity and one thing I have mentioned is I always have integrity. I am loyal and find it disloyal when I am asked about other clubs when I am the Watford manager. There is nothing that has changed in that respect.'

However, with Watford's Premier League parachute payments soon to evaporate, Rodgers admits that talks about available cash began to lead him off course and his mind began to drift along the M4.

'I spoke with a few people internally regarding finances, I knew it was going to be tight. My heart overruled my head. I felt Reading were a club that could fast track me and give me a chance of managing in the Premier League.'

So Rodgers went against his plan to continue 'learning the ropes at Watford' with his 'L plates firmly on' as he describes it, and chose to leave after just five-and-a-half months in charge. Cue the backlash.

Watford supporters were quick to remind him of the words 'integrity' and 'loyalty' which he had spoken about with some passion just days before. He refutes that he was 'leading supporters up the garden path', publicly saying one thing and secretly plotting another. 'That's definitely not the case,' he insists. Overall, however, he is now comfortable admitting that he shouldn't have made the decision to leave Watford.

'Looking back it turned out to be a decision that wasn't right and I could understand the hostility of the supporters,' he concedes. 'I'd probably given them a little bit of hope that we could move forward together and before they knew it I was away and had left them on their own again. I regretted the decision to go because I needed time to grow as a manager and at that time I couldn't have been at a better club than Watford. I should have continued with that.'

Malky Mackay learned of this latest managerial departure thanks to a call from Rodgers who told him that compensation had been agreed and he was leaving. Mackay says he was 'shocked' but he says he knew it was his time to step up and get the job on a full-time basis.

'I had a very good understanding of where the club was and a knowledge of the players, how the club worked, how it needed to work and how we should play. I don't think anyone at the time knew more about the club than me. I nailed the interview,' says Mackay.

He was officially given the job on June 15 and set about establishing a structure that would ensure survival in the league for the forthcoming season with the club's financial concerns becoming ever clearer.

Working with John Stephenson, the head of football business, Mackay knew that the model would have to be based on 'trading up' by unearthing rough diamonds and selling them on, while also giving youth a chance.

One such diamond was Danny Graham, who'd arrived from Carlisle on a free transfer. It was a deal that was agreed during Rodgers's reign and was a signing that would serve Watford well: in the striker's first season he finished top scorer with 14 league goals.

However, soon Mackay was told there needed to be a 'fire sale', with 'players being sold left, right and centre'. He turned to the loan market to try to plug the gaps left in the squad.

Henri Lansbury, from Watford's training ground neighbours Arsenal, hopped over the hedge at London Colney and joined the Hornets for a season, playing an influential role in midfield. He was one of two players to arrive from the higher echelons of the Premier League.

The second was Manchester United's Tom Cleverley, who'd been on the verge of joining Leicester City when Watford heard that the deal was off. It meant that Mackay made a call to Sir Alex Ferguson, who was a good friend of his father's from their days at Queens Park together. Mackay and Sir Alex agreed a season-long loan but the arrangement wasn't all that straightforward. Watford's financial constraints meant every penny had to be accounted for.

Due to a misunderstanding over a loan fee, Watford soon had to acknowledge that there wasn't the money available to take Cleverley for a full season, as Mackay explains: 'I wasn't looking forward to the second phone call. I called him [Sir

Alex] and told him the situation; he said "Okay, just take him for half a season." I then relayed that to the chief executive and he told me we didn't even have the money for half the season and it was at that point I almost swallowed my tongue. This is horrendous, I thought.'

It meant Mackay had to make a third awkward phone call to the most respected manager in the game, pleading poverty.

Fortunately, Sir Alex continued to understand Watford's plight. Mackay made a promise to the Manchester United manager. They agreed that once Tommy Smith was sold in the forthcoming few weeks, the full loan fee would be paid. Mackay admits he'll always be grateful for the leniency Sir Alex offered him as a manager just starting out.

Cleverley's impact was key during the 2009-10 season. He started 33 league games and scored 11 goals, the same tally as another loanee, Heidar Helguson, who returned to Vicarage Road for two spells that season from Queens Park Rangers.

Watford flirted with the top ten of the Championship in the first three months of the season before a decline over the winter. The seasonal turn coincided with a financial breakdown off the field. The club found itself in dire straits, with the owners Jimmy and Vince Russo demanding a repayment of around £5m that they were owed by the club.

It was during that period that Mackay became fully aware of the severity of the situation, as he recalls: 'Before Christmas of that year I remember vividly sitting with chief executive Julian Winter on a dark Friday afternoon. We were two hours away from administration. The Russo brothers had pressed the button. The staff that had worked at the club for years were ashen-faced. We were trying to stop it from happening.'

Thankfully administration was averted at the 11th hour, but the financial precariousness remained and meant an even tighter grip on the purse strings was assumed by the new board of directors made up of Graham Taylor, David Frandsen, Stuart Timperley and Julian Winter.

Their priority was finding a new long-term owner for the club; Mackay's job was to keep the club in the division while balancing his own budget. 'Every Wednesday we would speak together and try to make it work,' he says. 'They opened everything up and they knew where every penny was going. I couldn't go into those meetings and demand £500,000 for a player because I knew they would say, "Where are we going to get that from?" It was transparent between all of us.'

By March, Watford had slipped to within a place of the relegation zone and although turbulent waters had been negotiated off the field, they still had the challenge of staying in the Championship. This was eventually achieved thanks to a run of just three defeats in their last nine matches, which guided them to 16th, seven points above the drop.

Tailoring Watford's cloth to suit the worsening financial climate at Vicarage Road meant that Mackay spent much of that summer preparing for another campaign with few pounds to spare. He concedes that he knew what he was 'letting himself in for' but wanted to make it work.

He looked at every cost, trying to identify savings. It got to the stage where he was even re-writing the menu for corporate guests, removing the more expensive items from the list.

'I had been asked to make a huge operational saving and I remember sitting at my kitchen table with my spreadsheet and I was actually taking smoked salmon sandwiches off the sandwich trays, so I could spread the cost from the lounges elsewhere. We were constantly swimming uphill.'

The currents circulating within the players' pool told a different story. Limited changes within the squad meant that Mackay was able to build on the unity from the previous campaign. He noticed that many of those players had returned rejuvenated and undeterred by the club once again starting the season as one of the favorites for relegation. 'Danny Graham came back with a different mindset and I treated him as one of the more experienced players,' says Mackay. 'He and Adrian Mariappa took the bull by the horns and I wanted them to be the leaders in the dressing room alongside John Eustace. They all really kicked on, on and off the park, and kept the group together. They repaid the faith I showed in them.'

Both Eustace and Graham scored in an opening-day win at one of Mackay's former clubs, Norwich, in front of the TV cameras. That, though, was their only win in their opening five league matches, but then followed two strong runs. Starting in September they won five of seven league games including a 6-1 victory at Millwall, then in December they began a series of six straight victories which saw them sitting in the play-off places in the middle of January.

Due to Graham's predatory run he was a wanted man in the January transfer window. The same applied to the manager, who was offered the assistant manager's job at Newcastle then the manager's job at Burnley, both with an improved salary. He decided to stay at Watford, albeit with an improved contract, saying he had 'unfinished business' and wanted to do two years at the club. Graham would follow his lead.

'Danny could have gone in January, if he and his agent had kicked up enough of a fuss,' says Mackay. 'I had a chat with them and told him to stick with us and finish top goalscorer and get in the team of the season.'

Both of those targets were achieved by Graham, he was the Championship's highest scorer with 24 goals, the best goalscoring achievement by a Watford player since Marlon King had helped Watford to promotion with 21 in 2005-06.

Although Graham had also made the Championship team of the year, overall Watford had drifted towards the end of the season, winning just four of their last 21 matches and ending the season in 14th place.

The latter stages of the campaign had once again seen a change in ownership. Laurence Bassini took over on April 1, 2011. It would signal a large scale exodus of personnel from the club, including the top scorer and the manager, the latter feeling disillusioned with the direction the club was taking.

'It wasn't what I signed up for,' says Mackay. 'I was beginning to see something different. There were decisions being made that were different to how we would have done it before.

'There had been a stable group of people making decisions for the good of the club, but now you had a man who was an owner-chairman making his own decisions, which was his prerogative.'

Graham left to join Swansea for £3.5m while Will Buckley was sold by the owner to Brighton for £1m. Then Mackay was on his way. He was eventually given permission to talk to Cardiff in June and subsequently they agreed to pay compensation for him. Mackay's departure ended a six-year association with the club as a player, coach and manager. He was starting the next chapter of his managerial career with some valuable lessons having been learnt.

'You obviously have loyalty and you do the best you can,' he says. 'You hope to have a good rapport with the public and the players, but nowadays, quite easily, you can be called in and sacked despite all the good that you have done. So conversely a manager needs to look after himself.'

As with the departure of Brendan Rodgers, there was a degree of controversy after his exit, partly because Don Cowie, one of Watford's key midfielders, followed suit soon afterwards having reached the end of his contract.

Mackay says any suggestion of a 'Machiavellian plot' to run down Cowie's contract is 'laughable'. In contrast he states that due to the lack of clarity in Cowie's contract over an option to sign him for another year, he had been 'horrified' that the player was going to be able to leave on a free transfer that summer.

Due to Mackay's knowledge of Cowie's availability the player's move would never sit well with Watford supporters, who were not privy to the detail of the small print. It meant the manager's severance from the club with which he had a strong bond wasn't as smooth as he had wished.

Mackay explains: 'I was advised not to come out with a statement in the form of a goodbye letter in the local paper about my time, which normally happens, and I think the fans were upset that I didn't say how much I enjoyed my time at the club. Some people took umbrage that I didn't do that when I left. Hopefully, the fans judge me as a manager, player and coach.'

Not only did Cowie join Mackay at Cardiff but many of his back room staff followed as they 'didn't want to stay any more', Mackay says. One who stayed was Sean Dyche, despite the offer of a job at Cardiff. 'I asked him, but there was a possibility that he was going to get the [Watford] job. I always knew he had it in him. He had backed me to the hilt.'

Dyche did get the job, and he managed to surpass the league finishes of both Mackay and Rodgers, guiding Watford to 11th in the Championship in 2011-12. It was the club's highest finish for four years in testing circumstances on and off the field.

However, unlike his two predecessors he didn't have a chance to build on that or decide to leave of his own volition. Dyche was sacked and replaced when new owners arrived in 2012. Another manager given his first break by Watford, learned the hard way how loyalty works in football.

Adam Leventhal is a TV presenter, journalist, MD of 20Eleventhal Productions and Watford supporter. Following eight years at Capital Radio, combined with a broadcast journalism degree, he joined Sky Sports in 2003 and presents from sports events at home and abroad.

THE MATCH KICKS OFF

A large crowd has packed into Abbey Road to see England international John Barnes and the prolific goalscorer Maurice Johnston. But Stanton refuse to be over-awed and cause their visitors difficulties early on. George Reilly resorts to shirt-pulling...

Stanton start the game well and when Miguel Santina bursts across the halfway line to start a promising attack, Watford concede a free kick

Nick Cannon takes the kick and swings the ball wide, right into the path of Roy Randall.

But the visitors from the First Division are far from beaten and as the half wears on, the early ball to their speedy strikers begins to create chances.

But a great catch by Liam Rooney cuts out the cross and prevents an almost certain goal from the waiting Mo Johnston.

NEXT: There's a shock in store for Stanton players and fans.
Turn to page 215

7

Andrew French was Watford's press officer when the team reached the Premiership in 1999.

He was there, on the inside and behind the scenes during one of the most difficult seasons in the club's recent history.

For some it was the ultimate test of character.

Although the season ended with relegation, Andrew's account is far from doom and gloom.

But it does show what life is like when everyone at a football club is pushed to the limit.

WE ARE PREMIER LEAGUE

BY ANDREW FRENCH

When the final whistle went that afternoon in May at a sun-kissed Wembley Stadium, even amid the euphoria and the tears, many of us working for the club knew our lives were about to change. We just didn't realise how much or how quickly.

The rest of the day is a blur, metaphorically and literally. For the first time I dropped my professional guard and as television camera crews came into the dressing room to film the post-match interviews, I stopped being the press officer and joined in with the celebrations. I was impressed by the extent of the buffet in the corner of the dressing room. Unfortunately, as I tucked into the sandwiches, cake and lager, I could be seen in the background of the TV interviews.

After that, I was known as Sandwich Man.

We partied at Sopwell House long into the night. At one point, the players all gathered on the dancefloor, joining together in a big group hug. I can't remember the song but I do remember it was emotional.

I also seem to recall the hotel staff had to go out to get more Champagne.

Everyone was given the next day off but I got a call in the morning from one of the few staff that had decided to go into the stadium. Apparently some TV people were outside the ground. So I drove down to Vicarage Road – and got my first lesson in how my life as the club's point of contact for the media was going to be now we were a Premiership club. Parked outside the programme hut in Occupation Road was a large satellite truck. There were at least two reporters with microphones stopping people walking by, and because I turned down Occupation Road towards the offices a TV camera was thrust towards my car window in case I was someone interesting.

That summer was so different. People outside of football club life sometimes assume you just shut up shop when the final whistle of the season goes in May, and everyone regroups in early August. That's never the case – but even less so in the summer ahead of your first season in the Premiership.

It is the little things that stand out. One day I took a call from the Premier League's media office reminding me that we had to make allowances for the people from Panini during our press day.

Panini's sticker albums had been a part of my childhood. There was the ritual of collecting the stickers and swapping them at school, now I was helping to arrange the photographs that would be an indelible part of a million childhoods.

The day we got all the players and coaching staff together for the group photograph also served as a warning of the, often unintentional, patronising approach from some of those who were involved with top flight football. To some, we were still just 'little Watford'. The Premier League sent their photographic licencing people along to make sure the pictures fitted their criteria. They arrived just as Graham Taylor was orchestrating his players and staff to form three rows, seated, standing and the back row up on a bench.

Suddenly one of the Premiership staff interrupted what GT was doing, presumably assuming he needed help. A few minutes later, and after a quiet word between GT and the official, normal service resumed and Graham organised the photography session without any 'outside' assistance.

AUGUST

Long before the victory at Wembley, the pre-season trip to the Isle of Man to take part in the Steam Packet Football Festival had been arranged.

I was used to travelling with the team but it had been agreed I would stay behind. Watford's movements barely registered a flicker of interest among the media before the run to the play-offs but suddenly I was getting daily calls from newspapers and television and radio stations.

They wanted team news, confirmation or denial of transfer targets and quotes from the manager. When it emerged that Alec Chamberlain had injured his hand while on the Isle of Man we were taking several calls a day as the media wanted to know if the keeper would be fit for the opener against Wimbledon. Thankfully, GT was a great man to work for: he told me what was happening, advised of anything he wanted me to keep out of the media's reach, and left me to get on with it.

That management of the media also changed Fridays, the day when GT generally spoke to the media ahead of the weekend's game. This usually took place at the training ground and took no more than 20 minutes or so. There would be the local paper, a reporter from BBC Three Counties and perhaps a couple of agency men.

But with the demands of Sky and the national papers, we had to move press day to a suite in the Rous Stand at Vicarage Road. GT had to sit or stand in front of a backdrop board covered in logos whenever he was filmed and the event took more than an hour.

Anticipating the increased interest from the media, we installed a new Portacabin at the back of the old Family Terrace so that the post-match interviews could be done in comfort. We had made do with a small room near the players' tunnel but it would be too cramped if we had more than a couple of cameramen and a handful of journalists.

My memory of the opening game against Wimbledon was of some of the reporters from the national press turning their noses up at our humble media facilities, the new Portacabin and the old press box at the back of the East Stand. We had put in a new desk, better lighting and some TVs so the journalists could watch the action replays and we'd met with someone from the Football Writers' Association to get their input, yet I still felt we were being looked down upon by some. And I got the distinct impression one or two hacks from GT's England days were ready to put the boot in too.

Although it was a long midweek trip, I remember a sense of relief at travelling to Sunderland for our first Premiership away game. Life had revolved around Vicarage Road and the training ground for most of the summer so it was a welcome change of backdrop for the new adventure. If I didn't travel with the team, as on that occasion, I would generally try and see GT before the game, just to check whether there was anything I needed to be aware of.

He was unhappy that the referee was Jeff Winter, who was from Teesside, a bit too close to Sunderland for comfort. 'He's already been calling their players by their first names,' GT said to me. His mood was no better after the game: Winter gave a penalty as we lost 2-0.

The game at Liverpool was my first 'overnighter' with the players and staff. Where possible, GT liked to take the train to away games. The players travelled in tracksuits but took club suits with them for the matchday. Parking up at Watford Junction was wonderful – the town was still embracing the club's new status and as we walked through the station and onto the platform all sorts of people were wishing us luck. We met the team coach at Warrington Bank Quay station, and as we walked along the platform and out to get on board, we moved past a row of cab drivers standing next to their cars. The tracksuits gave away who we were, and one of them said: 'Like lambs to the slaughter.' Away trips followed a pretty similar pattern. We generally timed our travel to get to the hotel in mid afternoon. The squad then rested in their rooms for the remainder of the afternoon, although the likes of Luther Blissett, Kenny Jackett, physio Paul Rastrick and I would often meet in the lounge to chat and watch TV.

The players would eat first in early evening from a selected menu and then head back to their rooms. Then us staff would eat after they had all gone. Sometimes we'd stay up and chew the fat on current affairs and football – often GT would regale us with a seemingly endless repertoire of stories from down the years.

In the morning, players had the option to come down for breakfast or not. Those who did were eating cereal or fruit, nothing fried. Often we'd break the morning up by going out for a walk if the hotel had grounds or there was a decent open space nearby.

Then we'd meet for lunch: steamed chicken, pasta, scrambled egg, more fruit. After eating we'd go into a room for a team meeting. I was always impressed by the level of detail and information that GT, Kenny or Luther would have on our opponents. Okay, we were up against household names most weeks but the staff could detail their recent performances, tactics, formations and potential weaknesses without notes. Many of the players were renowned as jokers and talkers – but during these sessions they listened intently. Phones were off. No personal stereos. Just listening.

For many reasons, it was a shame the game at Anfield came so early – not least because little did any of us know that it was to be our first and last away win of the season. I sat in the press box during games, overseeing updates for the club website and looking after the club's interests as far as the media were concerned. As I took my seat, there were three or four journalists already in the row in front of me. Their Scouse accents gave them away as local reporters. One of them had a laptop open and had already written a few paragraphs. I had a look over his shoulder and read his opening line: 'Liverpool striker Robbie Fowler scored two/three/four as the Reds humbled newly promoted Watford with a four/five/six-goal thrashing.'

I said nothing but made sure Oli Phillips of the *Watford Observer* saw it. Without knowing it, we were a couple of hours away from shoving those words back into his keyboard, and down the throats of a few other doubters besides.

After the game, the media were keen to play on the fact that neither GT nor Watford had even taken a point from Anfield before. Tommy Mooney was a man in demand too but like so many of the squad at that time, a combination of being a nice guy and the novelty of the media glare meant he was happy to do the rounds of written press, radio and TV. It was a good hour after the final whistle before we headed back to the coach. Before I left the tunnel area, I took the chance to touch the legendary 'This is Anfield' sign.

The journey home on the coach was memorable. The players celebrated but without ever giving the sense that this was their cup final. A couple of bottles of Champagne appeared and were passed around. There was lots of babble on mobiles, and several times there were cheers from the players as Watford fans enthused on the BBC's 606 phone-in show. There were to be many trips home from the north-west and north-east where the coach's radio wasn't switched on and silence would prevail until at least Watford Gap. But this wasn't one of them.

After scoring the winner at Anfield, everyone wanted a piece of Tommy Mooney and he spent a lot of time doing interviews that week. It was the same when he scored the only goal against Bradford the following Saturday and yet he never baulked at requests. I had already seen first-hand that some of the Premier League's stars were less than co-operative with press requests, and so I was proud that although we may not have had the biggest names, we also didn't possess the biggest egos.

Results through the rest of August and into September weren't so good. We had a game at Leicester on a Monday night that was live on Sky. It was another occasion when we were subjected to the media equivalent of someone adjusting your lapels and tie while patting you on the head and talking down to you. We were at Filbert Street well before kick-off and as the players warmed up, one of the Sky floor crew came scurrying up to me. 'Can you help me with identifying your players? It's okay with other teams but none of us know who any of your lot are.'

SEPTEMBER

The first off-field landmark of the season came before the home game with Chelsea. We signed Nordin Wooter from Real Zaragoza for £925,000. It was a club record fee. Much was made of it in the press, comparing the 'haves' of Chelsea and their expensively-assembled squad of stars with the 'have-nots' of Vicarage Road, whose most expensive signing wasn't even worth a million.

Many will have their own memories of that win over Chelsea – Wooter's role in Allan Smart's winner perhaps. For me, Steve Palmer's awesome display in the heart of the midfield stuck in my mind. But seeing Tommy Mooney after the game was a sad moment. He had been injured after coming on as sub. His body language and the look on his face said he had a good idea that his season was over before it had really started.

Before the game with Arsenal at Highbury I was chatting to the players in the tunnel. One of them said that 'pink shirt man' – our sports psychologist Ciaran Cosgrave – had said: 'Get in their faces and look into the eyes of the Arsenal players'. The player said with a wry smile: 'Have you seen the size of them?'

After that game at Highbury, there was another little taste of the assumed Premiership pecking order. GT, as was often the case, was quite quick to emerge from the dressing room and we began to head for the TV interview area, only for a member of the Arsenal media team to tell us that 'Arsene likes to be first in the TV interview room'. We diverted to the room reserved for the written press with GT adding 'if that's alright with you'.

OCTOBER

Although we had been losing games, we still only had one defeat by more than a single goal – at Sunderland – on our record. And for half an hour at Old Trafford it looked like we'd be okay. But we were three down at the break, and some of the national press boys in the media suite were positively enthusing about the possibility of being able to write about Fergie's fledglings giving Taylor's boys a right whipping.

It didn't really happen: but what did occur was the dismissal – a harsh dismissal at that – of defender Mark Williams. He had quietly gone about his work since arriving on a free from Chesterfield and it was looking like another gem had been unearthed. But I remember GT saying as we headed to face the media – and he probably didn't know how prophetic his thoughts might be – that 'it will be interesting to see how Willo reacts to getting sent off at a place like Old Trafford'. He never seemed to recover that impressive early season form, made just eight more starts and joined Wimbledon the next summer.

We went to Coventry in late October without either Williams or Robert Page, and it became apparent that one of two youngsters – James Panayi or Darren Ward – would be starting the game partnering Steve Palmer at the heart of the defence. It was another game that was live on television. Panayi started, Ward replaced him at the break and we lost 4-0.

After the game, GT took me to one side in the tunnel as we waited to speak to the TV crews and said: 'Andrew, just make sure those two lads get on the bus.' It wasn't often we set out to stop the media talking to players but I knew what he wanted me to do. I always admired the way he was keen to make sure the younger players were looked after when the need arose.

Neil Cox was signed from Bolton shortly after that game. There was some great banter at the training ground when he arrived, with players asking him to re-create the moment that Nick Wright's overhead stunner cleared his curly locks on the way into the net at Wembley.

Next came Xavier Gravelaine, a mercurial and eccentric Frenchman. If ever there were two players from opposite ends of the co-operation spectrum, these two were it. Cox would do anything to help, Gravelaine was every bit as surly off the field as he looked on it. The Frenchman was the only foreign player I encountered who made no attempt to speak English.

NOVEMBER

Having lost six consecutive league games, the draw at Sheffield Wednesday was very welcome. But having led twice, there were bound to be questions about us throwing away all three points. GT said he wanted to try to divert attention away from that and onto the positives – we had ended a losing run and avoided defeat away from home.

After Tony Gubba's first question for the *Match of the Day* interviews, Graham burst into a chorus of 'Ee-ay-addio, we got a point.' It certainly made everyone aware he was feeling upbeat but as we walked back down the tunnel he said: 'I'll probably regret doing that in the morning.'

Because of the increased media demands, we had decided the players needed some formal training in how to deal with the press – particularly the leading questions, instant post-match interviews and regular attempts to get someone to say something controversial to fit into their story.

So, a couple of days after the 1-1 draw with Newcastle at Vicarage Road, all the senior players gathered at the ground. We had hired a professional media training company for the day, and they came armed with cameras, microphones and journalists from all facets of the press.

Players split into groups, and took part in mock TV, radio and written interviews. Every attempt was made to make the interviews realistic, so other players were kept away from each interview and the questions were related to the game a few days earlier against Bobby Robson's side.

The Watford supporters had booed the England striker, Alan Shearer, and that was among the topics aimed to catch the players out.

Later on, we all sat round to watch and listen to the interviews and praise the good and pick apart the bad.

Thankfully, it was only a training session or else Michel Ngonge would have made the news, big time. During his 'TV interview', he was asked why he thought the crowd had turned on Shearer. 'Because they are drinking before the game,' said Michel. The interviewer, either not believing his luck or not believing what Ngonge had said, followed up with: 'Are you saying the fans were drunk?'

There was no stopping Michel: 'Yes, I think so, they have drinks before the game and some of them were drunk.'

It was gently pointed out to Michel that calling your own fans drunks on television might not be a PR masterstroke.

DECEMBER

Sometimes, in the darker moments of a relegation season, fans wonder if the players and staff feel the pain of defeat as much as they do.

Had they been a passenger on the bus back from Selhurst Park after a 5-0 defeat to Wimbledon in December, they'd have been left in no doubt.

Getting onto a silent bus was the sign. Kenny and Luther were already in their seats. There was no chatter from the back of the bus. Graham got on after me, sat down and barely moved or spoke all the way home. There were no requests to turn the air-con up or down, or calls to change channels on the radio. The players stared out of the window. It was only a journey from south London to south-west Hertfordshire but in that suffocating silence it felt a lot further.

After a Boxing Day drubbing at Spurs, and having not won since mid-September, the 3-2 win over Southampton just before New Year was a real relief.

Working in the media area, you see a lot of the same faces every week because the newspapers and agencies would often send the same reporters to cover the game.

But two of the press box doyens I knew very well were Oli Phillips and Terry Challis from the *Watford Observer*. I had worked for Oli – the best teacher I could have had in the world of journalism. And I worked with Terry, whose quick wit had me in awe.

Watford's sequence of results had tested the resolve of Oli and Terry just as they had the fans but the win over the Saints provided one of those great press box moments.

Having been 2-0 up, we conceded two in as many minutes – only for Gravelaine to score what turned out to be the winner two minutes later. As the ball hit the net, Oli shot to his feet and let out a great long yell of 'Gravelaaaaaine'. Terry wasn't far behind him, and the pair high-fived – much to the amusement of most others in the press box, whose far more anodyne reactions to what was just another goal were interrupted by two large men whooping it up.

The Frenchman was gone, as quickly as he had arrived, almost a month to the day after that win over Southampton. To say he wasn't missed might be a bit harsh, but he wasn't the cheerleader among the players, and was something of a loner. He also had some peculiar habits. Travelling away to the game at Bradford in January, we stayed in a hotel in Brighouse – I only remember the place because the Brighouse and Rastrick Brass Band played on Terry Wogan's hit *The Floral Dance* when I was growing up!

Generally when we arrived at a hotel, players would head off in their regular room pairings. However, this time there was some debate. It turned out that as a new punishment for anyone who had a poor week in training, the 'prize' was to share a room with Gravelaine. Not only did he like to sit in the dark, but he was also partial to the odd cigarette – and he didn't like the window open because he found it too cold. I overheard a player saying that 'if it's not bad enough that he wants to sit in the dark as soon as you go back to your room after dinner, but then you hear him striking a match and all you can see is the glow of the tip of his fag, and then you get the smell of the smoke'. As Gravelaine only played in two away games where an overnight stop was required, that was one training ground ritual which ended before it started.

However, travelling with the players and staying overnight before a game also exposed me to things I just was not aware of. For instance, even though the players were on an agreed diet and their meals were structured to suit this, they would still chance their arm. I recall one Friday night the staff were just finishing their meals and the players had long retired to their rooms, when one of the reception staff sidled up to GT and said something. He sat back in his chair, smiled and said 'No lovey, tell them they can't.' One of the players had called down to room service and attempted to order a plate of chips and some ice cream. As with every hotel trip, the staff were under strict instructions that any requests from any of the players' rooms were to be relayed to the club's staff straight away. The players must have known this, but still they tried.

Kenny Jackett was the 'enforcer' on away trips. He would be the one who was dispatched to a room if there were any problems. And he was also the one who would carry out the 'random room checks'. That entailed occasionally popping up to the floor where the players' rooms were, knocking on a couple of doors and checking everything was okay. There was never any indication that anything actually needed checking upon, and I don't recall anything untoward ever being found. But it was a way of showing the players that if they did have any thoughts of doing anything other than watching TV, relaxing or sleeping, chances are they would probably be found out.

JANUARY

One thing I often got asked is what were the things that made me realise Watford were a Premier League club? How did the fact that the Hornets were now in the big time manifest itself? Well, signing a player for £1million was one of the moments when you took a step back and absorbed the moment. I'd been brought up on a diet of Watford signing players for small fees and then, generally, selling them on for more.

When Luther Blissett was sold to AC Milan for £1m in the 1980s, that was a 'wow' moment. I recalled having to find out exactly what a million was and how many zeros it had. But until January 2000, Watford hadn't signed a player for that magical seven-figure sum. We'd come close with Wooter, but now we were breaking new ground.

GT had already given us the name of the player: Heidar Helguson. A dozen years ago, the internet was not what it is now, and hunting for an Icelandic player plying his trade in Sweden was less straightforward than it would be today.

However, we did our digging and found out the sort of things the media would ask: Helguson's previous clubs, place of birth, position and height. And so the day arrived that Watford moved into the million-pound market, and when we got the nod that the deal was done, we began the process of firing the press release out. Today, the bulk would be done by e-mail and take seconds. In 2000, it was nearly all done by fax and took ages. As well as the media, we would also inform others with a vested interest, and one of those was club historian Trefor Jones. Not only was he a great source of information himself, he was also great for checking things – and within minutes of receiving his copy of the fax, he was on the phone. Clearly, our best efforts to interpret information that had been roughly translated hadn't worked very well. We had muddled some of the data, and were informing the media that Helguson was born in a place called 'Striker' and that his preferred position was actually a small Icelandic village.

We met Heidar soon after, and he is genuinely one of the nicest footballers I have encountered. Affable and funny, he was as popular off the field as he quickly became on it. The biggest shame for fans is that they seldom saw him interviewed on TV – but there was a very understandable reason for that, because he stuttered quite badly when speaking English. It was bad enough being the new boy in a foreign country when English isn't your first language without being stuck in front of a camera and exposing a speech impediment.

To his credit 'H' (as he became known) never asked to be kept away from the press but it seemed the best thing to do. That became a bit harder when he scored on his debut at home to Liverpool but because we ended up losing the game the media were quite happy to focus on the Reds. In fact, it's fair to say that as the season wore on, the media demands eased.

One thing we didn't discover when doing our homework on Heidar was that his wife had done a bit of modelling.

We may not have known, but *The Sun* did. And by the time we travelled to Bradford for a crunch relegation battle the next Saturday, they had unearthed pictures of Mrs Helguson in swimwear, and they were featured in their Saturday football pull-out on the morning of the game. There was some distinct giggling and nudging among the players as they gathered in the foyer of the hotel before the group walk on the Saturday morning. There were a few copies of *The Sun* among the players and soon everyone had seen the pictures. When H arrived, he was totally unfazed and had that look on his face of 'Yes my wife's a stunner, aren't I the lucky one.'

Helguson scored one of the goals that afternoon but it was to be a miserable outcome and we dropped to the bottom of the league table for the first time. We didn't know then that we would never move back up again. The 3-2 defeat started with a dubious penalty awarded by Paul Alcock, and I remember GT was still unhappy about it as we walked from the dressing room to the media room at Bradford. At that time, the TV interviews were held in a small room in one corner of the ground and to reach it required walking along the front of the main stand. By the time GT was ready to go and speak to the TV people, the ground had emptied. It was a dark and cold January evening, and while he was angered by the penalty, GT was quieter than usual. It was as if that grim, chilly walk in the gloom – albeit only about 80 yards – had been a reality check. At that moment, all the excitement of May and the anticipation of August felt a world away.

FEBRUARY

It was no better the following week. We were soundly beaten by a Paul Merson-inspired Aston Villa, and after the game GT did well to deflect from the one-sided nature of the game by talking about Merson, who he had given an England debut to almost a decade earlier.

Because the training ground and Vicarage Road stadium were quite some way apart, it was fairly rare to see too many of the players at the ground during the week. However, some of those who lived locally would pop in – and one such player was Steve Palmer. If he came to Vicarage Road, he would stick his head around the press office door. And he was also a prankster. He may not look it, and he certainly 'played a straight bat' in most media interviews, adding to the impression that he was a reserved character.

But he had a great sense of humour, as my press office colleague Richard Walker found to his cost one afternoon. We were both out of the office but had left our mobile phones on our desks. Steve dropped in, saw we weren't around and picked up Richard's phone. He then sent a text to everyone in Richard's phone which simply said 'I need you.' Unbeknown to Steve, Richard managed a football team and that text was on its way to all his players and their Dads, as well as to all his many family and friends. Steve then headed off home – and by the time we got back to the office, Richard's phone was hot with numerous replies ranging from 'Is everything okay?' to 'Have you lost the plot?' The phone buzzed all afternoon, and it took quite a while to work out what had caused so many of Richard's friends to be either concerned for his welfare or perplexed as to whether he had flipped his lid.

But if you are going to carry out such pranks, you have to be able to deal with the consequence, and to be fair to Steve, he took the revenge that we dished out really well. We went onto the internet and found a site that was a portal for catalogue companies and mail-order firms. We then ticked every single box in every single category on every single page, before entering Steve's name and home address. A few days later, he made another visit to the press office.

He walked in, laughed and said: 'Fair play boys.' We had signed him up to receive booklets, leaflets, catalogues and promotional material from hundreds of companies, and within a few days they arrived at his home, piling up on the doormat.

Steve said that one day the postman rang the door and, when he answered, presented him with a large sack saying: 'These are all yours mate.' A few years later, Steve said he was still getting brochures for 'Walking holidays in Bavaria' and booklets about 'How to make your own shoes.'

Another local boy was Paul Robinson. In fact, he didn't just live locally he was a Watford boy, through and through. I wrote about his footballing exploits for the *Watford Observer* when he was still a schoolboy, and he still had something of the cheeky schoolboy about him. He was funny, he'd pull your leg, he'd give you a bit of lip – but it was always just great banter.

I cannot ever remember having any sort of crossed word with Robbo. From a press perspective, he was also very good. Despite being one of the younger members of the squad, you could be confident that he could handle the media. They liked his cheeky-chappy manner and he seemed able to satisfy what the press wanted without ever straying into controversy.

MARCH

The hotel we stayed in the night before the game at
Newcastle in March had a cross-country track and assault
course in its grounds. We arrived early in the afternoon, and
there was still plenty of daylight left, so Kenny Jackett told the
players to take their stuff to their rooms and then meet back
in reception.

He had decided to make the most of the facilities and, after
a long journey north, the players would be off for a run to
shake off the lethargy of hours sitting in the coach.

We were all standing there in tracksuits and it became
apparent that the only person in reception wearing a tracksuit
but not planning to do any cross-country running was me. Both
Kenny and Luther would be joining in, and soon the players had
caught on and verbal pressure was applied for me to 'be one of
the lads'. In my early teenage years, I had been a half-decent
distance runner – but that was half a lifetime ago, and since
then I had discovered curry and discarded my bike in favour
of a car. I was not in good shape, but in the face of prov-
ocation from the first-team squad, I said I'd have a go. The
course wound around the hotel grounds, going up and down
hill, through wooded areas and was pretty muddy. We were to
do three laps, with each lap increasing in pace. I think bravado
carried me through lap one but even then I dropped through
the field, and when the pace was increased for lap two, I was
struggling badly. I made it back to the start but having slipped
to last place and feeling like my lungs would explode, I called it
a day as the rest of the group headed off for lap three at a pace
that, to me, looked like a full-on sprint.

I was still gasping for air when they finished, and was
subjected to plenty of ridicule – particularly as my face was a
nice shade of red.

We headed back into the hotel, but within a few minutes of getting back to my room, the fire alarm sounded. I assumed it was a test, but it wasn't – and soon staff came knocking at the door to ask me to evacuate. Assembling in the reception area, many of the players were dressed for a swim while others had changed out of their running gear. I was still in mine, as I hadn't mustered the energy to do anything. I was still very red-faced as I was greeted, in front of the assembled hotel guests, by Tommy Mooney, who boomed: 'Bloody hell Frenchy, your face has set off the fire sensors, son.'

That Newcastle hotel stay was also host to one of the funniest cases of mistaken identity I have seen. After eating on the Friday night, the staff went to one of the hotel lounges for a quiet drink. There was a bar adjacent to the lounge and it was hosting a function as it was packed full, with many of the guests spilling into the lounge area where we were sitting.

We were all wearing club tracksuits, and that generally made people have a squint to see who we were. It happened a few times as guests from the function came out to buy drinks, and tried to work out if the group of men in tracksuits were anyone significant. One group of women, slightly inebriated, were far less discreet, and stood at the bar gesturing and looking over in our direction.

Eventually one of them walked over and said: 'Are you footballers?' Kenny said we were from a football club, but we were the staff, and the players had long since gone to bed.

'But you're famous, right?' asked the woman. Without a hint of a laugh, Kenny said she may know some of us. The woman turned towards GT, and said 'He's famous, isn't he? Is he the manager?' Kenny said he was, and she might know him as he was once the manager of England. The woman turned back towards her friends and shouted to them: 'See, I told you... it is Brian Clough.'

The game at St James' Park ended in defeat, but the press
didn't get the story they wanted: a heavy home win with a sack-
ful of goals for media darling Alan Shearer. In fact, we nearly
nicked a point with Allan Smart going close, but eventually lost
1-0. Shearer had his chances but didn't find the net, and that
was due to a fine display from keeper Alec Chamberlain. It was
great to see him deny England's top striker, even if he didn't get
the credit his display deserved.

Victories were few and far between but the following weekend, we won again. The 1-0 success over Sheffield Wednesday
was our first three points since we'd beaten Southampton in
December. Smart scored the only goal late in the game, and
then wheeled away in celebration before striking a sort of
'shot-putter' pose. It wasn't instantly clear what the celebration
actually was, but he explained to the press afterwards that it was
an homage to the man on the Scots Porage Oats box. Smart
was a very proud Scotsman who had been known to don his
kilt at club functions.

The Monday after that win a call came through to the press
office that I thought, at first, was a wind-up. It was from the
manufacturers of Scots Porage Oats: they wanted to send Allan
a year's supply as a thank you for the media exposure the brand
had received in the wake of his winning goal celebration.

The only snag was that they really wanted a picture of Allan
with the 'Scots Porage Oats man', recreating the pose – and
both in their kilts. He was a little reticent at first, but Smarty
eventually agreed and so a few days later the actor who regularly
posed as the 'Scots Porage Oats man' arrived at Vicarage Road,
along with the company's PR people, some bowls and spoons,
and a photographer.

The two men recreated the pose from the box, as well as a
few other shots pretending to eat porage. The next day a copy
of the press release – with the headline of 'Smart gets his oats'

– was dispatched, and a lorry arrived at Vicarage Road with two pallets of family-size packs of Scots Porage Oats. Smarty took some, and the rest was shared among the staff and players.

Allan will always be remembered as one half of the 'Carlisle duo', together with Nick Wright. Of course, Wrighty has his name forever etched in Watford history for *that* goal at Wembley – although it cannot be forgotten (and Smarty doesn't let it) that both of the Carlisle boys netted that day. It is such a shame that injury meant Wrighty played only four Premier League games, and was to retire not long after. To go from the high of that overhead kick to the low of retirement in such a short space of time, especially when he was at his peak, would have tested anyone. But Wrighty was always cheerful, and his first-class character is epitomised by the way he has made himself a success again in 'civvy street'.

APRIL

If following the win over Wednesday with a point against Spurs gave any hope that we might climb out of trouble, that was quickly dashed by a 4-2 defeat at Everton. GT was a believer in omens, and we stayed in the same hotel as we had done for the game at Liverpool back in August. As usual, Ron the coach driver stayed with us. Ron was quite a character: a man with a silver-haired quiff and a strong Northern accent whose name was regularly heard on the way home from away games as players asked 'Ron, turn up the heating' or 'Ron, turn the radio down.' Ron always referred to GT as 'Mr Taylor' and having eaten dinner with us on a Friday night, would quickly head for his room with the words: 'I'm going to call it a day Mr Taylor.' After the pre-match lunch in the hotel, everyone gathered on the bus and Ron pulled away. The roads around Liverpool were particularly busy and eventually Ron turned off the main road and headed down some back roads. The further we went, the more we seemed to be heading away from the city and into residential areas. Even GT asked if Ron was sure where he was going, but Ron said he was and was just trying to get round the traffic. However, we eventually ended up in what looked a bit like Brookside Close, whereupon Ron admitted defeat. He had seen a car with an Everton sticker in the rear window turn off the main road and, assuming he was going to the game, had followed him. All the way to his house.

On another away trip Ron missed the turning off the motorway for our hotel for a pre-match lunch. With howls of laughter from the players, Ron carried on regardless and took the next exit – into some services. Still refusing to admit his mistake, he shouted over his shoulder that there was 'a bridge up here, and we can cross and get back onto the other side of the motorway'. Indeed there was a bridge: a footbridge for pedestrians. When we eventually got to the hotel and sat down for lunch, GT had got there ahead of Ron and put a piece of paper in his place with arrows pointing to his knife and fork 'just in case you needed any directions Ron'.

After failing to beat Derby at home, and with back-to-back home games with Arsenal and Manchester United looming, it became pretty obvious that we'd need to get something when we went to The Dell or else it was curtains.

Like Derby, Southampton were only just above the relegation zone. After the pre-match lunch, I can remember vividly GT's talk to the players. He stressed the importance of settling into the game and trying to add to the uncertainty of the home fans, who were very close to the pitch at the The Dell. He also warned of the threat of the Southampton substitute Marian Pahars, if he came on. It was ironic, then, that we were a goal down in four minutes before ever getting a foothold in the game, and were eventually killed off when Pahars scored a second 20 minutes after coming on to replace James Beattie.

The relegation coffin lid was shutting when we lost 3-2 at home to Arsenal. GT preferred to eulogise about Thierry Henry, who had scored twice, when the press were trying to get him to say that Watford should have had a penalty and David Seaman should have been sent off for holding down Helguson in the first minute, or that Patrick Vieira should have seen red for an apparent head-butt on the Icelander.

One thing that season taught me is how well GT played the media. They had an agenda several times during the nine months of life in the Premiership, but they never seemed to learn that unless GT wanted to talk about a subject, then he wouldn't. He had an uncanny knack of taking a direct and often very leading question from a journalist, and answering it so fully with the information and statements he wanted to make that the attempt to take him down a particular path were both thwarted and forgotten.

By the time Manchester United arrived at Vicarage Road the next weekend, we were already down and they had been crowned champions. It was still an eagerly anticipated fixture. When the fixtures were released months earlier, how many of us looked to see when the Red Devils would be in town? It was disappointing that the game was rendered pretty much pointless because the two clubs' vastly differing fates had already been sealed – and it became even more disappointing when we learned that United had asked that the plastic tunnel in the East Stand be pulled out before their players arrived to walk onto the pitch. I don't recall a reason ever being given, but I also don't recall any other team asking for this to be done. It effectively meant the United players could walk from the dressing room and onto the pitch without any supporters being able to get close to them. Draw your own conclusions.

GT had said in the week leading up to the game that he felt

United would use the opportunity to rest some of their star names. Squad rotation was less fashionable back then, and this seemed more of a chance to cock a snook both at him and Watford. United had won the league, this game was meaningless and they could still beat Watford with half a reserve side out. Sure enough, the likes of Jonathan Greening and Mark Wilson started the game (it was the latter's only Premiership started for United), while David Beckham was nowhere to be seen. The Hornets led through Heidar Helguson and may well have gone on to apply a small custard pie to some United faces, but the game turned on the double sending off of Micah Hyde and Nicky Butt with 25 minutes to go. United suddenly sprang into life and won 3-2.

Micah was one of a couple of players that I found quite hard work. Whether he was shy, or didn't enjoy the limelight, I was never quite sure. He once said he preferred to let his football do the talking, so it was perhaps the latter – but he was never someone who seemed happy to be dealing with the media, often giving brief, platitudinous answers. That made it difficult to approach him with any confidence and I was sometimes concerned about how he might react when asked to do something with the press. But I think perhaps he warmed to it over time as he was better the longer he stayed at the club. I thought he might stay in the Premiership even when Watford dropped out, and I remember GT saying in an interview that he felt Micah was someone who could remain in the top flight after we had departed. He never did, although he did play internationally for Jamaica, and I encountered him again when I was working for Charlton and we hosted a tournament in which Jamaica played. I was in the tunnel at The Valley when I heard a shout of 'Hey Frenchy' and there was Micah, walking over to shake hands. I was glad it was more dealing with the media he hadn't enjoyed, and not me personally.

The only player I thought didn't like me personally was Peter Kennedy. He really could be quite blunt to the point of appearing rude, and that wasn't just with me but with the media too. I could never really get to talk to him for long enough to work out what the problem was, but eventually I just put a line through his name when it came to considering players for various media duties. He seemed quite happy with that, and we remained on no more than nodding terms through the rest of his time at the club. So it was a big surprise when in the summer of 2001 and his move to Wigan was completed, he walked into the press office to say goodbye. I could count on one hand how many other players did that yet Peter took the time to do so. Not only that, he thanked us for all our help and even had a quick chat. I think it was the longest conversation I ever had with him.

It's no surprise that Alec Chamberlain has stayed with Watford since his playing days ended. He is one of the nicest footballers 'off the field' and I became friends with him and his wife, Jane. I remember them sending me and my wife presents when our first son was born in 2001. I now sit with my two boys in the Lower Rous – almost in line with the goal at the Rookery end of the stand – and we regularly arrive as Alec is warming up the keepers. He gives us a wave and often has a chat if he sees us: the emphasis being *if* he sees us, as he admits he struggles to see the stands from the pitch these days!

MAY

The penultimate game of the season, at Middlesbrough, is one I remember fondly. Not really for anything that happened on the field, but for the spirit and devotion of the fans. I'll be honest: I found the 19 away Premier League games pretty hard going and I was being paid to attend, and often enjoying a night away in a good hotel, mixing with the players and staff and not having to buy a ticket. For the fans – and especially those who went to all or most of those 19 games – it can't have been much fun at all. But fun was the operative word at the Riverside that day. I remember the 'We're out of your league' T-shirts that were made, the fancy dress costumes that were worn and the bemused looks on the faces of the locals around the ground as Watford fans celebrated all day despite having been relegated.

It was a story that the national papers seized upon, and there were a couple of columnists who sat in the away end that day to get a full taste of what was a very special afternoon. I was in the tunnel at the end of the game, and then went out on the pitch as the players went across to our fans and gave them a well deserved round of applause. Skipper Robert Page was very good that day – it was always a lottery asking a player something before a game and expecting them to remember it after the 90 minutes were over. But Pagey made sure at the final whistle that the players and staff showed due respect to the fans who had lit up the Riverside with their colour and song. It can't have been an easy season to be captain, as although there was the glory of leading the team in its first taste of Premier League football, Robert was also captaining a side where morale was often low and results were not good.

He was supportive to off-the-field staff though, Pagey – and was good to his word at the start of the season that as captain, if he could ever help the press office, we should ask him. He always seemed very aware of the bond between Watford and its fans.

Beating Coventry on the last day was a decent way to end a season where, once the shiny newness of being in the Premier League had gone, we were left with a realisation that staying up was a forlorn hope from quite early in the campaign. On a personal and professional level, I would not have wanted to miss it, and the experience of working at the country's most famous grounds and dealing with some huge personalities is something I will always be grateful for.

As a boy I stood on the corner between the Vicarage Road end and Shrodells, standing up on the railings at the back so I could see. I probably knew very early on that I would never actually play for Watford, so to represent the club in the way I did for our first season in the Premiership was about as good as it could get.

To be part of GT's staff, travel to away games with them, and share in some of their experiences was more than I could have hoped for when I was watching games with my Dad in the 1980s. Of course, I still had more years to come, but the likes of the Vialli season and financial problems meant I was never to sample such heady days with the Hornets again. May 1999 to May 2000 are 12 months I will treasure.

Andrew French, like many Watford fans, was born in Shrodells hospital and has supported the club ever since. A former sports editor at the *Watford Observer,* he was communications manager at Watford FC from 1998 to 2003 before doing a similar job at Charlton Athletic. He now works for online betting company, Betfair.

8

For many people, being a football fan is an integral part of their social life.

For others, like **Tim Turner**, it's a solitary pursuit.

Over the years, though, he's come to realise that when you're part of the community of Watford fans, you're never really alone.

YOU'LL NEVER SIT ALONE

BY TIM TURNER

Once a season or so, I go to a game at Griffin Park with my friend Stuart, a lifelong Brentford fan. The routine usually starts with a pint or two in one of the many pubs that surround the ground. At this stage we often bump into someone Stuart knows, even though he hasn't lived in the area for nearly 30 years.

Then it's on to the ground itself, where Stuart always stands in the same spot on the Ealing Road terrace with a group that includes his younger brother and various friends and acquaintances. After the final whistle we make our way to another pub, this time on Brentford High Road, where most of the customers seem to know each other. Stuart usually just stays for a couple of pints before heading home, but some of the others are clearly there for the long haul.

Now compare and contrast that with my own matchday ritual. On a typical Saturday I leave my home in south-west London at about 11 o'clock and drive to my mother's house in Bushey Heath, where she faithfully makes me fish and chips for lunch, just as she did every Saturday when I was a boy. I leave at 1.45 and drive to Watford, parking in one of the residential streets off Riverside Road, and I'm in my seat in the Rookery by 2.15 or so. After the game, I walk back to the car and drive straight home. When there's an evening match, the routine is even simpler: a train from Euston to Watford Junction, schlep across town to the ground, watch the game, back to the station and catch a train that takes me pretty much all the way home.

I'm not looking for sympathy here; it's just that my occasional visits to Griffin Park act as a sharp reminder that, for many people, being a football fan is a highly social activity. Whereas for me, it's mostly been a solitary pursuit – like stamp collecting or trainspotting, only with more swearing.

SATURDAY, OCTOBER 10 1970
WATFORD 0 CARDIFF CITY 1

In the beginning, I was a Spurs fan. In my defence, I was only seven, and my knowledge of football was limited to whatever I could pick up in the playground at Merry Hill Infants School in Bushey.

My best friend at the time professed to be a Tottenham supporter, so I instantly became one too. In hindsight, it wasn't such a bad choice; these were the days when Spurs regularly won trophies, thanks to a squad that included the likes of Jimmy Greaves, Alan Mullery and Pat Jennings.

This was only a passing infatuation, though it lasted long enough for Mum to buy me the late-60s equivalent of a replica shirt: a plain white, long-sleeved football shirt and a Tottenham Hotspur badge that she carefully sewed in the appropriate position on the left breast.

Then, in the spring of 1970, I found out that there was actually a professional football team in my local area. Watford had reached the quarter-finals of the FA Cup and were due to play Liverpool. (I must have seen this on the front of the *Watford Observer*, or maybe on the back page of my parents' *Daily Mail*.) I'd heard of Liverpool and my curiosity was aroused, so I asked Dad if he'd take me to the match.

He thought about it for a nanosecond and said no, it would be too hard to get tickets – and he was probably right, though

I'm pretty sure he had no intention of trying. But if I liked, he added, he would take me to a league match the following season.

Why wait so long? The Liverpool game was in February, and there were still plenty of home league games left that season. Maybe he was hoping I'd forget all about it. But I didn't, and so I made my first visit to Vicarage Road on a sunny Saturday afternoon in October 1970.

In the interim, I'd read about Watford's historic victory over Liverpool and, a few weeks later, listened on the radio to updates from the semi-final against Chelsea. The 5-1 defeat, after the scores had been level at half-time, felt painful somehow. I'd developed an affinity for this football team before I'd even seen them play.

That autumn afternoon, Dad and I walked up Occupation Road past the allotments, then through a turnstile, down some steps, up some more steps and into what I later learned was the Main Stand extension. I'd love to be able to say I remember every detail of my first exposure to live football, but I'd be lying. Anything I could tell you about the Watford team or their performance that day would be gleaned from the archives.

No, the impressions that stuck with me were purely sensory. First, the brightness of the colours: the orange of the seats, the green of the pitch, the yellow of the Watford players' shirts and the blue of their opponents'. (The next two teams I saw Watford play, Birmingham and Leicester, also wore blue shirts and white shorts, and for a while I had a confused notion that this was compulsory for all teams visiting Vicarage Road.)

Then there was the noise. I'm not talking about the total immersion of standing on the Kop, obviously; Vicarage Road in the early 70s was no more a cauldron of footballing passion than it is today. But I was initially taken aback by the individual shouts and cries from the people around us, along with the subtler rise and fall of noise as the action on the pitch ebbed and flowed. In fact, I have a feeling I came home from that first match complaining of a headache.

Finally, the smell. No, not the aroma of fried onions or Bovril – nothing so clichéd. My father smoked a pipe, and throughout the match the smoke kept blowing in my face. This became a constant feature of my early visits to the ground. Indeed, there were times when we swapped seats, only for the wind to change direction and continue to send the pipe smoke wafting painfully into my eyes. Like Watford's defensive frailties, it was just something I had to learn to put up with.

* * *

Dad wasn't a football fan at all. He was keen on sport, and when he was younger he'd been extremely fit and had played any sport going, from rugby to squash. What's more, he'd been good at all of them – a gene that missed me but was passed on to my brother. Dad was more of a doer than a watcher, and although he mentioned trips to Sincil Bank during his boyhood in Lincoln (you could go to a match with a farthing in your pocket and still have enough left over for a bag of chips on the way home, apparently), I never got the impression that he was a proper supporter.

Nevertheless, he dutifully took me to watch games at Vicarage Road for the next few years; not every home game, but one a month or so. In retrospect, he got the short end of the stick. During those years, Watford struggled in Division Two, got relegated, then found Division Three unexpectedly tricky and got relegated again. Even Division Four turned out to be quite challenging. We didn't see a lot of Watford wins in those years – not that I was bothered. I'd been hooked from the start, and the fact that my team never seemed to be challenging at the top of its division didn't really matter. I had no reason to expect anything better.

By the time I went to secondary school, I was deemed old enough to go to games on my own, and Dad returned gratefully to pottering in his shed on Saturday afternoons. This meant paying for myself out of my pocket money, so I moved from the Main Stand extension to the terraces – either the Vicarage Road end or the steps in front of the old Shrodells stand. There was a boy in my class who supported Watford, and I often met up with him at the ground. I'd love to say it was the start of a beautiful friendship, but in truth, Paul was just someone to stand with. As is often the way with school friendships, our paths started to cross less and less after a while, and eventually we drifted apart.

By now, Graham Taylor had arrived and what we would later realise was the Golden Era had begun. At school, this meant that, all of a sudden, I wasn't the only Watford fan around. Boys who had previously professed to support Spurs, Arsenal or Chelsea started wearing yellow, red and black striped scarves to school. I never went to games with any of them, though, apart from Paul. If there were any group trips to Vicarage Road, I wasn't invited, and I don't remember ever bumping into any of my classmates on the terraces.

Anyway, by my mid-teens I had someone new to go to games with.

TUESDAY, DECEMBER 9 1980
COVENTRY CITY 5 WATFORD 0

Nigel lived next door, and from the point of view of a timid teenage Watford fan looking to expand his horizons, he had a lot going for him. He was a year older than me; he passed his driving test soon after his 17th birthday and bought a knackered old Triumph Herald, and he somehow acquired the mechanical know-how to keep it running; he was stocky and muscular and looked like the sort of bloke you wouldn't want to mess with; he was a diehard Watford fan; and, finally, he was quite happy to give me lifts to games.

Not just home games, either. Over a period of two or three years, Nigel and his Herald took me to Orient, Chelsea, West Ham and Arsenal, to Luton (never again...), to Wolverhampton and Birmingham. Early in the 1990-81 season, we even drove down to Southampton on a midweek evening for the first leg of a League Cup tie that Watford lost 4-0. Sadly, Nigel was on holiday for the return leg, and must be one of the few Hornets fans to have seen the prelude to Watford's finest hour and not the denouement.

On this particular Tuesday afternoon, Nigel picked me up from the school car park. (My school, that is – Haberdashers' Aske's in Elstree. He went to Grange Park comprehensive in Bushey.) I was in the sixth form by now, so fortunately I wasn't in uniform. At a guess, I would have been wearing a sports jacket and trousers, with my parka over the top. In the back seat were two of Nigel's mates from school. There was a bunch of these lads that we used to stand with on the Vicarage Road end. I came to recognise the faces and learnt some of their names, but I rarely talked to them. I was nervous (bordering on scared) of most of them. Not that I ever saw any of them do anything dodgy, but they were all older than me and infinitely more streetwise. If it all kicked off – and in those days, away fans still occasionally tried to 'take' the home end – I had an uneasy feeling that they would run towards trouble rather than away from it.

The car journey up the M1 and M6 to Coventry was uneventful. We were in an optimistic mood, though. Now in their second season in Division Two under Taylor, the Hornets had already beaten Southampton, Sheffield Wednesday and Nottingham Forest in the League Cup, and drawn 2-2 at home against Coventry in the quarter-final. A replay at Highfield Road would be tough, but nothing they couldn't handle.

How wrong we were. Watford were soundly beaten 5-0 (I've still never seen a heavier Watford defeat) on a freezing cold evening, and we slunk back to the Herald thoroughly depressed. On the outskirts of town, before we reached the motorway, Nigel pulled up in a layby, went round to the back of the car and came back with a couple of six-packs of lager.

We spent the journey home supping lukewarm beer and listening to John Peel's Radio One show on the car radio. John Lennon had been killed the night before, and Peel devoted the whole two-hour slot to Beatles and Lennon songs which we sang along with, at first mournfully and then with growing gusto as the booze kicked in. I was 18 and I'd never felt more grown-up, or more alive.

* * *

Soon after the start of the following season, Nigel went off to university. Not long after that, his parents moved away and we lost touch altogether. In the Facebook era, the concept of 'losing touch' seems rather quaint, but the fact is that, in those days, if you wanted to stay in contact with someone who didn't live nearby, you either had to phone them or write them a letter. I didn't have Nigel's address or phone number, so – short of hiring a private detective – that was pretty much that.

A year later, in the autumn of 1982, I went to university as well. My timing wasn't great. That spring, Watford had done the unthinkable, the unimaginable, and won promotion to Division One. Although I was able to see the first few home games, I missed large chunks of that first season in the top flight, and the next three seasons as well. My last game before I left for Cambridge was an 8-0 demolition of Sunderland, with Luther Blissett scoring four of the goals. It was an astonishing result for a club that had been playing at this level for less than a month, yet it says something about how spoilt Watford fans were in those days that we took it in our stride.

Like many people, I formed some of my closest and most enduring friendships at university – but none of them were with Watford fans. The odds are that there were other Hornets at Cambridge during my time there, but I never met one – never spotted a yellow, red and black striped scarf in the street, never heard a cry of 'You 'orns!' in a crowded college bar.

So I contented myself with reading reports of Watford games in the papers and making the most of the occasional opportunity to watch the players on TV. In those pre-Sky days, this mainly meant internationals. I particularly remember the day England played Brazil in Rio in a friendly, which they won thanks to a remarkable John Barnes goal that involved him dribbling from the halfway line, beating almost the entire Brazilian team before calmly slotting the ball over the line. In the aftermath, I enjoyed telling the crowd in the college TV room how I'd seen his first team debut. I'm sure I gave the impression that we Watford fans got to see this kind of skill week in, week out – and it wasn't so far from the truth, at that.

In 1986 I graduated, and that autumn I started work and moved into the first of a series of shared houses in London. I always made a point of choosing addresses in the north-west (or, at a pinch, north) of the capital, so that it wasn't too difficult to get back home to see my parents – and, of course, the Golden Boys.

The new matchday routine I established at this time lasted for more than 15 years. On a Saturday morning I would catch a train to Watford Junction and a bus to Bushey Heath, where I would have lunch with my parents. Then I would borrow their car (fortunately, they never went anywhere on a Saturday afternoon – as far as they were concerned, the shops might as well have shut at one o'clock), drive to the game, and afterwards return the car to the family home, have tea and then cadge a lift back to the station. The matches themselves I watched alone, first on the Vicarage Road end terrace and then in the stand that was built to replace it, where you could sit where you liked, to avoid being stuck with anyone you didn't like the look of.

Just occasionally, though, I managed to cajole someone into coming with me.

SATURDAY, OCTOBER 23 1993
WATFORD 4 BOLTON WANDERERS 3

Although there's no great tradition of football support among my ancestors, there have been occasional spells when one of the family has followed his local team. In the 1930s, my maternal grandfather would apparently walk from his home in East Sheen to Griffin Park to watch Brentford play; as I've already mentioned, my father followed Lincoln City while he was growing up; and then there was me, the only one to turn childhood support into a lifelong passion.

But my younger brother had to be different, didn't he. He came along to a few games at Vicarage Road with me and Dad in the early Seventies, but, mysteriously, he never developed any attachment to the Hornets. Instead, on the day of the 1975 FA Cup final, he suddenly announced that he was going to support whichever team won the game. West Ham United beat Fulham 2-0, and so he became a Hammers fan. (He recently reminded me that he'd fallen off his bike that morning and had been ordered to rest, so I suspect some kind of traumatic brain damage may actually be at the root of all this.)

To his credit, he followed through on his promise and has been a West Ham fan ever since. Mind you, he's strictly an arm-chair supporter; he can count the number of Hammers games he's attended on the fingers of one hand. Indeed, he's never been much of a spectator. Like my father, he's one of those people who is much happier playing sport than watching it.

Nevertheless, one Saturday in the autumn of 1993, for the first time in a fair few years, he announced that he'd like to come to Vicarage Road with me. The early Nineties was an iffy period in Watford's history, and the team that day included such bit-part players as Simon Sheppard, Alex Inglethorpe and Julian Alsford. It wasn't a promising line-up, and sure enough, Watford leaked goals. Not long after half-time, Bolton were 3-0 up and Chris was doubtless wondering why I bothered coming back week after week.

And then there occurred the most miraculous comeback I've ever seen Watford pull off, as they worked their way back to 3-3 just before full-time and then, astoundingly, won the game with a Gary Porter penalty in the dying seconds. It was thrilling stuff, and you'd think Chris might have been sufficiently impressed to give Watford another try.

Not a bit of it: he hasn't been to Vicarage Road since. I'd like to think it's because he knows nothing can top the experi-ence of watching a team win 4-3 after being 3-0 down with 20 minutes left to play. But I know it's really because he simply hasn't got the football-watching gene.

* * *

The Nineties may have been a bit of a lost decade where the Hornets were concerned, but two things happened that changed my Watford-supporting experience for good, and for the better. The first was the spread of the internet. At the risk of sounding even older than I am, younger readers might find it hard to comprehend just how much this revolutionised life for football supporters, and particularly those of us who followed teams below the highest echelons of the game.

Before the internet arrived, gleaning news about your club involved combing the national newspapers and listening avidly to the sports news on the radio.

You could usually find a short match report in the Sunday papers, but the only other news that might be deemed worthy of a national audience was when Watford were involved in a significant transfer – and, being Watford, that usually meant we were selling one of our best players to a bigger club, so it was news you'd rather not hear. If it hadn't been for the *Watford Observer*, we'd never have learned anything about what was going on at the club outside matchdays.

The internet gave us an official club website, and with it the luxury of daily updates. More significantly, especially for an isolated fan like me, it gave us unofficial views, and particularly the Watford Mailing List. I must have read about it in the matchday programme or the *Watford Observer* and joined in 1998 or '99, and it became my new favourite thing.

The mailing list still operates the same way today. It is an exchange of news and views by email that is a cross between the letters page of a newspaper and a robust bar room debate. In the office where I worked at the time, I was the only person with an internet connection, and I would spend much of the day firing off responses to messages and engaging in heated debate with Watford fans I'd never met, but who I soon came to feel I knew intimately.

It couldn't last, of course. Soon enough I found myself in a job where I was actually expected to spend the working day working, and I switched to the digest version of the mailing list, which is essentially a summary of the day's exchanges to read in one go which avoids the time-consuming job of keeping up with a flurry of messages being volleyed back and forth in real time. It was much less exhausting, but also frustrating. I would read the digest email in the evening and discover that an entire debate on one of my pet topics had been started and finished while I was otherwise occupied, and that my killer argument had been put forward by someone else in my absence – and not as well as I would have put it, at that.

I still posted from time to time, but mostly late at night after a few drinks. More often than not, some rash statement I'd made would be picked up and hurled violently back at me, and as I'm not by nature an argumentative person, I tended to withdraw from the fray rather than answer in kind. Eventually I stopped posting altogether, unless I had the answer to a question someone had asked, or I'd spotted something unusual at a Watford game that no one else had remarked on.

That didn't diminish the value of the mailing list for me as an online community, though. I think of it as being rather like the House of Commons; there are those who are constantly up at the dispatch box, being witty and demonstrative and engaging in the cut and thrust of debate, and then there are those of us who occupy the back benches, and who mostly listen and occasionally bellow odd sounds to signal our approval or outrage at what's being said. But even backbenchers occasionally feel the need to step into the limelight and say their piece.

MONDAY, MAY 31 1999
WATFORD 2 BOLTON WANDERERS 0

It was a sunny Saturday afternoon, the start of a much-anticipated Bank Holiday weekend, and I was putting up shelves in the bedroom of my flat in Finsbury Park. On the radio, the Third Division play-off final between Leyton Orient and Scunthorpe had just got under way, and it seemed like the start of the build-up to Watford's own big day.

I was up the stepladder with the drill in my hand when the phone rang in the hall. It was my mother: 'Your father's just collapsed in the kitchen. I think he's dead.'

I won't trouble you with the details of the rest of that distressing day. (Though I still haven't quite found it in me to forgive the minicab driver I hurriedly hired to drive me to Bushey Heath, and who ran out of petrol on the M1, leaving me stranded on the hard shoulder in the afternoon sun, watching coachloads of victorious Scunthorpe fans making their way home while I waited for him to return from the nearest petrol station with a jerry can of fuel.) The point is that, at some point over that long weekend, the question arose of what I was going to do about the play-off final. There was nothing we could usefully do on Bank Holiday Monday (registering the death, arranging the funeral and the rest of it would have to wait for normality to resume on the Tuesday), so it was decided that I might as well go to Wembley as planned.

I felt more alone in the crowd than usual that Monday afternoon, especially as my ticket placed me up in the gods, surrounded by family groups who weren't inclined to sing and shout the way I wanted – no, needed – to. The match itself was both a distraction from my situation and a reminder of it, as I couldn't help thinking back to all those games Dad had taken me to when I was younger. And when Allan Smart scored that goal in the final minutes, I found myself yelling and cheering and crying all at once in a moment of pure catharsis. After the final whistle I stayed on as long as I could, singing along with the victory songs until I was hoarse.

A week or two later, I decided to try to write about all this – Dad's death, and how it had affected my experience of the play-off final – and it seemed the most natural thing in the world to do so in the form of a message to the Watford Mailing List. I wasn't expecting anything in return, but I got something anyway; a steady stream of kind, thoughtful messages acknowledging my post and the emotions behind it, from people who I'd never met and who didn't know me from Adam. It was extraordinarily moving, and for the first time I really understood what people mean when they talk about an online community.

* * *

The other thing that happened in the late-Nineties was the building of the new Rookery Stand, which then became the home end. Only now, instead of sitting wherever I wanted, I would be required (as a season ticket holder) to choose a seat that would be mine for every home game.

One sunny summer's afternoon, I made my way to Vicarage Road to audition seats in the new stand. It was an odd experience. The pitch was a vibrant shade of green, as bright and new as on that day in 1970 when I saw it for the first time, and was being watered by sprinklers. But there were no markings or goalposts, which was rather disorientating. It meant I had nothing concrete to base my decision on as I moved up and down the rows, and a few seats to the left and right, in search of the optimum spot. Finally I found a seat that suited me and went back down to the concourse to put my name to it. I've been there ever since.

The one thing I couldn't choose on that idyllic summer's day, of course, was my neighbours. I could have turned up for the first game of the following season to find myself sandwiched between a 20-stone racist and one of those people who believes referees deserve that special kind of abuse otherwise reserved for paedophiles. In the days leading up to the match, I tried not to think about this too much.

As it happened, I got lucky. To my left was a man a year or two older than me with a young son, and with whom I instantly established an easy-going rapport. To my right were a couple of quiet teenagers who were perfectly pleasant company, but who disappeared at the end of one season, never to be seen again. They were replaced by an older couple who have been there ever since. And so our little community in the middle of the Rookery Stand was established.

MONDAY, APRIL 14 2012
WATFORD 1 HULL CITY 1

I'm in my seat by 2.20, having no particular reason to hang around in the concourse once I've bought my cup of coffee. As usual, I'm the first to arrive, and I have the entire row to myself for a while. Time to read the programme and watch the players warming up. It pays to pay attention. Just a couple of weeks ago, an older guy who sits in the row in front of me got hit square in the face by a wayward shot from Troy Deeney during the warm-up.

The couple on my right usually take their seats about 20 minutes before kick-off. I know various things about them – where they live, where they moved to Watford from, where their daughter (to whom they text score updates during matches) is currently living – but I don't know the name of the woman, who sits next to me. That's one of the curious rules of modern football watching, I've noticed: if a couple have season tickets at a football ground, they will always sit the same way round.

My other neighbour leaves it much later. He has a genius for judging his arrival to perfection, such that the referee is often on the point of putting his whistle to his lips to start the game when he appears. Today he's not far off that standard, arriving as the players are taking up their starting positions.

The game is less than enthralling and the football is poor, so there's time to chat. We talk about the state of the pitch, the current situation with Saracens (the couple on my right are rugby fans as well), whether we're renewing our season tickets (we all are, of course), and occasionally even the match. With nothing much at stake, even the sending-off of Adrian Mariappa is merely a talking point rather than a source of anxiety.

When I say we talk, what actually happens is that I have alternate – and occasionally simultaneous – conversations with the people on either side of me. Sometimes I just make an observation and wait to see if either of my neighbours responds. Sometimes I'm just talking to myself – but then, I've always done that at football matches, even in the days when I stood on my own on the terraces.

The game ends 1-1, with Watford on top in the final stages, despite Hull having had an extra man for nearly half an hour. We all leave smartly at the final whistle, after applauding the players off the pitch, with the standard farewell: 'See you in a couple of weeks.' As it turns out, neither of my neighbours turn up for the Middlesbrough game, but no matter; we'll doubtless be reunited in August for the first game of the new season.

* * *

Back in the Nineties, reading Nick Hornby's *Fever Pitch* got me thinking about the varying levels of commitment of football fans. Hornby is at the fundamentalist end of the scale. In the book, he says that if his best friend was getting married on a Saturday afternoon and Arsenal were at home, then he'd go to the football match. (Mind you, these days the chances of a clash on a Saturday are probably fairly slight, thanks to Sky.)

At the other end of the scale are people like my brother, whose support of West Ham is extremely casual. As I write this, the Hammers have just won the play-off final and promotion back to the Premier League. I'm sure Chris is happy about this, but I doubt it'll make a great difference to his life.

And me? I'm somewhere above the average commitment level. I will go to every home game unless something comes up. That 'something' is occasionally work, but more often a family event. It feels like Watford occupies about the right amount of space in my life. I check the internet for news several times a day, follow the discussions on the mailing list, sometimes join in conversations about the team with people I don't know.

So, although I sometimes envy Stuart his social experience of supporting Brentford, I also think it might be a bit much for me. Not having any friends who are Watford fans separates that part of my life from the others and gives it a distinct character.

I got married eight years ago, and of the many special elements of that day, two things are relevant here. One was when Stuart, in his best man's speech, said that he knew I'd make a good husband because my loyalty was proven – after all, I'd stuck with Watford for 30-odd years. It got a laugh, but I took it as a compliment.

The other was earlier in the day, when the vicar pointed out that we were getting married, not just in front of God, but in front of the community of our families and friends. I don't have much time for God, but I am a great believer in community. And in this sense at least, it strikes me that being a football fan is like following a religion. As a Watford fan, I may not know any of my fellow devotees, but that doesn't matter; as a member of the community of supporters, I'm never alone.

Tim Turner is a journalist who lives in south-west London with his wife and a cat. He is the author of three novels, including *First Time I Met The Blues,* the story of three teenagers growing up in Watford in the mid-Sixties who form a blues band. For more information go to www.timturnerbooks.co.uk

9

The journalism of **Oliver Phillips** took generations of Watford fans behind closed doors at Vicarage Road.

Every Friday, the newspaper would be spread across laps and kitchen tables so every word could be absorbed.

Oliver looks back on more than half a century of watching the Hornets, from a schoolboy on the terraces to the doyen of the press box.

The first Watford match he saw, against Manchester United, was famous for The Goal That Never Was and as this account of the six decades that followed shows, football may have changed beyond all recognition and yet remains exactly the same.

SIX DECADES

BY OLIVER PHILLIPS

I was a convert to the principle of goal-line technology at the age of eight and since then have never changed my mind. Of course, the ability to determine immediately whether a ball had crossed the line or not, in all probability, had not been developed in 1950.

Yet it was more than likely I was not alone in resenting that fact. I should imagine every Watford fan among the 32,384-strong, then record crowd on January 28 1950, would have felt such technology would have righted a wrong.

The Blues, as they were, had drawn in the FA Cup the new power on the scene, Manchester United, a club that had spent much of the 1930s in Division Two until a chap called Matt Busby had taken over the also-rans at the end of the Second World War. Without the help of Middle East or Russian investment, Busby had propelled United into the top two for six seasons and ultimately their first title in 45 years. The former FA Cup holders were coming to Vicarage Road and I was to make my debut on the terraces.

I did not know it then but looking back I was never the same after that day. Football was frowned upon in my family and my sudden interest in the game had caught my parents off guard. I had watched a few matches on television where the quick-silver speed and ferocious shooting of Jackie Milburn had caught my eye.

The commentator had mentioned Wor Jackie had an

individual ability to complete a sliding tackle, collect the ball and rise in a fluid movement. As if on cue, he duly did that on the small screen: I was captivated. I followed his career to his retirement, through three FA Cup finals, and then picked up the fact he had a young nephew making his way in the game and followed his career. His name was Bobby Charlton.

Everyone, outside my household, was talking about the local side's big FA Cup tie, the biggest for years and eventually an uncle called in a couple of favours and took me.

I remember being stunned by the size of Watford's stadium – so much bigger than Chipperfield's – the atmosphere, the smoke, the hats and the noise. Another thing struck me quite forcibly: the extremes of anger and irritation that emanated from fans as I saw adults from an entirely new perspective.

At first sight, for an eight-year-old it was all quite daunting.

Then came the 35th minute when the acerbic Taffy Davies, deftly went past the magnificent Johnny Carey and lobbed the ball beyond the despairing Lancaster in United's goal.

The home crowd roared as the ball headed for the back of the net and even Aston's belated bid to head clear failed to kill the certainty, shared by Busby and many United players, that Watford had taken the lead.

Alas the view was not shared by Mr B.M Griffiths, the referee. He waved play on, United went on to win the game 1-0 and so a generation of Watford fans would readily recall 'The Goal That Never Was' right into their dotage.

I committed the name of Mr Griffiths to the department of my mind reserved for Dracula, Frankenstein, my French teacher and a chap called Adolf my Dad said I wouldn't have liked.

It was an education: I learnt that adults are not faultless; that life is not always full of long, hot summer days, honey and Mars bars and, despite the claim everyone had the right of appeal, not so little Watford.

Even so, I was hooked. Mr Griffiths went on to enjoy a distinguished refereeing career that included being in charge of the Matthews Cup Final in 1953, and my life moved on...

Well, I had no appreciation that Vicarage Road, which was in reality a ramshackle ground, would come to play such a significant role in my life. I liked writing, was enraptured with football, but my return to the ground was delayed by logistics and stints at boarding school until the family moved back to the town of my birth in 1956.

I was fortunate in that a near neighbour to our new home was Watford director Doug Broad. One thing led to another and I went to Vicarage Road as a guest, sitting on the bench and then in the box.

That provided the boost and quickly I made it back to the terraces where I remained for several years, becoming a regular among the Boys On The Bend along with a mate, Jim. I stood to the left of the Marie Celeste tea-bar (it never opened) on the unfashionable part of the ground also frequented by a young lad called Reggie Dwight.

THE 1950s

I can see Johnny Meadows, circa 1957, jog almost the length of the pitch towards the ball placed on the penalty spot in front of the opposition goal. He hardly missed a stride as he arrived and rolled the ball into the corner; and I mean rolled. I remember clapping and noticing others around me were all but doubled up at the manner in which he had taken the penalty kick. They chuckled, cheered and shook their heads for Meadows's spot-kicks were to be savoured for their sheer audacity.

Perhaps the modern athleticism of goalkeepers would enable them to dive the wrong way, quickly recover and come close to saving Johnny's slow-motion penalties, which always depended on the keeper guessing wrongly. However, they were not modern keepers and those penalties were that special.

Of course when old duffers such as myself, talk about the past, as I am now, there is always the question from the sceptical: 'Yes, very good, but would he have got away with that now?' Or 'Would that player have been such a success in the modern game?' Perhaps even the contention: 'He wouldn't last ten minutes in today's game.'

Such comparisons are futile. They played at the time they did, triumphed in that era against the relevant opposition and that was their aim. Their achievements delighted us then just as the achievements of modern players delight us now. After all, when we salute a great goal or a spectacular piece of dexterity or ingenuity today, we would not take kindly to someone tapping us on the shoulder and saying: 'But he won't get away with that in 2050.'

Meadows's replacement on penalty-taking duty was one Clifford Charles Holton, Big Cliff, The Big Fella, whose arrival kick-started the modern Watford story; the man who enabled the fans to stop recalling The Goal That Never Was as the near high-point of achievement and delight instead in the reality of FA Cup glory and promotion.

When Cliff stepped up to take a penalty, goalkeepers would have been comforted to know their insurance payments were up to date. He was the hardest kicker of a dead ball I have ever seen and, remember, or perhaps you don't, they were the old leather balls which, as Taffy Davies once described to me: 'On a wet, muddy day, those balls would get so heavy it would take two men to lift it for a throw-in.'

I can easily recall Cliff's sweeping passes inside the full back for the likes of Micky Benning or Freddie Bunce to run onto; his exceptional pace for a big man who was inclined to pace himself 'not just for a game but for a season' as he put it to me, and then there were those fulminating shots, not least the goal that helped knock top-flight Birmingham out of the FA Cup.

His influence inside the dressing-room was considerable. He was shocked on his first day to see the players gathered round the table waiting for the training kit. As it was deposited, the players dived in for the best of what were little more than rags. Cliff promptly persuaded the chairman to invest in new kit.

Suddenly a Fourth Division club was fashionable: they even had four-figure gates at the title-winning reserve team games. Here he was, a football giant who had stepped from Highbury and consideration for an England call-up to Fourth Division Watford at the age of 29 and scored 48 goals in one season.

Watford grabbed fourth place in the promotion race, possibly side-tracked by the brilliant FA Cup run to the fifth round, which helped them meet their HP payments on the Big Fella. They were not champions, they did not dominate or dictate the fortunes of the division so why all the fuss? That season was a classic example of how style is something you remember long after the exact results are forgotten – something I tried to pass on to young journalists for 40 years.

Cliff was too bright and had too much presence for the genial manager Ron Burgess, a great player in his day but unable to transfer into words what he knew, nor was he able to man-motivate. Mind you motivation in those days was a limited skill at best. Take Burgess's predecessor, the gin-soaked Neil McBain, who once asked Peter Walker to join him briefly on the team coach. Peter, whose great ability was at an inverse ratio to his confidence, was always in need of a pep-talk.

'Now laddie,' imparted McBain in days long before substitutes were allowed: 'I want you to give everything you've got in the first half. Don't stop for a moment. Do you get that?'

Peter nodded and McBain continued: 'Then, in the second half, I want you to do the same.'

Ron Burgess had only recently been a cultured wing-half hero for Tottenham and Wales. Then he was technically, if not effectively, Watford's manager. How sobering it was for a young journalist to pop into the ground during the summer and come across Ron and trainer Pat Molloy, decorating the inside of the reception hall: one of their summer tasks.

Management duties have changed over the years but so too has the game, the attitudes, diet, fitness and professionalism. Can you imagine a key winger, preparing to take on the top side in the division in an FA Cup replay, cycling home after being let off early from his shift at Odhams with cries of 'good luck' ringing in his ears?

Then, 'after having my tea', he cycled down through the crowds to Vicarage Road, continued down Occupation Road past the corrugated iron fence that surrounded the ground, where he joined Big Cliff and his colleagues for the key match. Back in 1960 Micky Benning, who along with Cliff was a part-timer, did not consider it unusual to be cycling down to play in a match after a day's work.

Ironically, that night he and his fellow winger Freddie Bunce had key tasks. They had to track back and help full-backs Bobby Bell and Ken Nicholas cut out the threat of Southampton wingers Sydenham and Paine.

That sounded pretty much like tactics. In 1959-60?

THE 1960s

Yes, it was the dawn of a new era, when tactics began to play an increasing and at one stage an almost obsessive part in the game. The days when you went out and tried to score more goals than the opposition were giving way to the need to concede fewer goals than your opponents in order to win. Teams started to give 'disciplined' performances.

These new trends were resented by the older profession-
als, who answered with undeniable logic, when instructed to
practice with their weaker foot in order not to be a one-footed
player, by drawing attention to the era's finest exponent: 'Well
Ferenc Puskas has only a left foot but it doesn't handicap him.'

Defending would become an art form and the days were
fast disappearing when managers would remind defenders
who strayed too far forward: 'Look, you know why you are a
defender. It's because you aren't good enough to be an attacker.
So stay back.'

I was in at the ground floor of the sea change in football,
particularly in England where Puskas and his Magical Magyars
had provoked a somewhat gradual rethink with their 6-3 win at
Wembley in 1953. Dismissed by some, perhaps with more hope
than belief, as a freak result, England's decline in the football
firmament was confirmed in the return match a year later when
Hungary ran out 7-1 winners.

It took a few years but the penny started to drop. By
1960 the new thinking had even reached the Fourth Division
and England won the World Cup six years later, with a team
described as 'the wingless wonders', with the greatest goalscorer
of the time, Jimmy Greaves, sidelined while the less prolific but
more industrious Geoff Hurst grabbed his chance.

How could this be when hitherto skill had been the quality
that opened defences, thrilled the masses and made the difference? Exquisite footballer and writer, Danny Blanchflower
remembered when Bill Nicholson shook his head and remarked
that Greaves had scored two goals and hardly broken sweat in
a Spurs game. Nicholson, who was the architect of the finest football I have seen until the 21st Century Barcelona came
along, was looking to build on his famed double-winning side
but Blanchflower crystallised the issue: 'What you want him to
do? Run about all afternoon and score none?'

Industry and the busily functional came into vogue; skill was to be welcomed only if covered in sweat.

In the early 1960s, players could no longer coast through games, turning on a cameo half-hour in an attempt to win the match and the plaudits. Watford saw many potential talents fall by the wayside because of suspect application and there are players who could and should have made more of their careers; from Mel Brisbane to Larry McGettigan, Charlie Livesey to Dennis Bond; from Craig Ramage to Roy Low; from Glyn Hodges to Graham French and some of Luca Vialli's signings.

Perhaps fans knew Big Cliff could turn it on and on other occasions loaf about, but he always stayed well on the plus-side. Typically when the Hornets appeared to be losing an important game, the chairman popped into the dressing room at half-time and offered a cash bonus. In those days of the maximum wage, it was illegal but it was not unknown. Cliff scored a couple straight after the interval and was heard to mutter during the second half: 'Fancy not telling us until half-time.'

He was one of those rare individuals in that he not only had a presence on the field but off the field as well. In the Holton era I can clearly recall the buzz, the belief that at last Watford were going somewhere when Cliff was there, but I, as the most junior reporter, happened to stumble on an exclusive story when, following a tip, I was sent to The Rest Hotel, Kenton, in September 1961.

I arrived in time to see Holton sign for Northampton. He scored a hat-trick that night at Crystal Palace and the first Watford fans knew of it was my piece in the stop-press and the back pages of the national papers.

Ticket increases, losing runs, unpopular chairmen such as Bonser, Petchey or Simpson; unpopular managers such as Dave Bassett; the invasion of the directors' box in the 1990s: none of them compared in the slightest to the furore that hit Watford when that news broke. For two seasons Watford lost their way, Burgess was sacked and then the Hornets regained momentum, achieving the highest points total in the history of the club to that date. But the disenchanted did not forget.

The new manager in 1963 was the authoritarian Bill McGarry, who took no prisoners, kept all the directors, apart from Doug Broad, at arm's length and was brusque to the point of rude. Yet, when comparing McGarry with Burgess, it was no contest. McGarry was organised and able to motivate. He also had that northern grit epitomised when it was suggested he faced a tough fixture at Vicarage Road and could lose. 'Lose at home?' he exploded. 'Do you want people to point at me in street? You don't bloody lose at home.'

This attitude together with a fair appreciation of the tactical necessities of the increasingly modern game brought him within touching distance of triumph and, even though they just missed out on promotion, they didn't 'bloody lose at home'!

He also introduced a theme to help bring an identity to Fortress Vicarage Road – the Z-Cars theme as the club established a record run of 27 home games without defeat.

Most importantly, McGarry derided and all but humiliated Charlie Livesey into producing the finest season by an individual that I have witnessed. Bill chided the striker at the concept of Charlie being 'a former boy wonder' playing in Division Three and that was the motivation Charlie needed.

A big man, with a dribbling ability second to none, Charlie was inspirational and he crowned that one afternoon with a goal against promotion rivals Oldham. He took on the entire defence, while Jimmy McAnearney ran unmarked to his left, repeatedly calling for the ball. Livesey finished with a superb shot and the majority of those there, including Jimmy, will affirm it was the finest goal they had ever seen.

Charlie, like Cliff before him, never celebrated goals. He

just walked back to the halfway line but did allow himself a question. Looking to McAnearney, he asked with irony and a deadpan face: 'Was there something you wanted to say Jimmy?'

It was my last season spent mainly on the terraces with my mate Jim but the fans were slow to warm to the promotion push. The residue of resentment over the Holton sale remained and the onlookers found it hard to embrace a concept that involved ten-men funnelling back and then, when gaining possession, following the manager's dictum: 'Kick it up to Charlie.'

Charlie, with his big backside, superb dribbling skills and exceptional acceleration, would bring the ball down and go walkabout while his colleagues streamed out of defence. In modern parlance: when the ball was played to Charlie, the ball stuck. Then when he had allies he would turn and head for goal, often, it seemed, treating his team-mates as no more than decoys.

Watford missed out on promotion that year, beaten by Coventry City and Crystal Palace, whose promotion their striker Holton regarded as his best achievement, 'because Palace were the poorest side in the division'.

Watford sold Charlie and the young, shy keeper who later became the assertive and confident Pat Jennings. I knew them both: Pat at the local coffee bar and Charlie, supping late-night pints at Bushey's Herkomer Club after the pubs had shut.

Drinking the night before a game? Well that was deemed almost acceptable compared to the old days when the trainer had to be sent up from Vicarage Road to drag the players out of the pub in time for the kick-off. In the 1960s, there was still a culture of drinking, wenching and gambling among footballers but the dietary constraints in modern days have since knocked the booze into touch.

The trouble with the likes of Charlie, with his market-trader pockets, was that he could do 'a little of this and a little of that' and probably earn more money than Watford paid him.

The career does not last long and there is no going back: the time is lost forever. Craig Ramage and others of that ilk have regrets they did not make more of their talent. Charlie, who played for Chelsea, England under-23s, Gillingham, Watford and got back into the top flight, albeit very briefly with Northampton Town, gained the subsequent realisation that he had, for one season, extracted the digit from his ample rear and delivered something equal to his precocious talent. That was confirmed when he chose to be cremated in a Watford shirt.

It was when McGarry left Vicarage Road in 1964 that I was given the opportunity to cover Watford full-time for the *West Herts Post*. I had made my first team debut some 18 months earlier, worrying how I would tackle the report. Not for the first or the last time, Big Cliff illuminated my football life scoring a hat-trick against Watford for Crystal Palace. I was disappointed for Watford with regards to the defeat but nevertheless grateful to Cliff: the report wrote itself.

I remember when first sitting in the press box back in 1960 and hearing all the varied opinions shouted in the direction of the press. I wondered if I would be strong enough to take the fusillade of criticisms which would head my way. I decided, where possible, to air all views while expressing my own, so, in effect, catering for most people most of the time.

'Some would argue' was the sort of line I would use to introduce the alternative thinking. Years later Steve Harrison, struggling as Watford's manager, pulled me up on that. 'How long are you going to hide behind expressions such as "others would say"? They are your views.'

He was so wrong. They were often the views I could appreciate but with which I usually did not agree. What I thought, I wrote: I found it simpler that way, although it won me few friends in the dressing room.

I was fortunate when assigned the Watford coverage. I

arrived on time for my first interview with the new manager, Ken Furphy, with questions already noted.

'You seem a bit nervous,' he said.

'It's my first day doing this job,' I confessed.

'Mine too. We'll have to struggle along together,' he replied. And we did.

Forty one years after agreeing to struggle together, Ken and his wife travelled up from Devon to attend my retirement bash. We had our ups and downs and he once disinvited me to a party because of a satirical article a colleague had written, which had included a parody of Ken's press statements claiming: 'There was a distinct period in the 12th minute when we were on top.'

It was a reminder that people can take themselves too seriously and later I embraced the more realistic antidote of Terry Challis's cartoons.

It was an interesting exercise for me, because I always sought the antidote to the professional viewpoint. You could be exposed so much to the inner 'professional' thinking, you could be in danger of losing touch with readers and the supporters. I realised that quite early on when a friend of mine, Jim, picked me up on a comment I made about feeling sorry for supporters.

I explained that they did not know the whole story and in saying that, I realised it was down to me to provide them with as much of the story as the laws of libel or respect for off-the-record information, could manage. In the days of the Shrodells and Main Stand enclosures, I would leave one of my sports assistants to cover the reserve game and circulate among the fans. I had been part of it once but I needed to keep my fingers on the pulse and plug into that terrace humour: more often gallows humour.

I always tried to hold the mirror up, not only to the club but the supporters. I saw that as the key facet of the job.

One facet I never came to terms with were mistakes: errors,

typographical or otherwise. I took them as a personal insult and an error spotted on Friday morning would haunt me until I was well into the next issue.

When we used to give players marks for their performance, we failed to spot that Vic Akers had been marked down as 0 instead of 6 in the team listing. Not only did I have to live with that error for a week but Vic must have felt even worse.

It is not for me to say whether 'this boy done well', broke even or should have done better. I agonised over so many things, sentences, articles, observations, judgements. You always took the job home with you. Put it this way, whatever the verdict, I know I gave it my best shot.

Of course, by the time I started to report on Watford, Taffy Davies had moved on but I was to meet up with him later. One of the first things I undertook upon taking over the full-time coverage in 1964, was to look through the archive files.

Every Wednesday afternoon I would focus on a season from yesteryear. I worked back to the war and then into the 1930s. I was able to draw on past comparisons and achievements and drop them into my articles, so giving this young upstart a smidgen of credibility.

So, I learnt about those of whom I had picked up the briefest of mentions. I learnt why, as a schoolboy, it was deemed significant by my contemporaries to catch a bus driven 'by Skilly' – the famous Williams, the Watford keeper with the safe pair of hands from before and after the First World War.

I also read of the then record-holder, whose goals and appearance totals seemed unbeatable: Tommy 'Boy' Barnett, of whom I later learned was a true great. I gleaned that from Taffy, who, it transpired, did not have a good word to say about anything with a Watford link. He tended towards the acerbic. Yet, he would enthuse about Tommy: 'The best player I ever played with: all action; all skill; all right foot. He made play and he made goals; scored goals. He could ghost past a player on either side, could dribble and he was as good a crosser of the ball as I have ever seen. He was the tactical leader.'

Boy Barnett remained a legend in my mind, yet I was to see those ancient records overhauled.

Ken Furphy was very much the young, green, eager manager, who had been no great shakes as a player and did not have the authority of a great playing career enjoyed by such international predecessors as Burgess and McGarry.

Furph, as he became known, was well versed in the new tactical thinking. His era commenced as the old school, while protesting the establishment of the new wave, was fading fast. Many wrote off Ken by yesterday's standards including George Harris who would have had an even better and certainly longer Watford career had he not misjudged Furphy's potential. 'I admitted to him years later: I got him wrong,' said George, one of my favourite players from that era.

George was probably among the best three headers of the ball the club ever had. He could also cross, take penalties and was prepared to work his socks off. He would have helped Watford to an even greater success in 1969, had he stayed but opted to join Reading.

Furphy had to convert a sceptical public who loved the likes of warhorse Duncan Welbourne, but while fans admired his commitment, they liked a bit of flair as well but were frustrated as work-rate seemed to take precedence. Furphy was there when the new thinking took root and he had to explain to an exasperated public why someone wearing a number three shirt did not have to play at left back.

It was the end of the old 2-3-5 line-up, which had held sway for decades, and it gave way to the numbers game, adopted by managers to fox the opposition when presenting the pre-match teamsheet.

Gradually Furph assembled a squad which included the commanding, majestic Keith Eddy, whose economy of movement bordered on the lazy but he was always in the right place when needed. I have related before how he finished a game of chess with me in an empty coach outside Gay Meadow before strolling into the ground and dressing room where he grabbed a progamme, lit up a cigarette and sat down unconcerned by his lateness.

Then there was a combative Tom Walley, who took no prisoners on the training pitch, let alone on match days, but the one probably remembered best was the mercurial Stewart Scullion, who dribbled for fun and was to cause striker Pat Morrissey to comment at half-time of a match during the 1970s: 'I gave Scully the ball after eight minutes and I aim to hold him upside down in the shower to see what he did with it.'

Scully, who beat five men twice within a minute and scored the quality of goal to rival Charlie's, was either brilliant or frustrating but hardly ever dull. He was pure theatre.

Furph's maxim was to contain and destroy and they deployed that tactic so well during the 1968-69 season that they gained promotion to the second tier for the first time.

There were heady moments that season, with Brian Owen scoring a goal after around 12 seconds; then scoring a freak goal which was 'in-off the floodlights'.

Watford were drawn against the European champions, Manchester United, in the FA Cup at Old Trafford. Scullion scored after two minutes with a thunderous shot but United pegged them back to force a replay.

That FA Cup tie replay, which saw Vicarage Road's attendance record from the previous United visit broken, prompted me to meet up with Taffy Davies about 'The Goal That Never Was' from the last time against United, so completing the circle from my childhood. Said Taffy: 'It was definitely a goal.'

THE 1970s

The decade opened with Watford fighting against relegation yet reaching the FA Cup semi-finals after a dramatic win over Liverpool at Vicarage Road. Furph was brilliant at one-off games, getting his tactics superbly drawn up and applied, schooling his players to the letter. 'When you went on the pitch, you knew what your opposite number would do. Furph was spot on. It [playing the game] was like reading a book a second time,' said Duncan Welbourne.

But behind the scenes, things were going awry. Chairman Jim Bonser held on to power, snubbed overtures from the equally rich, indulged his own petty dislikes with purges against various people such as one wealthy man who found his new seat was directly behind a pillar. He went to the club secretary Ron Rollitt to complain and Bonser, spotting this inevitable outcome, followed him and said: 'If you don't bloody like it you know where you can go.'

The Watford fan duly went to Luton, became chairman there and lauded it over the Hornets for a decade or so.

Bonser had been chaired round the Town Hall when Watford won promotion but his ultra conservative policies were based on his expectancy for Furph to continue to make bargain-basement signings but, while the manager had made a little go a long way, you needed extra quality in Division Two, and that meant extra funds. The chairman claimed the board was democratic, but three of them were business associates, two working out of the same Harrow building.

Sidney Lepard would be primed to make a proposal; Bonser would congratulate him on the worth of his proposal and second it. He would then turn to the remaining four, knowing two would vote for him, and deemed the decision had been arrived at democratically. 'You couldn't get anywhere,' fumed director Doug Broad. Bonser steered the club well to start with, secured a stand extension, a new lease and two promotions but then held on too long, overseeing the club's return to the bottom division.

Furphy travelled to Bonser's holiday base in the summer of 1971 and persuaded the chairman to agree to various individuals coming onto the board. The chairman then reneged, and the manager left the club. That was a sad day and I remember the photographer Mike Dellow took a symbolic picture of the sunset over Vicarage Road while awaiting the outcome of a board meeting. It proved a prophetic picture.

George Kirby came in with more positive thinking than tactical nous, and inherited the legacy of insufficient transfer investment. It was sad to see the chance lost, relegation back to Division Three and then, under Mike Keen, further demotion.

From the initial high of the Holton era, all the progress had been undone and the early 1970s were depressing. For my money, there was one highlight, a little sideshow postponing the otherwise unrelenting downhill struggle. Furphy had signed a young goalscorer who his successor, Kirby, inherited and did not rate. 'He is not courageous,' said Kirby of Billy Jennings.

When travelling with them to Luton to see a reserve match, George's wife Peggy observed this was a chance to see Jennings, of whom she had read so much locally.

'Oh, he'll score, Peg,' said George, as if that was just a minor facet to his game.

Former striker George spent most of his career, letting the centre half know he was in business, so the concept of a slightly lazy, non-physical striker did not appeal. He was not alone. His replacement Mike Keen had similar misgiving about Jennings – would you believe during a season the striker scored 29 goals?

Billy pointed out one day that he had accidentally bumped into the centre half during a match. 'They said in the dressing room that he was very wary of me after that. Did you notice anything?' he asked me, plainly bemused.

'No I don't chase everything or put my slight frame against great big centre halves. I score goals and to do that there is no point arriving in the penalty area either lame or exhausted.'

Billy was sold for the first six-figure fee in the club's history: almost double the previous record. Strange really, because 'he only scored goals', but Jennings would have been a terrace hero in the 1950s. He was a throwback; a man with a talent and if he was not the bravest of strikers, he turned that into an asset, attacking the ball with spring-heeled leaps much earlier in its trajectory, so avoiding the attentions of a defender.

Jennings was replaced by someone who supposedly was prepared to work harder and mix it with defenders. The result was relegation because, goalscorers, in my opinion, are born, not created and Watford without Jennings had little in the way of end product.

Looking back over the years we had Holton, Livesey, Dai Ward, Endean, Jennings, Keith Mercer, Blissett, Poskett, Mo Johnston, Paul Wilkinson, Gary Penrice and Kevin Phillips, who were natural goalscorers. Gifton Noel-Williams might have developed that way had not chronic arthritis limited his mobility but no one else until possibly the likes of Danny Graham were truly goalscorers as opposed to forwards who scored goals, like Colin West, Tommy Mooney, Ross Jenkins and Gerry Armstrong.

Neither Kirby nor Keen rated Jennings but I got on well with both managers, although neither had time for each other, and each of them suffered relegation. George believed luck and man-management were key components and tactics were less so. He convinced me, wrongly it transpires, for unfortunately George had no luck and his man-management did not prove too hot.

He did resent chairman Jim Bonser's spy-system: stooges who would report back to 'JB' as soon as they had anything to tell. George took a perverse delight in not answering his phone in the mornings, knowing there was an attempt to find out if he was in or late for work.

George took to me and remained a friend after his Watford days ended, whereas Keen and I got on extremely well but Mike, I learnt subsequently, went out of his way, believing that keeping me happy was pivotal. I thought his co-operation was out of respect, not concern and that was disappointing.

It was certainly unusual, sitting in Mike's office on a Thursday morning when the local evening newspaper rang and the manager would ask me what he should give them. I thought he did that because he liked me, not because he feared me.

Later Graham Taylor took over and access was far more restricted. 'Perhaps they needed you more than I do,' he told me curtly. Our relationship improved greatly over the next ten years, from what was an awkward beginning.

Mike Keen did find Terry Challis's cartoons something of a cross to bear and subsequent managers were caught in two minds initially, before settling down to varying degrees of disconcerted acceptance. I did not like cartoons in sport as a rule but those cartoons were great because they captured the terrace thinking and Terry never lost that despite years of sitting alongside me in press boxes up and down the country.

When Taylor left Watford that sad time in 1987, Terry caught the moment but stressed, he had both done a great job 'with our club'. He always stressed the temporary custodianship of 'our club', be it Elton John or Jack Petchey.

Even when Elton took over, there was little improvement at Watford but a year into his chairmanship, he was persuaded to persist in the pursuit of the Lincoln City manager, Graham Taylor. We all know that decision brought about the finest and

most successful period in the club's history, but the changes
Graham introduced off the field were almost as important as
his acumen in fashioning effective and exciting sides.

In 1977, the club was run by Ron Rollitt, the secretary who
also sold tickets. The staffing was of such a hand-to-mouth
nature that when Ron took receipt of batches of tickets for
big cup ties, he kept them under his bed at home for safety.
He had a part-time secretary (who worked mornings only), a
retiree helping out in the afternoon and, if there were maintenance problems on the ground, Les Simmons, the groundsman, would try to tackle it.

The tea and laundry lady, Molly Rush, still swore by
McGarry, because he had made sure she had a washing
machine instead of her cleaning the kit by hand as had been the
case for years.

In the dressing room area, there was the manager, coach,
trainer, physio and a part-time youth coach who did two
evenings a week and Saturdays.

In 1979, when Watford returned to the old second tier,
they had an assistant manager, a maintenance manager, a chief
executive, the club secretary, a marketing manager, a box
office manager and assistant plus a couple of full-time secre-
tarial workers. In addition they had an extra coach, an extra
physio and a full-time youth coach.

Graham brought about those changes and it could be
argued, for the first time in the club's history, it had a truly professional approach off the field as well as on it.

Those days have been well documented but unless you were
part of it, it is difficult to appreciate how the club changed, not
just at staffing levels or ground improvements or even their
on-field exploits. It was tangible: the heartbeat could be heard;
the belief coursed through all departments as we travelled on
a shared journey. We not only knew they were making mem-

ories, there developed an expectancy that was rooted in that knowledge and, what had been fantasies for almost a century, became reality.

The quality of the team assembled was impressive: from John Ward to Ed Coan; Caroline Gillies to Shirley Evans; Mike Sullivan to Ann Swanson and so many more. To the general public many were meaningless names but they all contributed to a vibrant, progressive club, one to be mentioned in Hansard and pioneering so much on and off the field.

The exceptional comedic qualities of John Ward and Steve Harrison enabled us to produce a series of memorable evenings at Bailey's, the town's premier nightspot which has undergone a number of name and identity changes since and is now known as Oceana. These were nights when the club let down its hair semi-publicly. One could not imagine such nights taking place at many clubs or, as far as Watford was concerned, in any other era. The best I could remember was when George Harris and Ron Crisp played guitars at the annual dinner in the early 1960s and keeper Dave Underwood, holding young Dennis Bond like a dummy, got the then apprentice to sing the high noted 'Ooooohhhhh' in Little Richard's *Tutti Frutti*, by grabbing a part of his anatomy.

Looking back on that era, it was the many little things which contributed significantly to the whole that have always fascinated me. Referring back to the 1960s, Barry Dyson came to the club in 1968 and hit a series of improbable goals in a run of 20 games, many of them fired from outside the box. Yet the following season his ratio dropped and his relative lack of industry (closing down and such like) prompted a row. 'If you want someone to run around all day, play Barry Endean,' Dyson retorted.

Furphy did just that and was rewarded with promotion with Endean, plucked from a pub side, the team's top scorer.

In 1978, having achieved promotion from Division Four with considerable authority, Graham Taylor was concerned that his strikers, Keith Mercer, Alan Mayes, Ross Jenkins and Luther Blissett might not be able to deliver. He began to monitor others, including Billy Jennings.

Now it could be argued he did this in order to spur on his existing strikers but I can reveal, knowing I was in regular contact with Billy, Taylor told me to pass on the fact they were watching him. Ultimately the manager decided against the player, because he did not get in there where it hurts – echoing the views of Kirby and Keen.

In the meantime, Luther, who lacked consistency, came through and was launched into the national spotlight with two headed goals at Old Trafford to knock Manchester United out of the League Cup. He admitted afterwards: 'You know me Oli, I can't head that well. I can't believe what I have just done.'

So the answer to Graham's goalscoring problem was staring him in the face but even Luther was not convinced he was the man, then.

Watford had won the title convincingly but if any of the sides assembled by Taylor was to be considered basic, that was most certainly the contender. There were some highlights but it was functional football. In the Third Division, we started to experience the first of many special nights with progress in the League Cup and, for a moment, what appeared to be runaway success in the league.

As Watford stuttered, Graham said he would drag them over the line but the character of that side was superb: victories at Sheffield Wednesday and the vanquishing of Hull at Vicarage Road one May night saw them through to Division Two.

While fans went home to celebrate, Watford's players and staff remained at the club. Bacon and eggs were served later: it had already become the pattern for the end of every season.

The decade finished with Watford playing in what is the Championship now. They struggled initially but survived. There were many memories still to be made but one occurred for me when crossing the roof of a stand at St James's Park on a narrow walk-way and entering the Newcastle press box. I do not like heights and was a little unsettled by the experience so I did not pick up on the fact that Terry Challis suggested I should slide into the bench seat first.

I did so, put my paraphernalia on the desk and was then offered a polite welcome by the journalist next door. I thanked him and then realised who it was: Wor Jackie Milburn, my schoolboy idol.

We talked every time I visited Newcastle, until he died. His hero status was never in question. Seventeen thousand fans attended his funeral.

THE 1980s

It is hard to believe now, in the light of subsequent triumphs, but there was a school of thought on the terraces and in the stands at Vicarage Road, that Graham Taylor was a good lower division manager but out of his depth beyond Division Three.

I received many letters on this theme as Watford struggled. Later Graham would contend he scrapped his old side a little too early (Joslyn, Garner and the others) and he shelved his 'strikers must be brave' yardstick when he brought in Malcolm Poskett to help fire them to survival, despite the fact he was no braver than Jennings. Subsequently, he also paid handsomely for Gerry Armstrong and allowed Ross Jenkins to go to the United States on an unofficial loan.

Blissett even played one season mainly in midfield and it seemed Watford were in transition and, as with Glenn Miller's search for his 'sound', Graham looked for the key line-up and perhaps even the approach. I have always believed happenstance plays a significant part in football. The band-leader found his sound when the trumpet-player cut his lip and Graham seized his own moment at Stamford Bridge.

The hitherto discarded Jenkins returned to a club where Nigel Callaghan had emerged, ready to fill the role on the wing that Brian Pollard enjoyed in the lower divisions; John Barnes (a left winger taking the place of Bobby Downes) was signed as an amateur and, at Chelsea one afternoon, Watford tore the opposition apart.

It began to fall into place. Luther had moved back into the attack, Ross was back and the format that had served so well in Divisions Four and Three, began to make inroads in Division Two. Graham moved Kenny Jackett into midfield to part-ner Les Taylor but his other big and, viewed at the time as an incredible, decision was to convert Wilf Rostron to left back.

Wilf continued to score goals, however, mostly at set-pieces after Barnes had won the near-post flick-on – a ploy Graham unashamedly lifted from Shrewsbury, who were managed by Graham Turner.

I remember Turner anticipating the criticism of the Watford style pointing out: 'They are not just haphazardly hitting long balls. They know precisely where they are hitting it. And the forwards know as well. It is very organised and the passes are hit with skill.'

There were a few rumblings about Watford's style but Graham was not surprised by this. When promotion was achieved and Watford were set to mix it with the best, Graham replied to my congratulatory letter by pointing out that we were heading for flak. The old international brigade would be turn-ing on this upstart with his brash style. Make no mistake the torrent of criticism that headed Watford's way was orchestrated to a significant degree.

Yes there were times when the style looked crass. Towards the end of the Division Three campaign, when they faltered, they looked as bad as their critics would later claim. I remember when Ian Bolton, who could hit a superb long, arrowing, accurate pass, commenting after being out with injury and watching a game: 'I knew Ross was ten feet tall but not that he was 30-feet wide.'

Yet within a year of reaching the top flight, Ross and then Ian Bolton had left the club. The concepts might remain but the execution had to be different because the personnel changed. Such subtleties were lost on the critics in the national press, some of whom were judged firmly in one camp. Just as the spies at Vicarage Road were marked down years back by their referring to Jim Bonser as 'JB', some of the Watford critics were noted for referring to Terry Venables as 'Venners' and seemed close to the rival boss, who was manager of Queens Park Rangers at the time.

Venables famously asked how a young boy going to school could practice playing the Watford Way, and answered only by kicking the ball as far ahead as possible and chasing after it. It was simplistic rubbish and I recall countering that a schoolboy copying Venables's QPR team would never make it to school, what with all the back-passing and playing offside.

Glenn Roeder, who later played for and managed Watford, recalled how he was injured and watched the QPR side he captained, for a few weeks from the stand. 'It was only then I saw the offsides and back-passes and realised the critics had a point. Sometimes you can be too close to things to see.'

I take that point, but whether close or distant, you cannot be excited by back-passes and offsides, whereas we at Watford were thrilled by the manner of victory not just results. Watford's playing policy was not simply wham-bam, and punting the ball upfield in hope, as the critics claimed was Taylor's approach. Ross and Luther, crossed over in the centre circle, then hared into the areas to receive the ball, played it back to the supporting wingers or midfield players and Callaghan and Barnes would take it from there. There was so much skill and talent, along with the pace and tactics. It was positive, produced goalmouth incidents, dribbling skills and boy was it exciting.

Subsequent long-ball exponents who did not possess the talent of Blissett, Callaghan or Barnes, would escape almost scot-free from criticism for the next 30 years, as they parodied the Watford Way with an even more basic approach. Dave Bassett, who spent many hours at Vicarage Road making notes, was the arch-copyist, but he threw in the offside game, stripped the approach down to the very basics and happily accepted his players earned bad disciplinary records. Watford, along with Nottingham Forest, had the best disciplinary record in the top flight over the years, until Bassett took over

Years later I heard Watford vilified by critics for their simplistic approach with a brutal, bullying centre forward, Ross Jenkins. It was nonsense: he was booked only once in his career, and even then somewhat harshly.

The Hornets were said to bypass the midfield with their long balls but the Hornets' faithful voted Les Taylor, a midfielder, player of the season!

Watford had the players with the energy to support the front men and they had the forwards who had the skill to open up defences after the opposition's midfield was bypassed. The object was to press the opposition defence, win the ball back in their half where they are vulnerable and look to turn the opponents as often as possible. In the end, as Graham pointed out, Watford's example improved the subsequent fitness levels of the old top flight. Closing down became *de rigeur*.

It was at times such as these that I pinched myself. What a great start to a career I had with Watford: Cliff, Charlie,

McGarry and then Furphy. Then came the Kirby and Keen days when people sympathised with my having such a dreary job (their view, not mine) only for Elton and Graham to come along and change the whole perspective for us all. Before long, people were asking: How did you get a job like that?

Yet for all the great memories, one of the most pleasant things to happen to me in the course of covering Watford was to meet Tommy Barnett in the early 1970s and become something of a friend over subsequent years. I have no hesitation in naming Tommy as the nicest and humblest footballer I ever met. He could never understand why people remembered him and in such detail. But he was grateful for it: 'It's very nice, really,' he conceded in his Lancashire accent. 'I owe it all to you for the articles, Mr Oliver.'

He never seemed to quite grasp that the articles only brought to life what he had achieved.

He delighted in Watford's rise up the league and watched his records surpassed, and I know he would have been very touched to see that Graham, Luther Blissett and I attended his funeral in 1986. Along, of course, with Taffy, who told Graham in his usual dismissive manner: 'When I played for Watford, a coach was something you travelled to games in.'

Good days and you can never really exaggerate how good they were. From Darlington's The Feethams, at the end of August 1976 as Watford sunk to 92nd in the Football League after losing 1-0, to exactly six years later, travelling to witness a 4-1 win at Southampton in the top flight.

I remember driving back from that game so exhilarated and arriving home where my wife Ellie had taped The Last Waltz concert film by The Band on video. I could not sleep after that game, so I sat and watched the film right into the early hours.

That summer Watford sold their England international striker, Luther Blissett, for £1m. There are two facts in that sentence which, had you predicted them in any of the previous six decades, would have had people falling in the aisles. Luther left and when ready to depart for Milan that summer, I happened to see him and his family drop off at Vicarage Road *en route* to Heathrow airport. For Luther all roads led to Watford and so it proved.

We had ten years of almost constant success and excitement. Such moments as sitting in Sofia watching the Balkans light fires on the terraces as Watford won in extra-time before the largest crowd the Hornets had ever played before at that stage, and then seeing the club knocked out of the UEFA Cup in icy, picturesque Prague. It was not the defeat that was so memorable but the fact that three days later, in early December, travelling up to Manchester on the train, I heard myself saying to a fan: 'I don't believe the season will just fizzle out after Prague. We'll probably reach the FA Cup final or something.'

I am not trying to highlight my ability as a prophet but the fact success was such a matter of course under Graham, I all but expected a fresh barrier to be overcome – such was my faith in the man. I was not alone.

The marvellous experience of the FA Cup final, Elton's tears; Luther's return, another run to the FA Cup semi-final, a great new stand but then...

After every high, came a low and when Graham read the signs of disenchantment at the top, he took a punt, asked Elton if he could apply for the Aston Villa job and was disappointed to have his suspicions confirmed when the rock star gave him the thumbs up.

Graham was shaken by the ease with which Watford were prepared to let him go. He had half-expected his request to shake Elton out of his self-absorption and cause everyone to refocus and reaffirm their vows. As he left Elton, he was quickly followed by the star's manager, director John Reid, who caught up with Graham and assured him: 'We won't be asking for compensation.'

How was that for greasing the wheels to expedite the manager's departure?

There was a school of thought that suggested Watford's progress under Taylor had provided Elton with millions of pounds' worth of free publicity, giving him the image of an ordinary guy with the chance to indulge his favourite club. But with Watford in the top flight and finding it harder to make further progress, the club became a financial drain in the view of John Reid, who sought to distance his star from the club.

Either way, Graham moved on and, while we were told it was business as usual, the standards dropped almost as quickly as the team. It was appalling to witness the structure of the club being dismantled until, in reality, it became an over-staffed, almost rudderless version of the 1977 Watford Graham inherited.

THE 1990s

The 1990s saw the 'unofficial centenary of the club'. That was in 1991, just ten years after the real centenary: a date which had been unearthed by Trefor Jones, as we cast around for some 100th milestone.

By then I had seen many magic moments and favourite players such as Big Cliff, George Harris, Charlie Livesey, Dennis Bond, Dave Carr, Stewart Scullion, Duncan Welbourne, Keith 'Fast' Eddy, Billy Jennings, Luther Blissett, Nigel Callaghan, Ross Jenkins, John Barnes, Les Taylor, John McClelland, Ian Bolton and Tony Coton. There were latter players who I enjoyed such as David James, Craig Ramage, Dave Bamber, Neil Redfearn, Micah Hyde, Richard Johnson and Neal Ardley, but perhaps it was an age thing. They did not resonate in the same way as my earlier preferences.

The first six years of the 1990s were quite dire in comparison to what we had experienced over the intervening years from 1959. The club appeared to be going nowhere. After Taylor, Watford made a succession of managerial appointments that ranged from the ill-advised to the desperately hopeful such as Bassett, Harrison, Lee, Perryman and Roeder, while Graham struggled with England.

I believe there were those associated with Watford who drew comfort from his international travails, while they seemed to spend the time at Vicarage Road attempting to dodge his shadow while dissipating his legacy. With every passing year Watford demonstrated how much the halcyon era had been down to Graham's leadership and acumen. He might have assembled a good team but they proved to lack direction without his leadership.

Dave Bassett had been the wrong choice as manager, a knee-jerk appointment (essentially made by Elton and Muff Winwood) without sufficient thought deployed, as if they had forgotten what the club stood for in that one May weekend. His cause was not well-served by the hurried nature of his appointment. Fans were still reeling from the departure of Taylor and to have Bassett thrust upon them with the 'King is dead! Long live the king!' approach, was just too crass for words. Elton had other pressures at the time, we now appreciate, but he certainly got that very wrong.

Bassett had little time for me as an individual, although in fairness he was always available to me as a manager. I could understand his thinking but to blame me for orchestrating public antipathy – 'The Yuppies have got me out,' he said – was perhaps a delusional self-defence mechanism. He made so many mistakes.

The biggest was opting for revolution instead of evolution, coming in and changing the culture and the staff of an organisation that had run effectively for a decade, so he lost the dressing room.

Steve Harrison followed, admitting later that he feared he was not cut out for management after the first day and knew it for a fact within a week. Colin Lee came next, promoted from the youth management and was too inexperienced, then Steve Perryman laboured in his wake, given the additional burden of Jack Petchey's version of chairmanship.

The club continued to take punts on possible potential with the appointment of Glenn Roeder, probably the most openly honest occupant of the managerial hot-seat at Vicarage Road before Ray Lewington. I do not mean to infer the others were less than honest, but some felt it was not wise to be too open while Glenn and Ray could not play it any other way but dead straight. If that was perceived as weakness, what a sad world.

One could give a stream of anecdotes on those years but in reality it was a dreary succession of failure and a sub-standard approach. Some of the people employed by the club were beyond belief and the old guard was whittled away. I did the same job for 40 years but when asked why I changed things every year, I would explain: 'To keep the revolution hot.'

I feared becoming settled and content, going through the motions. Some people were guilty of that at Watford. They no longer went the extra mile for the cause and there was no one around to question why.

Perhaps one moment crystallised it for me and perhaps for you. Taffy Davies, who was 20 years with Watford, died and his funeral cortege was set to pass the ground. Nothing was being done, no one seemed to care: the club had fallen away from community and heritage, while protesting to the contrary.

Happily, the moment was saved. A member of staff rounded up a few injured players, a couple of reps, someone from the maintenance staff, admin and kitchens, lined them up outside the ground opposite the Red Lion and hoisted the Watford flag to half-mast. Taffy's widow expressed her gratitude for the club's support.

As they used to say, things had come to a pretty pass: keeping faith with the community and heritage had been engineered and organised totally by groundsman Les Simmons. Someone was still carrying the torch.

That, to my mind, said it all about the period between the First and Second Coming.

Ten years after he left, Graham became the team manager once again and many of the old standards returned along with the old success. However, the free-scoring style and those extra qualities that made the Eighties so special, proved elusive. He gave Watford two successive promotions but the burden of the past and the debt to Petchey proved too much to 'plant' the Hornets in the top flight as he had done first time around.

He later remarked it took the 1990s board five years to become tired of him whereas the 1977-87 board had taken ten years. But it was not just Taylor's style and approach that they misjudged. There were those on the board who did not appreciate that the likes of Tom Walley who, with his occasional malapropisms, his customary swearing and passionate haranguing of his charges, was the stuff of legends and very successful; not some old-school buffer past his sell-by date.

If Watford or the fans ever forget the contribution of Tom Walley, be sure that one group never will. The number of his former players, including some big names in the game, still beat a path to Tom's door, anything up to 35 years later. He was, and still is, The Man for many who passed through Watford's youth system, whether they made it in the game or not.

As Nigel Gibbs once put it: 'If Tom held you against the wall by your shirt collar and shouted his professional philosophy in your face from six inches, you knew he thought you had a chance of making it. He cared enough. That was the only consolation.'

Perhaps there were members of the board who felt Graham was effective in the lower divisions but mistakenly thought his approach outmoded in the upper echelons: a knock-on from the England saga. An irony really when you think they took over the club still owing the money to Petchey, which Graham's acumen and Watford's progress enabled them to pay off and therefore assume ownership of the club.

Graham read the signs and retired, too early I thought, and so it proved. One cannot doubt he was badly scarred by the England experience and felt truly let down by Wolves.

The Second Coming was not as memorable as the first, but there were great memories, not least that play-off final and the manner in which ten years of muddled thinking and repeated mediocrity were rolled back. The days of hand-to-mouth policy decisions were suspended and the club had standards once again as the name Watford became something to be reckoned with, as it had been before.

One should also remember that the sale of Kevin Miller largely financed the club's promotion to what is now the Championship and then they reached the Premiership with little more than plundering relegated Carlisle United's resources and coming up with Nick Wright and Allan Smart – hardly names to conjure with yet, within a year, they were the goalscorers as Watford won promotion to the top flight at the old Wembley.

Many Watford fans were happy to note Graham nailed his colours to the mast of attacking football. 'Working with the defence bores me,' he said. That he should have come out fighting again after licking his wounds in the Watford administrative offices, took courage and he demonstrated he still had the managerial Midas touch before eventually putting himself back into the national firing line with his prolific media work. It goes without saying his career did not turn out as he would have wished. Winning top honours with a big club was to elude him. It is said you should never go back, but Graham did and many, many Watford fans were grateful for that.

THE 2000s

The board looked set to prosper from the investment. The debts were paid and the company was going to be floated. Graham left the club with a base firmly established. But hold on! What is going on?

Had I been doing the job too long and lost my touch? Briefly I did think I had lost my way and perhaps misjudged the situation. That was when Gianluca Vialli took over. I felt like the boy in the story of the emperor and his new clothes. I saw naked stupidity and I could not see anything else.

Some fans adopted more positive attitudes than logic told me was due. I felt very alone when I was tipped off certain directors had encouraged a spate of letter-writing to the paper.

It was a ruse to offset what they deemed my less than enthusiastic attitude towards what they considered the sexy, new, foreign concept. That had been sparked by the example of Fulham's success under Jean Amadou Tigana, which included an annihilation of Taylor's Watford 5-0 the previous Boxing Day, prompting the view that GT was old hat and 'foreign' was the way to go.

In the end the emperor proved to be naked after all, as Watford suffered from possibly the worst and undoubtedly the most costly managerial appointment.

Of course Watford had a number of unsuccessful managers, yet despite the flaws apparent before or after selection, others could see the thinking behind the appointments, which is something that eluded me from the day I heard of Vialli's arrival.

The Italian was less qualified as a coach than Blissett and Jackett, the outgoing coaches and, in fact, was due to take a coaching badge that summer. Vialli had no knowledge whatsoever of the First Division and his experience was gained at the very top level as a player and as a manager with a hefty budget.

It was even claimed he signed players at Chelsea without having seen them. That may well have been a false accusation but, upon seeing the players he signed for Watford, it gave the claim some credence.

The assurance that his coach Ray Wilkins would make up the shortfall on knowledge on the division was not encouraging as Wilkins had failed as a coach and manager up until that time. As it happened, often Ray did not know what the team was to be on a Friday or even a Saturday before the players were told, so his influence was peripheral at best.

Communicating with the directors at the time, it was as if I was speaking to converts who had seen a vision. They seemed entranced and in awe of their appointee, as if all will and reason had been lost. As Graham Taylor remarked: 'Every time Luca Vialli walks into the boardroom, the directors get a collective mental erection.'

A year or more after the debacle, one of the directors admitted to me: 'I now think on reflection, Graham was spot on.'

I have no doubt on that score. Graham asked me what I thought on the evening of Vialli's appointment. I said I did not feel good about it and he said he felt exactly the same.

The board lost their way after Graham left the first time. History was to repeat itself and the concept of entertaining Vialli with pasta, rubbing shoulders with big names and being flattered by Vialli's acceptance, was all too much for the directors who were in love with the vision and the celebrity and did not see the reality.

I am not one to hold grudges and while I had a stress-

ful time during Vialli's season in charge, I did feel sympathy
for Haig Oundjian, the vice-chairman, who having flown
back from Paris to Stockport, stood staring into space in the
directors' box at Edgeley Park after another Vialli debacle.

I deduced things had become a touch flaccid.

Vialli was the first manager I dealt with who was not
available to the *Watford Observer*. That was his initial standpoint
and he eventually and begrudgingly agreed to phone me every
Wednesday, at an unspecified and variable time, which meant I
spent a season of Wednesdays at code red, unable to take on
any other duties that took me away from a phone and laptop.

It was an awkward and undesirable time but gradually Vialli
opened up, although whether this was trust or the feeling he
needed an outlet for his views as it became plain his season was
badly adrift, is something only he will know. He had the courtesy to ring me while I was on holiday in the Pyrenees when
he was sacked but, while I quite enjoyed our conversations
towards the end, it could not be disguised that my misgivings
were well founded.

The incredible waste of money in the transfer market, in
addition to the settlement of his contract and the crash of the
anticipated cash-cow, ITV Digital, left Watford on the verge of
extinction. Like a punch-drunk boxer, they staggered round the
ring, recovering briefly only to take another punch.

Next, we had the crisis of the summer of 2002, with the
ground sold and the fans rallying round to keep the club alive.
What was initially a pro-active Supporters Trust was formed,
fans put in their hard-earned cash but the club lurched to the
Crisis of 2003, caused, we were informed, by the nebulous
'hole' in the accounts.

There were at least a couple more flotations, which brought
in people with no interest in football whatsoever (something I
always regarded as a danger) and the by now castrated if well-

intentioned trust was reduced or duped to the verge of point-less endorsement of the club's unfortunate stances.

The man given the chance to survive under a repeatedly reduced budget was Ray Lewington, one of the nicest men I ever met in the game. He did well to balance the books, reach two cup semi-finals and steer the club to survival despite the inner rancour and the resentment felt in the dressing room towards the chairman and, subsequently, his acolyte. Every year Lewington saw his budget cut still further and then had to watch his successor operate with significantly greater resources.

Ironically Adrian Boothroyd owed something to his prede-cessor. When Simpson and Tim Shaw took responsibility after the Vialli and ITV Digital fiasco, other directors cut their losses and washed their hands of the club. That included Elton John but Simpson showed restraint in not criticising the star.

That was wise on his part. Elton appeared to have little time for directors. He enjoyed the likes of Jim Harrowell, Geoff Smith and Muir Stratford in the original and most successful board – all Watford fans from birth. Elton seemed to share the view with his former manager that too many directors were in the game for the wrong reasons and he was not that bothered to try and find out which was which.

So Elton continued to phone the occupant of the manager's seat as he had done for years and established a good relation-ship with Lewington, his only real point of contact. Sympathis-ing with the likeable manager's predicament, Elton opted to fund Mark Devlin's transfer and wages.

When the budget was cut again, Elton talked in terms of buying several players. Ray drew up a short-list but Elton's management said such a move was impossible, so the short-list was ditched and Ray soldiered on with the much smaller budget, reduced yet again in planning for the 2005-06 season.

Elton then came back with the offer of a concert which the

club jumped at. But they earmarked the profits to pay for buying back the ground, which Elton did not want, as he announced on stage in the summer of 2005. Simpson, loathe to upset Elton in case more funds were to be forthcoming, engineered a still further improved budget for Boothroyd, knowing full well the new manager was being called regularly by the rock star.

Lewington never received anything like Boothroyd's budget and never got to spend the money three years of talks had brought about but his successor did profit from it.

The pity was that with a little more relaxation of the purse-strings, Lewington might well have made a better fist of chasing a play-off or promotion spot. Certainly the dressing room was behind both him and Nigel Gibbs, a fact underlined by Heidar Helguson's willingness to sign a new contract under Lewington just weeks before the axe fell. 'With a little shrewd recruitment, we could move on,' said 'H', as the striker was known.

In that final season, Ray's cause was hurt by the defection of the extremely underpaid Neal Ardley to Cardiff, a player under-rated by the public. The side was never the same after starting the campaign so well.

I ceased covering Watford's games, freelance activities apart, in January 2005 and while I kept in touch with Ray on a weekly basis, I was no longer covering the club in general. The way Simpson and Ashton behaved was such that it made the break somewhat easier than I expected.

Mind you, I had experienced past problems at the top. Bonser stopped talking to me for the last two years of his chairmanship although he did a series of interviews with me later. Petchey considered having me banned from the ground; Steve Perryman said we no longer had a special relationship but within a few days dropped the idea and Vialli told me he would not talk to me one-to-one yet, after a meeting, overturned the stance. Simpson banned the *Watford Observer* over an article on the sale of Elton John concert tickets, in which I played no part in the writing. He invited the editor down to the club, made impossible demands and, I am told reliably, related that he and Ashton kicked each other under the table when they saw the consternation their stance caused.

Simpson resisted overtures to broker a peace deal but once a national newspaper featured the row and questioned what Elton would make of it all, Simpson contacted me and agreed to a speedy rapprochement.

You did not need to have an O-level in body language to see that Ashton was less than happy as Simpson and I knocked out a joint statement putting the row to bed. They were not to forget and attempts were made to hound the *Watford Observer* into submission in what appeared to be a matter of policy over the next four years. One only has to look at Kevin Affleck's reflections elsewhere in this book to see further examples of the manipulation and outrageous behaviour perpetrated in an effort to bring that about. It never seemed to strike them that their reign would be over one day, and the story would be told.

RETIREMENT

When Ray was called in early one morning he knew the outcome. When Simpson tried to explain and justify the decision, Ray declined to stay and listen. 'There's no point,' he told Simpson with his usual honesty. 'I won't agree with any of it.'

It was put about by the powers that be: Ray had lost the dressing room. Vialli's former henchman, Terry Byrne, in regular touch with the players, stressed there was not an ounce of truth in this and told the chairman so.

Watford went on and enjoyed the influx of relative riches and the illusion of success, and I watched from afar as the unhappy triumvirate of Boothroyd, Ashton and Simpson, led the club to fresh and near-terminal financial disasters. Their cringe-making decision to feature themselves on the front cover of the match programme suggested they truly entertained an inflated view of their own significance and infallibility.

That was in the future, technically off my watch but, as my retirement approached, I did not like the vibes emanating from Simpson and I regarded Ashton... well, I tried not to.

He talked a good career but after checking out his time at West Brom, my opposite number in Birmingham assured me that whatever Ashton might have done at the Hawthorns, it had happened well under his radar.

Sadly those portents I feared proved accurate: Watford and the fans are still picking up the bill. So, upon reflection, when it came to my retirement I could see that my career involved perfect timing for me: coming in with the Holton era and leaving before the Simpson-Ashton regime imploded.

A couple of years into retirement, working in the garden in France, a sentence came to mind and I jotted it down. Some 18 months later I used it as the truthful introduction to a celebratory article: 'Logic dictates there must be those with a good word to say about Mark Ashton, it is just that I have never met any of them.'

Yes I did enjoy that moment, not just for myself but for Kevin Affleck, Anthony Matthews, a legion of ex-employees and many more who were, to my mind, treated shabbily.

The wheels had started to come off when they axed as directors the Russo brothers, who did much more good for the club than was credited. They enabled Watford to buy back the ground and purchase Marlon King who spearheaded the promotion campaign, although this particular piece of happenstance caused some to believe misguidedly they had the magic touch. Later the Russos got rid of Simpson and Ashton and cut the deficit. The experience cost them a pretty packet and when they were about to be used and abused again, they dug their heels in. The club's future was never actually in jeopardy, for all the posturing, but the Russos made sure they did not blink first. Fair play to them.

Beyond all the politics and dark sagas, the team still played football and, from afar, one incident set me thinking. That was when the Hornets met Reading. I read the referee had awarded a goal against Watford after the ball went wide of the target. Everyone knew it was a miss except for the referee. I thought of goal-line technology and Taffy turning in his grave.

From The Goal That Never Was to The Goal That Should Not Have Been and still no technology.

END OF THE ROAD

Some 55 years and a couple of months after that 1950 tie with Manchester United, I found myself virtually alone on a Saturday evening in Vicarage Road. The fans had long since left, the ground staff and players, the directors and staff had also gone as I collected an armful of telephones and walked down from the press box.

I smiled a goodnight to the cleaner. We knew each other by sight over a number of late Saturday evenings but I did not draw her attention to the fact it was to be the end of our nodding acquaintance.

It was my last game covering Watford. I stood at the entrance to the tunnel, savouring the occasion. A door slammed shut in the eddying breezes that frequently sends waste paper scurrying around the stadium. I was alone and able to reflect and indulge in the emotion of the moment at a place where I seemed to have spent half my working life.

Of course there were memories of myriads of trips, the obligatory pre-match curries and good friendship as various friends and colleagues accompanied me to away grounds. Every ground had a special memory or two.

An empty ground on a Saturday night is a desolate place but, as I was alone, it served ideally as an empty picture frame and I spent some time colouring in the montage of memories from yesterday and yesteryear, the changes and comparisons, each vying for attention, for I had spent over 44 years close to the breeze-block heart of Vicarage Road and 41 years very close. I have touched on many of those memories here.

I thought of the personalities, the moments, the delights and despair, the amazing changes I had witnessed. Of any 40-year stretch in Watford's history since 1881, I had reported on the best, the most exciting, controversial and progressive.

Also I took time out to recall a short-trousered boy with a snake-belt who had caught the bug many years ago. I looked over to the place where I had witnessed that 1950 injustice. With no one to witness me I was able to indulge my *déjà vu*.

The irony is that unknown to me, my old mate Jim from our days on the terrace, was waiting for me at the top of the steps. He had popped over from his home in Denmark and happened, to his surprise, to catch my final game and the on-field presentation to mark my retirement.

He stood in Occupation Road for an hour and saw my hat first as I climbed the steps and left Vicarage Road for the last time as a journalist.

'A lot of memories, Oli, old pal,' he said. Then, spotting I was swallowing hard as he spoke, added: 'Take your time to reply, Ol.'

I accepted the offer.

Oliver Phillips is Watford born and bred, a Watford fan who covered the club until 2005. He then retired to France in part to 'break the all-consuming intense connection with Watford FC, which has been an integral part of my life'.

STANTON TOWN 1 WATFORD 0
Half-time

New chairman Dave Dawkins is determined to have his say on team selection during the club's pre-season friendly against First Division Watford.

Harry Cannon faces a showdown with his supremo at half-time. Although a goal up against the side from Vicarage Road, it's obvious changes need to be made.

Strikers George Reilly and Maurice Johnston – the team's FA Cup heroes last season – look set to rip the Stanton defence apart following magic on the wing from England star John Barnes.

It's obvious that Stanton's struggling full-back George Baranski has to go off – but who replaces him?

Both chairman Dawkins and Harry have their own ideas and they face a tense dressing room discussion...

The crowd is mystified as Dawkins takes Harry Cannon's seat on the bench

WHAT'S GOING ON, BERT? THERE'S NO SIGN OF THE MANAGER.

BEATS ME, NOBBY. AND—LOOK—JOE STOREY'S COME OUT FOR THE SECOND HALF. HE HASN'T PLAYED FOR AGES.

Unseen, Harry takes a seat at the back of the stand.

RIGHT, DAWKINS, IT'S ALL YOURS. LET'S SEE WHAT YOU CAN DO.

Watford's tactics are clear from the start... to play on George Baranski, who struggled to match the pace of England winger John Barnes in the first half

In the dugout

YOU SHOULD HAVE LET HARRY REPLACE GEORGE WITH BRIAN HOWLETT AS HE PLANNED, MISTER DAWKINS.

I KNOW WHAT I'M DOING BURNHAM. JOE STOREY WILL DEAL WITH THIS CROSS.

cannon

10

The dynamic Aidy Boothroyd steered Watford to the Premiership in 2006.

But less than two years after the high of promotion, the club was once again on the brink of financial ruin.

How did it happen?

Kevin Affleck was there, reporting events for the *Watford Observer* and trying to get to the truth.

For the first time, he tells the full story of how things unravelled so spectacularly.

However you remember that period, you simply have to read this account.

TROUBLE AT THE TOP

BY KEVIN AFFLECK

Aidy Boothroyd celebrated his 40th birthday in February 2011. Ben Foster was among the guests at the party held at the Ricoh Arena in Coventry. I was not invited. I was not alone in that.

The invite was not extended to Graham Simpson or Mark Ashton either. Five years earlier chairman, chief executive and manager had posed for a photograph that filled the cover of the matchday programme. It was intended to be a display of unity. 'I work for great people and, as a manager, you need that,' Boothroyd once said.

The fact the club's former executives were not uncorking the Champagne to commemorate Boothroyd's fourth decade demonstrated how spectacularly their relationship unravelled. The unwavering loyalty of the triumvirate was palpable in the early throes of the two seasons I spent covering the fortunes of Watford Football Club. This was the realisation of a boyhood dream and so I decided to write a journal so I could, one day, accurately look back with great affection. That was the plan.

The following are extracts from my journal and recollections from some of the people who lived through one of the most turbulent eras in the club's history. I started the job in the summer of 2006. Watford had just won promotion with a play-off final victory over Leeds and were about to tackle the Premiership. I didn't have a professional relationship with Boothroyd at the time. I thought we were starting with a clean slate.

THURSDAY, AUGUST 10 2006

I'm told Boothroyd is uncontactable all day. Left a
message anyway and, to my surprise, he calls. We have a
good chat but he warns me if I criticise Simpson or Ashton
he won't speak to me exclusively on a Wednesday [as was
the arrangement between the manager and the *Watford
Observer*] and that I will just come to press conferences.
Seems very defensive about his bosses and determined to
lay down the ground rules early. He told me that Richard
[Walker, the press officer who resigned that summer]
putting in a good word stands me in good stead.

I admired Boothroyd's loyalty to the men who had plucked him
from obscurity and parachuted him into his first managerial
job. It was reciprocal. Ashton stormed furiously down from
the directors' box in the East Stand to support his manager
when Boothroyd became embroiled with Fitz Hall, the Crystal
Palace defender, which sparked a melee in the incendiary play-
off semi-final.

Boothroyd seemed unusually defensive about his bosses
but the excitement of working closely with a manager who had
earned rave reviews for masterminding an unlikely promotion
the previous season outweighed any reservations I had about
the peculiar dynamic among the club's hierarchy.

Ben Foster played a central role in the 2005-06 promotion-
winning season, and it was an exclusive interview I secured that
summer which caught the attention of the editor at the *Watford
Observer* and resulted in the offer to swap my role as Saracens
correspondent for the job covering Watford.

In that interview the goalkeeper, who had been on loan
from Manchester United, told me of his desire to return for a
second season at Watford.

I had loved working with some brilliant, innovative, forward-thinking and professional people at Saracens. The media access to world-class players was something I only truly appreciated as my football reporting career developed.

If the likes of World Cup winners François Pienaar and Tim Horan or Thomas Castaignede, the French maverick, didn't take your call first time they would always ring back. I rubbed shoulders with these household names and many more when invited to travel with the official team party to Tokyo and Biarritz. There was no need to submit expenses when I travelled on the private plane with the team to Newcastle and Leeds for games. Saracens picked up the bill.

It was therefore with a heavy heart that I told my contacts at Sarries I would now be reporting on the landlords at Vicarage Road. It was a no brainer, though. Watford was the team I supported as a child. I travelled the country with my father and later as a teenager with my cousin and friends to see the Hornets play. A dreadful goalless FA Cup third round draw in Scarborough on a bitter January day in 1995 tested the resolve of my youthful enthusiasm as did the FA Cup semi-final with Tottenham Hotspur in 1987. 'Who is Gary Plumley?' I persistently asked my father.

On the flip side, I recall the 1-0 victory at Oxford United in 1991 that ensured Watford avoided relegation to the third tier. Maybe it was the magic of the atmosphere on the tightly-packed concrete terrace or the memory of Steve Perryman ordering his players back out onto the pitch to thank us for our support amid repeated chants of 'The 'Orns are staying up,' I don't know but that balmy day at the Manor Ground remains one of my fondest.

Now it was my responsibility to deliver news to the same fans I had stood on various dilapidated terraces with and shared sweets with on a Mullany's supporters' coach. A video on the coach seemed like such a treat. I was thrilled at landing the

Watford job at the age of 27, my family – several of whom are
season-ticket holders – were delighted and I thought it would
be an unforgettable experience, albeit a daunting one attempting to fill the sizeable moccasins of Oli Phillips whose copy I
had raced home from school on a Friday, every Friday, to read.
I even eschewed the usual bike preferred by most paper boys so
I could digest the sport sections of various newspapers on my
circuitous delivery round.

The fact Watford were in the Premiership when I began the
job was the icing on the cake. Boothroyd navigated them there
after replacing Ray Lewington. Boothroyd and Colin Calder-
wood had been the only two interviewed by Simpson, Andy
Wilson and the Russo brothers, Jimmy and Vince. Ashton did
not sit in on the interview as it was felt it would constitute a conflict of interests as it was Ashton who recommended him to the
Watford board after their paths crossed at West Brom.

The budget for Boothroyd's first full season was £3.25million,
around £500,000 more than Lewington had been allowed. The
budget was in a other stratosphere when Watford reached the
Premiership and the season after that.

Boothroyd wanted to bring back Paul Robinson and make
him his first signing following that remarkable promotion. It
would have been a smart move. Apart from Helguson, it was
difficult to think of a more popular player among the fans.

Boothroyd and Robinson knew of each other from their
time at West Brom although Boothroyd had never coached the
left-back. Watford's bid for Robinson never got past Jeremy
Peace, West Brom's canny chairman, and Robinson only heard
about the interest later, through his agent, Rob Segal, and was
never officially told about the offer.

Had he been, it would have presented a dilemma for the
former St Michael's school pupil. Robinson and his wife,
Caroline, have deep Watford roots. Robinson's parents, Mel and

Sandra, his brother, Mark, and sister, Joanne, all live in the town while his father-in-law is a season-ticket holder. But Robinson had settled in the Midlands with his young family and the fact Watford and West Brom had swapped divisions may not have been sufficient incentive.

'I never got a chance to speak to Watford,' Robinson says. 'It would have been a tough decision so, in the end, it was good I didn't have to make a call on it. I stayed and really enjoyed it at West Brom and we won the Championship the season after.'

I played representative football with Robinson; he marauded forward from left-back while I minded the shop at right-back. There was only one of us who was going to carve out a career as a footballer. Our paths eventually crossed again when I was dispatched by Oli in my early career as an apprentice reporter to source player reaction in the tunnel at Vicarage Road. Robbo would happily stand and chat about the game while others, having seemingly showered in expensive aftershave and carrying their designer washbags, swaggered past.

SUNDAY, AUGUST 13

Boothroyd was hostile and abrupt in the press conference following the friendly with Chievo. Not as charming as normal. He walked out of the changing room with his wife and kids and asked me who I was waiting around for. I was waiting for some players to get their post-match reaction. Boothroyd didn't even say goodbye. Seems to be blowing hot and cold.

My first official visit to the training ground at London Colney in my new role was ahead of the Premiership opener with Everton. I had been to the training ground before to interview, among others, Paul Mayo and Jermaine Pennant.

Pennant's high-specification Audi TT stuck out like a sore

thumb back then. Now the car park resembled a showroom of high performance cars, emblematic of the club's new lofty status. With players awarded 30 to 40 per cent pay rises, this was clearly now a Premiership club and the excitement around the training ground was palpable as we converged in the back room of the canteen to discuss the match at Goodison Park.

I suffered a scenario every reporter dreads when my voice recorder ran out of batteries. I didn't take notes as I wanted to listen intently to what Boothroyd was saying. Only once had this happened before, in an interview with the then Saracens head coach Rod Kafer. He was sympathetic and kindly agreed to re-stage the phone interview. I didn't fancy my chances of asking Boothroyd to repeat himself so I borrowed the dictaphone of Tom Collomosse, the agency reporter, and went outside where it was quieter to transcribe the interview.

FRIDAY, AUGUST 18

Receive a phone call from Richard Walker who says Aidy has called him to say we have got off on the wrong foot. Why he phoned Rich I'm not sure as he no longer works for the club. Boothroyd, he says, accuses me of eavesdropping and sniffing round the changing rooms after the game against Chievo. He accuses me of being ambitious. Find that strange as he strikes me as the ambitious type. I was offended and try to call him back. No answer. Left message but he didn't call back. I find out Boothroyd had a meeting with the chairman and Iain Moody [Watford's press officer]. My name comes up and, apparently, Boothroyd is convinced I'm out to 'nail him'.

I travelled to Merseyside for the Everton match by train as did Ashton. Tony Francis wanted to travel with him to do a piece for his *Daily Telegraph* column but Ashton refused. Watford lost at Everton but impressed with their work ethic and had good grounds for a point.

SATURDAY, AUGUST 19

Got a wry smile from AB as he walked into the post-match press conference at Everton. Wary of asking anything too probing as I didn't want him to show me up on my 'first day'. This is probably what he wants though so I give him a couple of gentle full tosses about how unlucky his team were, which they were.

'I remember that hand ball against Chris Powell that never was,' says the striker Darius Henderson, recalling the 2-1 defeat at Goodison Park on the opening day. 'We quickly learnt the Premier League can be cruel and it ended up being a tough season from start to finish.'

West Ham were next up. My dad is a West Ham fan who talks wistfully about the days of Trevor Brooking and Alan Devonshire so I got him a ticket in the away end. There is always something special about a game under lights at Vicarage Road. It's difficult to quantify. The atmosphere in and around the ground is just very different; it seems charged from the outset and does not need an incident to rouse the fans. A classic example I remember vividly was the victory over a Leeds United side featuring Eric Cantona in 1992.

MONDAY, AUGUST 21

Press conference at training ground ahead of the West Ham game. I asked a couple of questions, including if Boothroyd reads the papers. They were very complimentary about his team at Everton. 'I don't have time to read all of them but make sure I get a copy of local one, it's the most important.' He says it with a smile. Good banter.

Watford threw the kitchen sink, the dishwasher and the fridge freezer at West Ham and should really have won all three points. It was strange seeing Alan Pardew, then the West Ham manager. Last time I saw him was in the opposition for a Sunday League National Cup match in Southend. He played sweeper and was the best player on the field by a distance. It made me wonder how good he must have been at the peak of his playing career. Pardew has a reputation for possessing an inflated opinion of himself yet I found him very forthright and transparent in the press conference.

TUESDAY, AUGUST 22

Relayed to Boothroyd in the press conference how Pardew said Watford should have won the game. I got a good response. Later he walks past with Iain while I'm talking to Tony Yorke [then director of communications]. Rather embarrassingly and unsolicited, Yorke stops him and broaches the subject of our relationship. I wish he hadn't done that. I'd heard whispers Boothroyd is not too fond of Yorke so he probably wasn't the best person to be acting as a mediator. Boothroyd shakes my hand and agrees, albeit reluctantly, to set-up a meeting. I have a chat with Iain and he said we might be making progress and Boothroyd might 'have got you wrong'.

Manchester United were next up. This was what being in the Premiership was all about. For a preview piece for the paper, I called Tony Coton to talk about the progress made by Ben Foster, who was ineligible for the match, and Coton's affection for Watford. Coton always seems like he would rather be anywhere else than on the phone and his voice rarely raises above the gruff Midlands tones but he talked at length and answered every question.

I got to the ground early so I could see the United players warm-up at the foot of the now disused Family Terrace. The last time I stood in the Family Terrace I was probably trying to petition the female steward on the gate into allowing me into the seated family enclosure, which seemed to a schoolboy as glamorous as the directors' box.

Now I strolled along the same route with my media pass, round the back of the East Stand, sailing confidently through every checkpoint and then up the wooden stairs to the make-shift press box. It was like an assault course. The press box was bursting for the game with United and most of the big hitters from the Sunday papers were there. Many were not impressed at being left out of breath after the ascent to the back of the stand. The rugby correspondents at the national papers enjoyed red wine in the same media room at Saracens games and some were spared the climb to the press box and were allowed to sit near the dugout instead.

The increased media presence and a sell-out crowd intensified the pressure on Richard Lee, who was playing his first game in the Premiership and had the onerous task of keeping out Cristiano Ronaldo and Wayne Rooney. The charming and eloquent goalkeeper had played in Boothroyd's first three games in charge but felt he hadn't done himself justice. He was still recovering from a ruptured bicep when Boothroyd arrived and was troubled by a knee problem that required surgery in the summer. 'I shouldn't have played through injury,' Lee says.

Lee was told early on by Boothroyd that he would not be part of the plans for his first full season in charge. Lee's agent arranged a move to Blackburn Rovers where he was reunited with Kevin Hitchcock, who left his position as Watford's goalkeeping coach in 2004. The deal would have been made permanent had the clubs agreed a fee. Watford wanted £1million. Blackburn were prepared to offer £250,000.

'Swapping being number one at a Championship club for number three at a Premier League club probably wasn't the wisest thing,' Lee says.

Even though he failed to play a single first-team game that season, Blackburn tried to make the deal permanent but again could not agree a fee. Lee knew it was time to return to Watford when he learned Blackburn had signed another keeper, Jason Brown from Gillingham, while he was on a paddle boat on holiday. Lee returned to the club knowing Boothroyd had reservations about his kicking and his size. Now he had to stand-in for Foster, who possessed a sledgehammer of a left foot and commanded his area with great assurance, against the eventual champions who had scored eight in their first two games. Even if United didn't exploit any perceived weakness, Lee knew he'd be replaced the following week regardless. It struck me as a thankless task.

SATURDAY, AUGUST 26
Boothroyd is in a foul mood post-match. I asked him about the decision to bring on Matt Spring, who gifted Ryan Giggs one of the two goals, and he is very defensive.

There is a picture of Giggs rounding Lee in the home of the goalkeeper's parents as well as a more positive image of him thwarting Park Ji-Sung. He could have framed the prints of the several smart saves he pulled off to deny Louis Saha too.

The United game is not one Darius Henderson will want reminding of. He missed the kind of chance that would have been easier to score. He missed an even simpler one against Charlton Athletic weeks later. 'They [the chances] still give me nightmares,' Henderson says. 'The United one was tough as it kept getting highlighted every week but the Charlton one hit me harder. I had never been as low after a game. Missing those chances has probably made me a stronger person, a stronger character. But I still should have scored.'

The immediate aftermath was not the time to request an interview with Henderson. Neither was it the time, it appeared, to arrange this suggested meeting with Boothroyd

MONDAY, AUGUST 28

Ask Iain to set up my meeting with Boothroyd. No joy. Said he was too busy as it's nearing the end of the transfer window. Fair enough.

MONDAY, SEPTEMBER 4

Ask Iain to set up meeting with Boothroyd. Iain said Boothroyd is stalling over meeting and 'is in no rush to set up meeting'.

WEDNESDAY, SEPTEMBER 6

Ask Iain about meeting again. He said: 'Aidy agreed to it at the time but doesn't see any point in it now.' Iain said it's not worth calling him.

It did not require an intermediary to speak to Tommy Smith on the cusp of his return to the club. Boothroyd had not had the opportunity to persuade Robinson to come back but he had successfully orchestrated the return of another member of the team that defeated Manchester United in the FA Youth Cup fourth round replay in the 1996-97 season.

Smith talked happily and eloquently about overcoming the boo boys at Vicarage Road. He seemed to have matured from the player I was told made an impulsive decision to leave the club after being dropped in favour of Michael Chopra for the FA Cup semi-final with Southampton in 2003.

He sent a text the day the interview was published to say

how pleased he was with the story heralding his return from Derby County. He was smart enough to recognise the role the local paper could play with the supporters.

THURSDAY, SEPTEMBER 7

Boothroyd came out with this at press conference before the Bolton game. 'I think the power of the media – you cannot get away from it. If I read everything that was written, watched every programme that was on and listened to everybody's opinion then you'd drive yourself mad. With that comes more pressure and the ability to switch off and maybe not read. We had interest for the last three weeks of last season but this is another level. It's not a problem, in fact it's something I quite enjoy.'

The focus on the development of Vicarage Road and the East Stand, in particular, had sharpened with the unexpected windfall from the Premier League. I had requested interviews with club executives and senior management at the club to get an update but with no success.

I decided to report the story from another angle by speaking to Dorothy Thornhill, the Mayor of Watford. Her passion for the town was obvious as she said she was instrumental in keeping the club at Vicarage Road when the possibility of the club relocating had been explored. The editor recognised the significance of the story and pushed it up to the news section. Ashton found out before publication and called Thornhill, reducing her to tears apparently. She phoned our editorial manager and tried to retract what she said. I reluctantly rewrote the intro.

FRIDAY, SEPTEMBER 8

I expect a backlash given yesterday's events but Iain says Ashton is not that unhappy with piece.

A third successive trip to the north west, this time to Bolton, does nothing to embellish Watford's points tally. The games all followed a depressingly familiar theme; Watford huffed and puffed but found their own house blown down by a late goal, this time a Gary Speed penalty. It was cruel.

SATURDAY, SEPTEMBER 9

Boothroyd is rude post-match at Bolton when I asked two questions about Danny Shittu being Watford's outstanding player and about trying to take the positives. Feel he is trying to belittle me in front of the national writers.

While I was on a training course in Southampton Iain sent a message to say how unhappy the club was with a piece a news reporter at the paper had written about the club buying the Red Lion pub on Vicarage Road. I hadn't even written a word that week yet they were still unhappy. The magic of the dream job started to wear off. I was not looking forward to seeing Boothroyd at the home game with Aston Villa.

SATURDAY, SEPTEMBER 16

Things come to a head with Boothroyd after he gives me a one-word answer in the post-match press conference after the Villa game. We become involved in a heated exchange on the stairs on the way down from the temporary media centre at the top of Occupation Road. He told me my 'questions need to be better'.

'I don't tell you how to do your job so don't tell me how to do mine,' I responded.

We have a blazing row on the Family Terrace, of all places. Iain attempts to mediate. I pluck up the courage to tell Boothroyd he is trying to bully me. He thinks I'm

trying to 'nail' him and that 'the paper has an agenda'. I
counter by saying I would be pretty foolish in my first
season in the job trying to nail someone who the fans
think walks on water. After a heated 20 minutes we shake
hands. My phone rings three times later that night display-
ing a number I don't recognise. I eventually answer and, to
my surprise, it's Boothroyd. He apologises. He says: 'You'll
do for me,' and 'You're on my bus.' I'm not sure quite what
bus that is but am presuming it's a metaphor. He tells me
to work at resolving the agenda he feels the newspaper
has with the club and he'll do the same at his end. I know
the paper doesn't have an agenda but I reason it's not the
time to start arguing again.

The *Watford Observer*'s biggest sale for years came after the play-
off win over Leeds so it is beneficial for the paper if the club
performs well and there is positive news to report.

But the paper performs a different role to the club website
and has a duty to the club's supporters – their stakeholders – to
accurately report events from the boot room to the boardroom.
Sometimes those stories will not be positive but, as David Cam-
eron said, local newspapers 'strengthen our democracy, holding
the powerful to account'. Or, as Boothroyd succinctly put it in
July 2007: 'The *Observer* is as essential to Watford Football Club
as Watford Football Club is to the *Watford Observer*. We need to
work together so that the *Observer* can sell newspapers and we
can communicate as well as we can with our fans.'

With the town's football team in the Premiership, the
adopted rugby club in the top flight and town's flagship golf
course, The Grove, hosting the American Express Championship, there was no better time to be a local reporter than in
2006. A friend of mine had two spare tickets to watch the golf
at The Grove so, as a gesture of goodwill, I offered them to

Boothroyd. I called him on the number he gave me at the start of the season but it was switched off. I tried later and it was still off. I remembered to save the new number he rang me on after the Villa game so I called that. It rang this time but he didn't answer so I left a message.

MONDAY, OCTOBER 1

Got an email from Iain. 'Aidy has gone mental because you've got his new phone number. We're under strict instructions not to give it to anyone at all. I won't ask you where you got it from but I'd advise using it sparingly.'

I reply: 'That is absolutely pathetic. He rang me from that number three times – the first two times I didn't answer as didn't recognise the number – when he phoned to apologise after the big bust-up following the Aston Villa game, so, funnily enough, that's how I got it. And what's wrong with the local paper having the manager's number? Only phoned in an attempt to be nice and offer him some golf tickets. Wish I hadn't bothered. He didn't even have the courtesy to ring back and say yes or no, or thanks anyway.'

I have the phone numbers of, among others, four rugby World Cup winners, international footballers and various club directors but it is an unwritten rule in journalism that you don't betray the trust of your contacts by handing out their numbers. I even stored Boothroyd's number under a different name after my friends got hold of my phone and threatened to ring him. I was understandably apprehensive at seeing Boothroyd after the Fulham game. He thanked me for the offer of the golf tickets and said there was no problem having his new number. 'Just don't give it out to anyone,' he said.

The game with Fulham proved a seminal moment in the

season. It was Watford's best chance yet of claiming that all-
important first victory but their failure to protect a 2-0 lead
exposed their flaws. It also opened the first fault lines in the
boardroom. The Russos felt Boothroyd should be fired. That
would have been impulsive and premature as Boothroyd had
earned plenty of latitude for his achievements the previous
season. Simpson apparently said to Jimmy: 'Are you mad?'
Things were never really the same again in the corridors of
power. The vote of no confidence from the vice chairman and
his fellow director filtered down to Boothroyd and he barely
spoke to the Italian brothers again. More than 18 months
later, I discussed with Boothroyd the prospect of the Russos returning to the club as owners. 'That will be the worst
thing that ever happened to the club,' Boothroyd said. When
this was relayed to Jimmy, he said: 'Tell Boothroyd, when
I come back he's fired.' It was one of the more humorous
moments of my time covering the club.

TUESDAY, OCTOBER 3

Text Boothroyd to ask when is a good time to call him
and he phoned me. Have an okay-ish chat. I asked what he
thought of the recent coverage and he said: 'I know you've
got a job to do.'

I struck up a good rapport with *Daily Telegraph* columnist
Tony Francis, who wrote a weekly column on Watford's Premiership experience. He is a broadcaster, has commentated
on World Cups and is a skilled writer and author. When he
spoke, with great humour and insight, I listened. It's fair to
say he began to sense paranoia at the club. He told me he got
approval from Dorothy Thornhill and Simpson to sit in the
directors' box for a match but that Ashton blocked it.

The first hint of a crack in the relationship between

Boothroyd and Ashton surfaced when I was told that Boothroyd was furious about the colour of Watford's new commemorative midnight blue away kit. Privately, he fumed at Ashton and his girlfriend, Sarah Winning, who worked in the commercial department, about the new kit. Boothroyd believed blue was a passive colour and the antithesis of the fire and brimstone approach of his team.

This was a commercial setback as some fans had paid nearly £40 to wear a shirt they thought the likes of Marlon King would be wearing away from home. So, publicly, Boothroyd endorsed the kit, saying his son, Nathan, proudly wore one but he did not explain why Watford did not wear the strip at Charlton Athletic. So I attempted to provide transparency in a news story. Boothroyd responded by attacking the newspaper and me in his weekly newsletter to the fans. He described the kit as 'wonderful' yet it was not worn at Liverpool in December either, the next time Watford were forced to wear an alternative strip. He also suggested we were 'trying to sell newspapers' by reporting the speculation, fuelled by postings on the club's own message board, that Marlon King had missed the game against Charlton for disciplinary reasons. I wrote a commentary piece in response, highlighting, among other things, the need for transparency.

SATURDAY, NOVEMBER 4
Got a text from Iain to say Boothroyd wants a meeting.

I met Boothroyd at the training ground the following Tuesday. He was armed with a copy of the paper and said he only read the comment piece that morning. He felt the headline – Tell us what you really think, Aidy – was an example of 'the agenda we have against him' but he said he 'liked' me. I stressed the need for him to trust me and suggested he put this to the test by opening up more, talking more off-the-record and helping me write more insightful copy. It was all very amicable. He asked me to stay for lunch and I sat with him and the coaches, chewing the fat. We talked about his interest in the goalkeeper Mike Pollitt had Foster not been allowed to return.

THURSDAY, NOVEMBER 9

At the press conference before the away game at Chelsea, Boothroyd asked why I didn't call him yesterday as he said I could call on a Wednesday from now on. I told him his phone was off for most of the day and he said to leave a message and he'll always call back.

WEDNESDAY, NOVEMBER 15

Tried to call Boothroyd but his phoned was switched off. He got a message to me via Kate, his personal assistant, and Iain saying sorry but his phone was out of service. Nice touch.

Results continued to go against Watford in their worst start to a season for 16 years. They were beaten by a late Kanu penalty at Portsmouth, and Boothroyd had a real rant at the ref. Then came a truly dreadful performance at home to Sheffield United. I discussed with Neil Price, who played left-back for Watford in the 1984 FA Cup final and was working as a forthright radio summariser, and Tony Francis how the writing looked on the wall already.

In between times, Boothroyd remained helpful. He answered his phone on the second ring on his day off and seemed happy to chat, despite having new wardrobes fitted at the family home in Bromsgrove. He talked about the need to get the stadium rocking ahead of the Sheffield United game and I agreed to help with a bang-the-drum back-page story imploring the fans to get behind the team. I told Boothroyd that was an example of how we could work together. He appreciated it and talked of getting Alan Smith and Helguson in on loan and dismissed the rumours of David Healy, Ade Akinbiyi and Carlton Cole signing in January. He also gave me advance warning of Richard Lee's new contract while shopping in Sheffield ahead of an FA Youth Cup match.

The game against Newcastle on December 16 will not go down in the club's history as particularly significant. It was an unremarkable 2-1 defeat that followed a similar pattern to the ones that proceeded and followed it that season. It did, however, provide the setting for the start of arguably the messiest boardroom battle in the club's storied history.

The opening of the January transfer window was looming and I felt I needed an executive to discuss the club's recruitment policy. Were they resigned to relegation and so intended to save the promotion windfall? Or were they going to spend in a bid to launch a relegation rescue act?

With Ashton and Simpson unavailable, I decided to call Jimmy Russo, the vice chairman. Our relationship didn't get off to the most auspicious of starts. He asked me to call him back, which is usually a polite way of someone saying they don't want to speak. Undeterred, I called back and Jimmy clearly thought I was someone else. 'For a minute, I thought you were that bloke from the paper,' Jimmy said. I almost hung up through sheer embarrassment but I plucked up the courage to admit, indeed, I was 'that bloke from the paper'. It broke the ice and Jimmy spoke candidly, sensibly and with all the hallmarks of a successful businessman thereafter.

'...we will be as active as we can be within reason', Russo said in an interview published on December 15. 'We will push the boat out as much as we can in order to secure our safety for next season. Aidy will get all the support he needs. He is a

reasonable guy and knows how far he can go. But we are cus-
todians of the football club and if we don't do it right there
won't be a club...

'The easiest thing to do is go and borrow a shed load of
money, spend it and then get relegated,' Russo continued. 'Look
at Leeds United, how many millions did they blow, and for
what? We are not going to spend next year's money, we aren't
in a position to do that and we wouldn't do that as it would be
reckless. Watford have been down that road already in the last
five years and we don't want to do that again.'

FRIDAY, DECEMBER 15

Got a call while in bed from Iain at 9.03am on my day off
saying: 'Graham and Mark have gone mad about the Russo
story.' Can't believe it. It's not even controversial. Starting
to wonder if it's all worth it.

The Russos made their own way to away games and when they
met Simpson at St James' Park things were decidedly frosty.
Simpson thrust a copy of the paper in Jimmy's direction and
told him to read it. Jimmy said he would read it in his own
time. They had further words at half-time and Simpson told
Jimmy not to talk to the press. Jimmy felt this was over the top
and characteristic of how Simpson had changed following promotion. The Russos felt he had quickly forgotten it was their
money that helped save the club and then been solely respon-
sible for buying Marlon King, the catalyst for the promotion-
winning season, for £500,000 from Nottingham Forest.

MONDAY, DECEMBER 18

I was forwarded an email from a source outside the club.
Email was originally sent to Ashton by Stuart Higgins, the
former editor of The Sun, who the club are employing at

great cost on a consultancy basis.

The email from Higgins read: 'I have spoken to Iain about the Russo piece in the *Watford Observer* today and I understand your concern and anger. However in this case, I do think it is unfair and unrealistic to expect the paper to give us advance information on anything they run, given they have an editorial freedom to pursue stories involving the club or people concerned with the club without our approval or knowledge.

'However, in this new era of co-operation it would have been nice to give us a heads up. More importantly, Jimmy Russo should know that he is not entitled to speak to the media about the club's activities without authority from Mark or without the knowledge of the press office. He is absolutely in the wrong in doing this and deserves – in my opinion – a severe ticking off and a none too subtle reminder about his responsibilities.'

I called Jimmy on the Tuesday. He had no problem with the story. He said it was 'excellent' and that I was doing a 'great job'. He said to keep the call between me and him. 'You'll need me in the future,' he added.

I grew to like the straight talking Jimmy and Vince, who is the younger brother by three-and-a-half years. They had a reputation for meddling in recruitment when Lewington was the manager but I found them both very warm, passionate people who, despite being Chelsea season ticket holders, continue to hold a deep affection for Watford, even though they are no longer directors. They travelled to watch the team play at Blackburn and Plymouth after they had been removed from the board.

Their sprawling houses in Broxbourne and the two red Ferraris Jimmy keeps in his garage are the products of their multi-million pound salad growing business in Essex, but I am always struck by their humility. I find them very down-to-earth individuals, proud family men and I enjoy their company.

The Russos came in for unfair criticism from those not in full possession of the facts when they resigned from the board in December 2009 and requested the return of their £4.88m loan, which was payable on demand. This was standard practice but Watford were not in a position to pay back the money because it would have plunged the club into administration.

As the brothers explained in a subsequent letter to Elton John, they would 'never have allowed the process to proceed'. It was a game of brinkmanship in an attempt to get Lord Ashcroft to come to the table. Ashcroft's representatives were unreceptive to a business plan presented by the Russos in November 2009 that indicated the level of financial rescue package required.

The Russos were prepared to convert their loan, at that time £2.6m, and invest a further £650,000. Fordwat, Lord Ashcroft's company, was asked to put in £3.25m but rather than inject cash offered support only through a rights issue.

On the morning of the annual general meeting in December 2009, the Russos were advised that Simpson had appointed Fordwat's nominated proxy, Andy Wilson of Strand Partners, to also act on his behalf.

This meant 53 per cent of the votes were secure and their intention was to remove the Russos and their advisor, Robin Williams, from the board. The Russos jumped before they were pushed.

'There was no way we were going to sit there and be humiliated given our total commitment to the club,' the Russos told Elton in a letter.

Julian Winter, who was then chief executive, and Graham Taylor were flabbergasted at the Russos' decision, which is surprising. If the Russos knew they were going to be voted off then you suspect, as non-executive directors, they did too. Taylor called Jimmy Russo 'a bad man' in an interview, but subsequently apologised in a private meeting at The Grove.

I met Jimmy in person for the first time at Anfield in December 2006. He seemed nervous about being seen talking to me. I remember that game because Foster played, much to my surprise, as Boothroyd told me he wouldn't be ready after a knee problem that I'd been told was set to rule him out for the entire season. He underwent knee surgery on his return to United. Some at Old Trafford felt Foster was naïve and misguided to play through the pain barrier.

I started to get the impression Boothroyd was just telling me the stuff that suited him. I understood the need to surprise the opposition but I'm sure Rafa Benitez wasn't losing any sleep over whether Lee or Foster played in goal for Watford.

I went to Australia that Christmas to watch the Ashes, a trip booked before I was handed the job of covering Watford. I stepped off the plane at Heathrow on my return, switched on my phone to get a text from a source saying Dave Hockaday and Chris Cummins had been sacked.

Boothroyd was not in a great mood after a shocking performance at home to Liverpool. The game was live on Sky and any players who were thinking about joining would have thought twice after watching that.

However, Watford had lined up a move for Collins John, the Fulham striker, offering him personal terms that would have eclipsed the eye-watering package given to Ramon Vega in 2001.

I didn't ask a question at the press conference as I had been away and was not sure what had been going on. All the talk had been of Ashley Young leaving. I got a text from a source saying that Steven Gerrard had told Young to 'get out of here' as they came off the pitch at the end of the game at Vicarage Road.

The speculation over Young's future had started to reach fever pitch. Some in the boardroom were apparently prepared to accept £5m for him but others felt they could draw Aston Villa and Spurs into a bidding war.

Spurs offered Calum Davenport, a central defender that Boothroyd had previously been interested in, plus cash.

Notorious for their brinkmanship, Spurs had apparently told Young not to go anywhere and to sit tight until closer to the end of the transfer window. They were hoping to strike a better deal as the deadline loomed.

I called Young to find out the latest but he declined to talk.

THURSDAY, JANUARY 18 2007

Had a disagreement over the phone with Scott Field [Watford's press officer]. Young, for some reason, had phoned Field to tell him I called him and Field phones me to say I shouldn't have called the player. I strongly disagreed. Field then sent me an apologetic email and gave me the heads up over where Young was going. I was really grateful as my lead story originally had Young going to Spurs whereas Villa was the most likely destination.

I travelled to Villa with Iain in a club Saab. I really enjoy his company. He is a multilingual, smart and intelligent guy who I respect enormously. Malky Mackay clearly rates him highly. Moody joined Cardiff as head of recruitment and when he was having difficulty securing outstanding money he was due from Laurence Bassini and his trusted aide, Angelo Barrea, Mackay gave him £1,500 out of his own pocket to compensate.

So many media officers obstruct rather than facilitate, but the 18 months Moody spent as a football writer meant he was sympathetic towards the press. He became increasingly influential at Watford after they finally recognised his talents in recruitment and player liaison were under used in the media department. He became football operations manager after the FA Cup semi-final defeat to Manchester United, drawing on the experience of working for the agent Athole Still and his top client, Sven Goran Eriksson and working with Jacques Santini during his brief spell at Tottenham.

Despite being a trusted ally of Boothroyd's – he later offered him a job at Colchester – and an influential figure, Iain never sought the limelight and went about his job with minimal fuss, troubleshooting, firefighting and acting as a conduit between the football and administration departments.

In early 2009 some of the club's salaries were leaked and it was a surprise to learn that Moody was paid £20,000 a year less than other administration staff such as Field, Michael Jones and Katie Wareham, who could have been said to be more firmly in Ashton's camp.

Meanwhile, on the pitch the injuries began to bite and resources were thin. I was sitting with Iain having a meeting before the home game with Blackburn Rovers and Boothroyd popped his head in. We had some good banter. I told him: 'I've got my boots.' He said: 'You might need them.'

It took until January to secure a one-on-one interview with Simpson. We sat in his office overlooking the car park at the foot of Occupation Road and he spoke from the heart about being a custodian of the club. There was no trace of management-speak. Simpson spoke with the same conviction and passion as he had at the Bill Everett Centre in 2002 when he highlighted the grim state of the club's finances.

He and Tim Shaw had dug deep into their pockets to save the club, and I admired him for that. Perhaps it was his career as an actor in the 1970s that made him difficult to read but it was tricky to get an accurate insight into his character.

I was never quite sure if he was the sort of dour uncle who, at a family party, might ask sternly if you were knuckling down to your studies before offering unsolicited advice about the wisest route home or the fun uncle who tells racy jokes and slips a folded bank note into your top pocket with a wink and a 'make sure you spend it all on sweets'. Apart from painting a picture of the hard sell he, Ashton and Boothroyd gave Collins John in that very room earlier in the month, he didn't give much away.

He didn't mark my card over any signings so it was just as well I left the interview to find a message on my phone saying that the club had expressed an interest in Steve Kabba and Keith Gillespie.

With a history of heavy gambling Gillespie was the type of wayward player with a point to prove that Boothroyd often favoured but the deal fell through.

Kabba did arrive but I knew it wasn't a signing to excite the fans. Kabba was deemed surplus to requirements by Sheffield United, a club Watford were promoted alongside and were now locked in a relegation battle with.

The fact Watford were signing the peripheral players of their fellow strugglers was indicative of how they had spent time treading water since they routed Sheffield United at Bramall Lane during the run to the play-offs. Kabba turned out, as expected, to be a huge disappointment and never found favour after telling Boothroyd early on in his Watford career that he didn't train on Sundays. Boothroyd always called players in on Sundays for a warm-down session.

FRIDAY, JANUARY 26

Aidy phones out of the blue at 5.30pm. I miss his call. Call him back but no joy. Find out the following day that he's got the hump about me saying he doesn't admit it when he gets things wrong tactically. Doesn't approach me with it,

comes via Scott and Iain. Remember him saying earlier in
the season that he does things face to face and doesn't go
through a third party. He told Iain I was sheepish in press
conference before the West Ham game. Don't think I was.
They win at West Ham so he's in a good mood.

Man United rested Rooney and Ronaldo against Portsmouth
but I suspected it was not to keep them fresh for the midweek
game against Watford. Sir Alex Ferguson must have thought
about handing them another game off after seeing the Watford
team sheets. I almost spat out the delightful food I was devour-
ing in the press room at Old Trafford when it emerged Chris
Powell was going to be stationed in central midfield.

Signed for £10,000 a week after Boothroyd failed to get
Robinson, Powell found himself out of favour after just four
league games of the season, as evidenced by Boothroyd not
even looking at, let alone acknowledging, the defender when he
was sent off at home to Sheffield United. Yet here was Powell,
at Old Trafford of all places, lining up in midfield against
Michael Carrick.

Harry Forrester, the promising teenage midfielder, travelled
with the team that day. Boothroyd would have been better off
playing him. I remember discussing with Neil Price the notion
that Boothroyd had lost the plot tactically.

I asked Boothroyd a question about his curious team selection in a press conference room at Old Trafford so vast it could
have doubled up as a cinema. Even Boothroyd's own media
team felt he didn't answer it well.

THURSDAY, FEBRUARY 1

Boothroyd returned my call and we talk about home game
against Bolton. He opened up and said he would like a
meeting to discuss how he plans to take the club forward.

I welcome it with open arms. I text him to say I'm able
to write a more insightful piece if he opens up instead of
giving me crumbs. He texts back a day later to say: 'Thanks
for text but headline in paper not helpful.' I reply saying
headline – We tried to sign big names – was actually
positive. His reply: 'The perception of fans is not the same
as my players. Not paranoia just important to respect all
points of view.'

Watford were absolutely shocking as they lost against
Bolton. Boothroyd was abrupt and short in the press conference, as he had been after the corresponding fixture earlier in
the season, and storms out early. He brought cake to his following press conference as an apology.

WEDNESDAY, FEBRUARY 7
Received text out of the blue from Boothroyd at 8.20am
on a snowy morning telling me Foster is in the England
squad. Text him to say: 'Thanks – I'll call you later'. He rings
me to say he's off on holiday and can I speak to him now.'
All good.

I met Boothroyd in a coffee shop in London Colney on
Tuesday, February 13. He told me who his summer transfer
targets were and believed I should, in exchange, reveal who my
sources were. It doesn't work like that and he was naïve to think
it did. Exposing sources goes against the grain of being a journalist and I told him that I would never reveal off-the-record
information he had told me so I wasn't about to do it with
other sources.

He asked how I found out that he only let Hockaday do
set-pieces in training. He said only an insider would know that.
The thing was, he and Ashton had alienated so many current

and ex-employees that people were queuing up to help me, but I didn't tell him that. He finished by telling me he thought I lacked respect for authority. I disagreed. I got a call from Iain afterwards saying Boothroyd had just 'sung my praises' to him.

WEDNESDAY, FEBRUARY 14

Boothroyd called me as he says his phone is going to be off for the rest of the day. Progress indeed. Talked openly and I enjoyed the conversation. It's starting to resemble the chats I recall Oli Phillips having with Lewington.

Boothroyd was an hour and a half late for the press conference ahead of the Ipswich FA Cup game. Not great as it's deadline day. I try to continue the period of goodwill by handing him the Ipswich team that their local journo had got from Jim Magilton. Boothroyd called me at 8.15am on the Friday to say 'thanks for info, much appreciated,' and says Malky Mackay is going to be out injured. The paper was already in the shops but it was good story for the website.

Watford beat Ipswich with a late goal from Damien Francis but leave it very late. Feeling emboldened by the improved relationship with the manager, I lead the press conference and Boothroyd answers well. He apologises afterwards for not letting me know about Foster and Jordan Stewart being ruled out through injury too but said they were Friday injuries. That's fair enough.

Watford have a tradition for fielding fine goalkeepers and Foster continued the trend. Watching him during the Premiership campaign was a privilege. As a schoolboy I used to station myself at the bottom of the stand directly behind the goal so I could get up close and witness the art of Coton, David James and Kevin Miller. Foster established himself in their company

during his two years at the club and few players at Vicarage
Road can have received the kind of standing ovation he did
after he returned gingerly to his feet following treatment in the
midweek game at home to Wigan.

United, Foster's parent club, were thrilled by his progress
at Watford. According to Coton, United found Boothroyd and
Alec Chamberlain very professional, particularly when it came
to promptly sending the monthly DVD highlights of Foster's
performances to United. Boothroyd's friendship with Richard
Hartis, a coach at United, played a key role in landing Foster on
loan for two seasons. Once it became clear Foster was going
to be sent on loan after being signed from Stoke, Coton and
Hartis ensured there was only one place he was going to.

The way Foster was instructed to launch the ball from one
end to the other meant you were always in danger of suffering
neck ache that season.

Fortunately, I made a point of not always following the ball
but watching the manager and the activity in the dugout and
technical area. You can always catch up on a replay of the game
later but the body language and behaviour of the manager is
not replayed on TV. I remember the tactic paid dividends during the following Championship season when I spotted Smith
was handed a written note by Boothroyd during the second
half of the game against QPR. Akos Buzsáky strolled into the
space Smith vacated and scored at the far post.

Boothroyd provided a fascinating sub-plot after the home
game with Wigan when he remonstrated with a fan as he walked
down the tunnel. I spotted the fan was wearing a distinctive
jacket so I ran outside to try to grab him for a chat as he made
his way home.

I didn't know who the fan was but with my eyes peeled for
his jacket, I zig-zagged through the crowd in a scene straight
out of the film *Crocodile Dundee* and found him.

He was furious. He said Boothroyd invited him to 'come and sort it out downstairs,' but stewards intervened. He said Boothroyd's wife, Emma, got involved as well. The fan gave me his number and I said I would call him the next day. I got back into the ground and walked past Boothroyd who was in deep conversation with Field. The conversation level dropped down as I walked past.

Boothroyd called the next day and I talked to him about the angry fan. He responded with some good quotes but said he'd prefer it if I didn't mention his wife. I didn't give a guarantee as I'd already spoken to the fan and he mentioned Boothroyd's wife. After a chat with the editor we agreed to run with the story on the front page as Jane Parr, our excellent photographer, had captured a great picture of Boothroyd gesticulating to the fan. We located a picture of his wife to use as an inset. I told Iain, out of courtesy, that we were going to use a picture of Emma. I was called downstairs by Iain before the press conference to preview the game against Everton and told by Boothroyd that he is 'not into threatening people but I don't want you using a picture of Emma or my kids'. I subsequently found out from Iain that he actually said: 'If a picture of Emma appears I won't fucking talk to him again.'

Boothroyd was happy to pose with his wife and kids outside the town hall when they won promotion yet, according to him, we weren't allow to run a picture when it is associated with a negative story. Following an editorial meeting we reluctantly pulled the picture of Emma as a gesture of goodwill. We ran the story, though.

FRIDAY, FEBRUARY 23

Anxious about Boothroyd's reaction. Received a text from him. 'For what it's worth I thought the *Observer*'s coverage of the spat and the games was excellent,' it read.

Thursdays in the *Watford Observer* office is always frantic and fraught because it is deadline day. The back page and inside left-hand page are invariably blank at midday which can cause angst among some and exhilaration for others.

I like the thrill of deadline day and was comfortable with having blank pages so late because it meant we had space to put in all the news from the weekly press conference, which was held on a Thursday. But any delay would reduce the time I had to write around 1,000 words. The closest I ever came to missing deadline was after the play-off defeat to Hull City the following season. I filed a considered match report and an end-of-season post-mortem from the pre-admission lounge at St Albans hospital minutes before it was time to go down to theatre for surgery.

THURSDAY, MARCH 1

Boothroyd called me just when I needed him to before deadline. Told me Clarke Carlisle is going on loan to Luton and says that is because he wants to try to get Leon Barnett in the summer. Good conversation. I find out from a source at Charlton that Ben Thatcher is going to be out this weekend. I relayed the news to Boothroyd. 'Cheers pal,' he replies. 'Tell them fuck all.'

Boothroyd was late for a press conference again and the large press pack, who descended on the ground to preview the FA Cup quarter-final with Plymouth, were not impressed. Instead of moaning about the timekeeping of the manager, I noticed John Barnes milling around waiting to be interviewed by a TV camera crew and plucked up the courage to ask if he minded talking about the 1984 semi-final with Plymouth. Considering I did not start watching football until the 1986 World Cup, I could not draw on any anecdotes of the game but my family told me all about that cup final. Barnes seemed to enjoy talking about that period of his career as much I did interviewing my first Watford hero.

FRIDAY, MARCH 9

Woken by a call from Boothroyd at 9.15am. 'What is my reaction to the paper going to be?' he says.

'Don't know?'

'You tell me,' he retorts. 'What's my reaction going to be?' he repeats.

'Is there a problem?' I ask.

'Should there be?' he says.

'No, I don't think so,' I say.

'Good,' he says. 'I really like you Kev, we'll have to meet up again, see you Sunday.'

Bizarre conversation.

I phoned Iain to ask him what that was all about. It turned out Iain had the same one with him. Apparently he rang me, changed his mind about it half way through and then didn't know what to say when I answered. Turned out problem was with Terry's Challis' cartoon.

I text Boothroyd: 'Why didn't you just tell me what the problem was? Hadn't – and still haven't – seen cartoon. Good luck on Sunday.'

He replies: 'No problem at all, all part of being a manager. Thanks for text.'

My suspicion that the pressure started to get to Boothroyd was gathering pace. He arrived in March 2005 and impressed the players with his boundless energy, innovative ideas and eternal optimism. One described him as a 'breath of fresh air'. 'He made the players feel good,' said another. Boothroyd was very hands-on and enthusiastic on the training ground, focusing on the number of entries into the final third of the pitch made by his players, the shape of the team and he was meticulous in his preparation. He fostered a learning environment at the club and would abruptly stop a team meeting and turn it into a auxiliary classroom by posing a hypothetical question. For instance, he would split the players into small groups and give them ten minutes to formulate a game plan for what to do tactically if they were 1-0 up with ten minutes to go but had a man sent off.

He managed to convince the raft of signings, who all arrived with a point to prove or a career to salvage, that promotion was a realistic target. 'He said we were favourites to go down but if we got everyone believing, that we could get promoted,' Henderson says.

But he stretched his credibility in the dressing room the following season when the players learned via the press he felt European qualification was an attainable goal. He felt the template used so successfully in the Championship could be translated to the Premiership.

The players he recruited for the Premiership season and the subsequent one in the Championship were not indebted to Boothroyd for resurrecting their careers in the same way the summer signings of 2005 were. They were not as malleable or receptive to his methods.

For example, he endured a fractious relationship with Jobi McAnuff, who felt constrained by the shackles placed on the club's wide players. The winger signed from Crystal Palace in June 2007 for £1.75m but, less than two months later, found himself out of favour and on the bench for the final pre-season friendly.

The following month, Boothroyd signed Adam Johnson from Middlesbrough on loan. The simmering relationship between Boothroyd and McAnuff boiled over following the final home game of the regular 2007-08 season, against Scunthorpe. According to sources in the dressing room, McAnuff spoke out following the 1-0 home defeat against a side who had already been relegated and the players were locked in the dressing room for more than an hour as they undertook a frank exchange of views.

Earlier in the season, Boothroyd stunned even the seasoned players in the team when he lashed out at Jordan Stewart. Jay Demerit, the captain, intervened only for the manager to turn on him too.

'He [Boothroyd] started to develop an edge to him,' recalled one player. 'He had a very positive take on the world when he first arrived but it wasn't the same atmosphere when we started to struggle.'

The departures of several people from the backroom team – Nigel Gibbs, David Hockaday, David Dodds, Chris Cummins and chief scout Mark Stow – began to lead to the creation of a culture of fear at the training ground.

Meanwhile, Keith Burkinshaw, Boothroyd's experienced assistant told friends how disappointed he was that the club explained his departure as being solely down to the ill health of his wife.

SATURDAY, MARCH 10

Watford somehow burgle a 1-0 win at Plymouth in the FA Cup. Foster is magnificent. I shake Boothroyd's hand afterwards and offer congratulations on reaching the semi-final. Bump into the Russos afterwards. They must be dedicated, coming all this way to watch the game when it's live on BBC. I grabbed a lift to Devon with Iain and Scott but we broke down on the way home after running out of petrol in the club car. Relations with the media team are at a season high.

WEDNESDAY, MARCH 14

Boothroyd called me back on his day off. It feels like I've
inconvenienced him. Asked him about him being linked
with England under-21 job. 'I haven't spoken to the FA and
even if I had, I wouldn't tell you.' Bit abrupt.

TUESDAY, MARCH 27

Got an email from Moody who says Boothroyd is unhappy
that I have criticised Doyley in an interview I did with
Tommy Smith. 'AB wasn't happy to see one of his players slagged off in an interview with another one and I'm
inclined to agree with him. An interview piece is no place
for journalistic opinion.'

My reply: 'It's hardly slagging him off. Sports writing is
full of journalistic opinion, Iain. If the paper, or any papers
for that matter, did not have any opinion or comment it
would just be like reading a press release or something on
a club website. Is Aidy therefore going to give me praise
for sticking by and supporting Henderson all season,
praising Jay at every opportunity and saying how well
Foster has played this season? It cuts both ways, although
appreciate Aidy has to defend his players. If Lloyd was any
good, why has he hardly played in 2007? Think we'll have
to agree to disagree.'

Some seasoned writers in the press box for the home game
with Chelsea remarked Boothroyd was getting a bit too big for
his boots when he picked a fight with Jose Mourinho. It was not
only the Portuguese alchemist who riled him. In the press conference ahead of the away game at Middlesbrough I asked him
about perhaps playing Richard Lee instead of Foster as Lee is
going to be playing in the FA Cup semi-final and could do with
some match practice. Boothroyd laughed it off and made out

it was ridiculous idea. Things became heated when I asked him
if he feared his credibility as a manager would be damaged if
he took Watford down. He said he didn't have an ego and then
made out I was being really negative. In a diversionary tactic he
asked other journalists to have a word with me as I was, apparently, 'too negative'.

It was difficult to see the positives from a woeful display at
the Riverside. It was their worst performance of the season,
which was saying something, and Gavin Mahon, the captain,
was cast as the scapegoat when he was dragged off at half-time.
The look on Mahon's face spoke volumes when he emerged
in his tracksuit after the break and boarded the coach. The
national writers were not impressed with Boothroyd either
when he named King on the bench for the FA Cup semi-final
with United after saying in midweek he 'had no chance' of
being fit. 'As if Ferguson is going to be bothered about King
playing or not,' says one.

Boothroyd's apathy for the press was evident again when
he arrived late for another press conference, this time ahead
of the away game at Blackburn. I asked him about the situation with Shittu, who was dropped for the FA Cup semi-final,
the biggest game of the season. He was uncomfortable about
the line of questioning. 'Danny might come to me but if he
does I won't be telling you,' he snapped. It was therefore a nice
change when the club put up Burkinshaw and Carlisle for the
press conference after the defeat at Blackburn. Burkinshaw said
the performance was not good enough, which was a refreshing
display of honesty.

THURSDAY, APRIL 26

Text Jimmy Russo to ask him for off-the-record chat as
heard whispers that Ashton has supposedly been offered
a job at United. He rings me. He clearly has reservations

> about Ashton. Jimmy said he has done his research on me
> and that he knows 'I'm on his side'. I'm not on anyone's
> side but Jimmy seems to be a force for good.

I found Ashton a shadowy, nervy figure who seemed to exhibit an abnormal sense of paranoia. The only time I was afforded an audience with him he brought along his trusty administrative allies Michael Jones and Katie Wareham. There was a feeling Ashton exaggerated any apparent interest in him from Manchester United to strengthen his position at Watford. Jimmy Russo told Simpson: 'If he is that good, then let him go.'

The interest in Ashton never amounted to anything but he did receive the sort of salary a United executive might envy in 2007-08 – more than £900,000, which was more than David Gill, his equivalent at Manchester United, was reportedly paid.

Without the usual legal or accountancy background of most chief executives, many insiders at the club felt Ashton was out of his depth and relied too heavily on agents based in the Midlands and expensive consultants to perform his role. Catalyst, the management consultancy firm, was recruited by Watford in the summer of 2007 for a year at an eventual cost exceeding £1m. Mark Reynolds, the Catalyst executive, became a key decision maker.

SATURDAY, APRIL 28

Things come to a head with Boothroyd again. Told by Scott Field that Boothroyd wants two minutes with me outside after the press conference at Sheffield United. Said I called him 'befuddled' in my Man City match report. I didn't. I said his thinking was muddled when referring to the substitution of Douglas Rinaldi, who was the best player against Man City. He said I should show him more respect. I said he should try to give me more information then I would be able to write more informed, insightful copy. He said why should he give me more? I say he doesn't have to but it would help both of us. I added that surely he had had worse stick from the national press this season, particularly from Tony Francis. 'He's limited,' says Boothroyd. After the final game of the season against Newcastle, Boothroyd presented Tony with a urine sample bottle as he felt he had taken the piss out of him all season.

WEDNESDAY, MAY 2

Met Field in the Watford Café before press conference ahead of the Reading game. He said Aidy wanted the relationship to work but I think he is just a puppet and he thinks Aidy and co can do no wrong. Pointless exercise really as we just seem to be going around in circles. Told me I should start ringing Boothroyd again in midweek. I said it's a waste of time as he is really abrupt and not as charming as he is in press conferences. Went to press conference. Boothroyd okay. Why didn't he just meet me instead of Field?

THURSDAY, MAY 10

On the advice of Field, I called Boothroyd first thing on Thursday morning. He answered the call and we chat away. He reported back to Field and said, apparently, that I had only asked him four questions. I can't win!

WEDNESDAY, MAY 16

Call Boothroyd but get no answer. Leave a message but he doesn't call back. I find out we [the *Watford Observer*] are being sued by the football club over an open letter written by Steve Simmons, the former financial director, questioning the make-up of the board. No wonder he didn't call.

2007-08

Following relegation from the Premiership, Watford initially made a good fist of bouncing back at the first attempt. They started strongly but there was a watershed moment in early November when West Bromwich Albion, who eventually were promoted, took them apart 3-0 at Vicarage Road.

The 2007-08 season can be neatly divided into two parts; pre-West Brom and post-West Brom.

Victory over the Baggies would have opened up a 12-point lead at the top of the table. Watford had taken the division by storm with ten wins out of 13 league games.

'We felt unbeatable,' says Henderson. 'Went in at half time 1-0 down against West Brom and the fans were always with us, but they started booing. I was thinking: "But we are nine points clear." I heard it and a few of the players mentioned it at half-time and after the game. We went from being unbeatable to wondering where our next win was coming from. We drew so many games in a dreadful run. The West Brom game was definitely a turning point.'

Watford only won eight of their next 34 matches.

The West Brom game marked the return of Robinson for the first time since he left in 2003. 'The reception I got gave me goosebumps,' Robinson said. 'But I remember the crowd jumped on their backs. That wasn't fair as we were unplayable that day. It could have been more than three. We were just told to win the battle first and we really paid attention to detail on set pieces. We dealt very well with that. We knew they fancied their chances. They went on a downwards spiral after that while we got a lot stronger.'

The future and form, or lack of it, of the strikers, was a theme of that season and Henderson was a central figure.

'The gaffer pulled me on the first day of pre-season and said

I was down in the pecking order and that Preston had come in for me,' Henderson says. 'He told me it might be in my interests to speak to them. It was a bit of a shock.'

Henderson went up to the north west to speak to Paul Simpson and his assistant but decided the move wasn't for him. His availability alerted others and bids from Sheffield United, Fulham and Leicester landed on the club's fax machine in Wolsey Business Park, the temporary office they used in Tolpits Lane at a cost of more than £1m while Vicarage Road was being refurbished.

Boothroyd wanted to regenerate his forward line by signing DJ Campbell and Helguson but he made the mistake of overplaying his hand by telling Henderson he was surplus to requirements before having his replacement secured. Henderson became disaffected, restless and agitated for a move to Fulham. He was appeased with a significantly improved contract which catapulted him among the club's top earners. 'I went from being shown the door, to getting a new contract,' he says.

The rise awarded to Henderson was indicative of the money gambled that summer to secure promotion at the first attempt. Where most clubs cut their cloth accordingly following relegation from the Premier League, Watford's wage bill rose from £16.7m to £17.6m. Mart Poom, Matt Jackson and Jobi McAnuff signed contracts worth more than £10,000 a week each; Martin Hunter and Dick Bate were added to the coaching staff on six-figure salaries; John Stephenson joined to head up recruitment on a similar package; psychologist Keith Mincher saw his contract upgraded from part-time to full time; the number of performance analysts tripled to three and £200,000 was spent on IT to support match analysis. Sean Fitzpatrick, the former All Blacks captain, was paid, according to a source, a 'huge amount' to give a motivational speech to the squad. Former England rugby union backroom members Dave

Aldred and Dave Reddin were hired on a consultancy basis. Reddin played a role in the expensive revamp of the home team dressing room, using the positivity created by inspiring quotes and images in the England dressing room at Twickenham as the template. Dave Bassett was also paid £1,500 per week as a consultant to Boothroyd, who would visit the former Watford manager at his house in Denham.

Money, it appeared, was no object that madcap summer, as evidenced by the financial commitment to sign Nathan Ellington. Ashton led the negotiations to sign a player languishing in West Brom's reserves for £3.25m with a further £1m based on appearances on a four-contract worth £10,000 per week. One source said the salary was £12,500 per week once bonuses and appearance fees were factored in. I remember choking on my pre-match hot dog at Southend when word reached me about the deal for Ellington. To put it in perspective, the highest-paid player during Lewington's era was Helguson on £4,000 a week and £2,000 a game and the club was losing money then.

Ellington was no problem in the dressing room, according to his teammates. One player said 'he kept himself to himself', another said he was 'a good lad', while two described him as 'down to earth'.

Yet it quickly became apparent to the coaching staff Ellington had lost the edge which made him a mobile and prolific striker at Bristol Rovers, Wigan and then during his early days at West Brom.

Some felt he had lost his edge after marrying his Bosnian wife who is, so I'm told, the dominant figure in their relationship. It is also unclear whether Watford were aware Ellington converted to Islam three years earlier but two weeks after he signed, Ramadan started and he fasted during daylight hours for the next month. I remember being taken aback by the reception Ellington received warming up in front of the West Brom fans.

Returning players, by and large, are never warmly received but the greeting from the Baggies faithful bordered on vitriolic.

'Of course I heard it,' Robinson, a former teammate of Ellington's, says. 'I was surprised but that's part and parcel of football. I know he took it personally and found it very tough.'

Ellington was signed in August 2007 but by March the following year it was clear the move was not working out. It quickly became apparent to those based at the training ground in London Colney that Ellington was not at the mental or physical level Boothroyd anticipated. His agent, Tony Finnigan, called me in a fury when Ellington was substituted during the home game against Norwich. He felt his client had worked harder than Henderson and was being made the scapegoat for Watford's faltering promotion bid. 'I'm getting him out of here,' Finnigan blasted.

Whether Ellington was signed to complement, supplement or replace King was unclear but with Watford's promotion charge stuttering, Simpson apparently felt it was time to accept an offer from Fulham for King.

Simpson and Ashton both arrived grim-faced at the training ground in London Colney after King's move broke down, a sign of their desperation to begin balancing the books. Boothroyd also went to King's house in Boxmoor on the Saturday night to discuss the next move. With the help of his agent, also Finnigan, his move away was resurrected, this time to Wigan for a smaller fee than Fulham were going to pay.

Boothroyd called to ask if I could play down King's degenerative knee problem in the paper and then, in exchange, he would give me details of the deal to sign Mat Sadler. I said he had overestimated the power of the paper and that any club would find out about the state of King's knee in a medical. Boothroyd was probably relieved that the story of King once arriving for training after a big night out had stayed in house.

King had been banished to the bench as punishment for the next game, against Reading on March 11, 2006.

Talking of medicals, Collins John, King's temporary replacement, failed a medical at Watford yet his loan deal was still sanctioned. If failing the check-up was not bad enough, an administrative mix-up meant the club had to pay six months of his five-figure weekly salary instead of three. One of the players was shocked at how 'overweight' John was when he reported for training. His bi-weekly trips back to Holland to see his family did little to aid his rehabilitation. His three starts and two substitute appearances cost the club in the region of £1m.

Given the financial extravagance, the joy on the faces of Ashton and Simpson at Blackpool on the final day of the regular season was probably more one of relief.

Ten days later, after a 6-1 aggregate defeat to Hull City in the play-off semi-finals, Simpson drove home from Humberside with a member of the senior management team and agonised all the way about sacking Boothroyd.

2008-2009

Watford started the following season shakily, with four wins from their first 14 league games. The chairman eventually felt the urge to pull the trigger following the 4-3 defeat at home to Blackpool in November. It was probably not as bad a result as it had appeared because Blackpool went on to clinch promotion via the play-offs at the end of the season.

Boothroyd's departure was dressed up as mutual consent but it was about as far from mutual as you can get. He was summoned to a meeting with Ashton, Simpson and operations director Paddy Flavin after the Blackpool game.

Boothroyd was presented with a dossier of alleged failings, which was used as leverage to reduce his compensation payment. By the end of his time at Watford, Boothroyd was estimated to be earning an annual salary of between £600,000 and £700,000 and it is said he had a two-year compensation clause in his contract, which had been inserted by Ashton when they were getting on well.

In addition, he had, with good reason, been given a bonus of £500,000 for winning promotion. There was a clause in his contract that would earn a further £500,000 had he kept Watford in the Premiership. He received the bonus despite the club being relegated. He left immediately after being fired and said goodbye to the players and the staff at the training ground a couple of days later.

'I wasn't overly surprised when he was sacked. So much had gone on,' says Richard Lee.

The damage had been done long before and the foundations for Boothroyd's exit had already been laid.

He started pre-season for the 2008-09 season aware he had to trim the size of his squad and jettison some big earners on the periphery, but was under the impression there was no pressure to sell his leading players. The goalposts were shifted when Boothroyd was in Austria leading a pre-season training camp and heard Henderson had been sold behind his back.

'Aidy said the club had accepted a fee from Sheffield United and it was probably worth going up to speak to them,' Henderson says. 'I didn't want to go. He said it was the club's decision as financially, they were not in the best shape. I told him I was happy and didn't want to leave. I asked if I stayed, would I still be wanted.'

Henderson again headed north to speak to the bidder and, this time, he accepted the improved terms on offer. He felt the time was right to move, even though he had a young family and the barn he was renovating in Markyate was near completion. 'I felt if Watford were a selling club, and not buying, I'd be better off at Sheffield United as they had ambition,' Henderson says.

The sale of Henderson weakened Boothroyd's position and dramatically changed the dynamic of his relationship with Ashton and Simpson, who were absent from a monthly senior management meeting in July when Alastair Ferguson, the finance director, talked about the prospect of administration. Ashton hit the roof and things imploded internally and externally. Boothroyd and Ashton barely spoke after that.

I wrote a story for the *Watford Observer* on July 25, 2008 revealing the possibility that the club could fall into administration. This story was much maligned. The key phrase was 'face the prospect of administration'.

This explosive news reached me via a trusted source. My information was that Boothroyd was told by an intermediary that everyone in the squad was up for sale as the club sought to raise £10m by the close of the transfer window at the end of August.

The fact they did not enter administration was down to the sales of Henderson and Shittu contributing £4m; Smith would have been sold had he agreed to join Stoke City. There was a new bank facility, designed to buy some time until the end of the January transfer window, when it would be due to be repaid, that accounted for another £4m. Throw in the £750,000 insurance pay-out from Damien Francis's retirement and the club was just £1.25m short.

Ellington would have been sold had it not meant they would then have owed West Brom the remaining £1m on the balance of his original transfer. Instead, he was loaned out twice, with Watford subsidising £3,000 of his weekly wage.

For the second time in a year, the club instructed expensive libel lawyers and threatened the paper with legal action in a bid to dilute the administration story. They did not have a leg to stand on and received no apology from the paper, no settlement or compensation. I was simply reporting to the fans what had been discussed by the finance director in a management meeting.

Several months later, after I left the newspaper, and with the threat of legal action still looming, Simpson requested a face-to-face interview with the sports editor of the *Watford Observer*.

Simpson gave no guarantee of funding the new East Stand, talked about the prospect of more player sales the following January and discussed the prospect of the club going into the red in a matter of weeks.

In January 2009, the threat of legal action against the *Watford Observer* was dropped. 'As a club we acknowledge that we have made mistakes in the past, in respect of our relationship with the newspaper...' chief executive Julian Winter said. He added that 'the club should be less sensitive to fair adverse criticism which will inevitably arise from time to time'.

Jimmy Russo, who was not the source of the original story, validated the article in an interview on the front page of the paper on December 4, 2009. 'You broke the story last year that the club was £10m short and actually it hasn't changed much,' he said. The Russos saved the club from administration three times in 2009, including once in November with an injection of £1m half-an-hour before funds were due. Fordwat saved the club from administration a fourth time after it paid a loan due to the Russos after the brothers resigned.

Russo was the chairman when he appointed Malky Mackay as his first manager when Brendan Rodgers joined Reading. Mackay had already been caretaker after Boothroyd left.

Watford's former goalkeeper, Tony Coton, had applied for the job and was interviewed by Simpson and Ashton at Simpson's house. On the trip down from Manchester, Coton heard that the little-known Rodgers was already the front-runner but carried on anyway for the interview experience as it was the only managerial position he'd applied for.

In the interview Coton said he would make Mike Williamson from Wycombe his first signing. Simpson led the interview process. Ashton 'sat there and didn't say a word', according to Coton. As the former goalkeeper expected, Rodgers was appointed but he did receive a courtesy call from Simpson informing him he had not been successful.

Rodgers arrived yet almost resigned in a matter of weeks after feeling the job was not as Simpson and Ashton had presented it. Rodgers then had to work against a backdrop of boardroom instability. Within a week, Simpson resigned after the Russos said they would revisit the details of some boardroom business conducted back in 2005.

Simpson was prepared to call the Russos' bluff at the extraordinary general meeting called by the brothers but blinked first. He instructed Richard Fennells from Strand Partners, the company Watford's major shareholder Lord Ashcroft has a significant investment in, to call the Russos. They had convened at The Grove hotel with their legal advisor, Robin Williams. The two parties met in an executive box directly above where the fans had gathered for the EGM and the Russos were asked what they wanted in exchange for their silence. They wanted Simpson to resign with immediate effect and Ashton to follow in two weeks.

Simpson fell on his sword amid an emotional speech, which was probably the wisest option. There were also some shareholders in the room, including a former club executive, who had some searching questions that would have rendered the EGM the most dramatic and contentious in the history of the club. Those questions were not aired.

Ashton followed suit a fortnight later. As he loaded his car in the car park, he was greeted by a furious member of staff who had driven from the training ground just to tell Ashton he 'physically despised' him.

I'm led to believe Simpson apologised to Jimmy Russo immediately after the EGM, presumably for the way the brothers were jettisoned after they helped rescue the club. Jimmy accepted the apology but they have not spoken since.

It finally brought the curtain down on one of the most tumultuous periods in the club's history. Sometimes I wonder if winning promotion to the Premiership in 2006 was the worst consequence of that heady day at the Millennium Stadium. Would the lessons of a valiant defeat to Leeds have been of greater benefit to Boothroyd's promising career and the longer-term future of the club?

What was the legacy from the tens of millions of pounds generated by promotion? Expectations became unrealistic.

In October 2006, Boothroyd said: 'Next year we can maybe go after a £5m player and the year after that maybe a £10m or £12m player. At the minute it's £3m tops.'

The club lost touch with its roots and money was frittered away as easily as Boothroyd's team came to concede possession. I certainly know a few fans who would have traded those memories of Cardiff to avoid the subsequent financial uncertainty and boardroom instability.

Kevin Affleck is a former deputy sports editor of the *Watford Observer*, where he spent two seasons as Watford FC correspondent and more than three seasons covering Saracens RFC. His work at the paper resulted in multiple regional and national awards. He spent three-and-a-half years working in the United Arab Emirates as deputy sports editor of *The National*, an English language newspaper.

11

In 2001, Watford hired Gianluca Vialli as their new manager. The supporters were excited. Of course they were.

But as we all know, it turned out to be an expensive and ultimately doomed attempt at a glamorous make-over.

A year later, Vialli was gone, leaving behind a towering pile of receipts.

So it was perhaps understandable that some fans welcomed the latest Italian takeover and Gianfranco Zola's arrival with a little more caution.

Lionel Birnie looks at why the Vialli experiment failed and talks to one of the few genuinely bright spots of that season, Milan's European Cup winner, Filippo Galli.

THE ITALIAN JOB, PART ONE

BY LIONEL BIRNIE

Maine Road, Manchester
Saturday, August 11 2001

Before the arrival of the Middle Eastern billionaires, before the nouveau riche surroundings of the Etihad Stadium and Roberto Mancini's extravagant gestures and elegant suits, Manchester City were more of a spit and sawdust sort of club.

They played at Maine Road, which was smack in the middle of Moss Side, one of Britain's roughest, toughest housing estates. The imposing Kippax Stand towered over the terraced houses like a giant climbing frame for grown-ups.

As you parked on the estate, kids in tracksuits would dart out from nowhere, palm outstretched for 50p or a pound, and say: 'Mind yer car, mister?' And you gave it because you knew there was a chance your car might be keyed or, worse, up on bricks by full-time.

The stadium itself was vast, home to one of the widest pitches in English football. In good times, this suited City's expansive, flowing play. In bad, it enabled the visitors to carve great holes through their midfield and defence.

Something about the place was edgy and dangerous. While Anfield always felt like The Beatles in their clean-cut early days, or the ever-so-twee Gerry and the Pacemakers, and White Hart Lane couldn't be more Chas 'n' Dave, Maine Road embodied the spirit of the Gallagher brothers long before

Oasis were born. The swagger, the defiance, the couldn't-give-a-damn attitude that hung over the place as persistently as the Mancunian drizzle.

When the crowd unleashed its guttural roar, deepened and made more rasping by the years of frustration, the force of it could rock you back on your heels. The fans would have you believe that Manchester City was the club that the real people of Manchester supported. Shameless FC.

City had suffered plenty of bad times of late. They were up and down like a broken lift as the millennium approached and turned. Relegated to the third tier for the first time in 1998 they hauled themselves back up to mere mediocrity with two late goals in a play-off final against Gillingham. That match happened – in the rain, of course – the day before the sun shone on Watford's play-off victory over Bolton, which lifted them to the Premiership.

You may well be wondering by now what all this has to do with Watford.

Well, on Saturday, August 11 2001, Manchester City faced Watford in the opening game of a Division One season that was to prove pivotal for both clubs. City were the bookmakers' favourites for promotion and Watford were very close behind them.

The media had gone giddy for the potential clash of styles. Manchester City were big and famous and had just appointed an ex-England manager to drum them back to their rightful home, the Premiership, with guts and gusto.

Watford, perennially unfavoured by the press, had swapped another former England manager and his supposed long-ball fetish, for the patient passing of an Italian aristocrat's beautiful game.

Before the early evening kick-off, the managers and captains of the two sides met in the referee's changing room for the pre-match briefing. The contrast could not have been starker.

For Manchester City there were Kevin Keegan and Stuart Pearce, the epitome of the British bulldog spirit with hearts pinned on rolled-up sleeves, passion oozing from their pores.

For Watford, two Italian sophisticates, Gianluca Vialli in his grey schoolboy's jumper and fat tie, and 38-year-old Filippo Galli, with a style and poise that was diametrically opposed to Pearce's in-yer-face attitude and clenched fists. They were two calm, softly-spoken Italians with European Cup-winning pedigree and they thought they could tame and then outwit the wilder excesses of Division One with grace and guile.

Watford were betting the house on winning promotion and attempting to alter the DNA of the club in the process. With the former Chelsea manager at the helm and an influx of players used to more glamorous surroundings, they couldn't fail.

That was the script, anyway.

Ninety minutes later, Vialli's expensively assembled team looked like a group of nursery school children who, thinking they were on a trip to a petting zoo to see the animals, wound up at the London Dungeon. Manchester City stretched Watford to breaking point on their big pitch and exploited the gaps ruthlessly as they brushed them aside, 3-0.

Nine months later, we awoke with a thumping hangover. For a fleeting moment we thought it must all have been a dream and felt a wave of relief, which rapidly gave way to a rush of nausea as we set bleary eyes on the detritus of the excess, the empty Champagne bottles and a tower of scrunched up receipts.

This match between Manchester City and Watford turned out to be much more significant than a mere showdown between the pre-season favourites. For Watford, it came to symbolise the game's folly. Maine Road had witnessed an Italian-inspired revolution and all but crushed it underfoot in one evening.

There weren't many bright spots that season but few would pass up the opportunity to watch a player who demonstrated Galli's composure. After one of his early displays it struck me that I'd never seen a Watford player do so much by doing so little. As my dad said to me: 'Imagine how good he must have been when he was 28.'

So, how did a former European Cup winner with Milan, a contemporary of Baresi, Maldini, Costacurta, Gullit, Rijkaard and Van Basten, end up at Vicarage Road?

This is the story of that season, a year when Watford tried to step across the chasm that divides the haves and have-nots and came a cropper.

* * *

What a bewildering few months it had been. That spring, English football went mad, and Watford were right at the centre of things, with their underpants on their head.

A television company called ITV Digital wrote down a number with a lot of noughts on the back of a napkin and football's executives could not believe their luck. They held out their pockets and filled them with television's magic beans. Even the kids in Moss Side offering to watch your car for a quid knew the value of having a cold, hard coin in your hand better than this lot.

But they were dizzy with ideas. Many of them were football's nearly men, in charge of clubs that had not cracked into the elite. Some had already enjoyed a drop or two of Premiership elixir on the tips of their tongues and they lusted for more. So they abandoned their critical faculties, ignored the trifling questions about who would pay a hefty monthly subscription fee to watch Bradford City and Crewe and Grimsby and, yes, Watford, and they signed away their futures.

The big clubs had been wallowing in money for the best part of a decade and now that cash was going to cascade downwards thanks to the wonders of digital television. All the clubs had to do was tilt their heads back, open their mouths and swallow as much as they could.

The Football League's three-year deal with ITV Digital was worth £315million. No one paused to ask whether this was viable. Watford's match at Manchester City was the first to be shown by the new channel but just a month later, the official viewing figure for Nottingham Forest's match against Bradford City was less than 1,000. As *The Guardian* pointed out, the rights for that match cost the station around £1.2m, meaning 'it would have been cheaper for the channel to drive each of its viewers to the ground, put them up in a five-star hotel and give them all £500 spending money'.

ITV Digital's mascot, a knitted monkey, may well have been a metaphor for the whole thing.

* * *

When you look at the club's long history, Watford were uniquely placed to avoid taking the potentially ruinous path. After Graham Taylor had masterminded back-to-back promotions to the Premiership, they were financially sound. Relegation, and the meek battle to avoid it, had been disappointing but the club was in excellent shape.

Immediately after relegation, the fans were given good reason to hope for a quick return to the top flight when Taylor added Espen Baardsen and Allan Nielsen from Tottenham for a combined fee of £3.5million. Some supporters grumbled that it was the sort of cash Taylor should have splashed trying to retain, rather than regain, Premiership status. That, of course, avoided the obvious point that any team battling for its life at the bottom of the Premiership is trapped in a sort of parallel transfer market – a Supermarket Sweep version of the real thing where the doomed and the desperate are spurred by the ticking clock to grab at anything they can. Often, they only realise when they get home from their shopping spree that they've ended up with the rubbish no one else wanted.

Taylor's pragmatism and his careful negotiation of choppy waters was admirable, even if it did not excite some of the more demanding fans.

The arrival of the two Scandinavians provided an impressive, if short-lived, impetus. Watford started the season at a hectic pace and, while they were not always effervescent, they were effective, getting the job done in a manner that struggling or recently ejected Premiership sides tended to when up against Division One opposition. They rode their luck sometimes but bulldozed their way to the top of the table and by mid-October the season had condensed into a two-horse race. It looked like a fight between Fulham and Watford.

A 3-0 home defeat to Manchester United's reserves in the League Cup at the end of October was like a sudden dose of heartburn. The bitter taste of the previous season's Premiership experience rose in the throats. Perhaps the players were demoralised by a glimpse at their futures. It certainly seemed that way.

The season tripped up in late autumn, stumbled and fell head-first with a 5-0 defeat at Fulham on Boxing Day, before tumbling in agonising slow-motion down a seemingly bottomless ravine. They weren't even in free-fall, it was more painful than that, as they bumped off the sides on their way down. Unbeaten for the first 15 league matches, they won just eight more and by March, promotion was still a theoretical possibility but the team's form made it look improbable.

Towards the end of March, Taylor announced his plans to

retire at the end of the season. Perhaps he did it to spur the players on to one final, unlikely push. Maybe he recognised that the team needed a major overhaul and he didn't want to start another two or three-year rebuild, or perhaps he sensed the vibe in the boardroom that the directors wanted to go in a more glamorous direction. Or maybe it was a combination of all three factors.

With Taylor on the way out, the list of possible successors was long but one name quickly emerged as the favourite. On April 3, Gianluca Vialli was in the directors' box to watch Watford's 3-0 win over Nottingham Forest. Talks were already underway and the secret was about to get out.

* * *

If this was a television documentary, rather than the chapter of a book, this is the point that we'd cut to a dinner party scene. The camera would pan round to show a group of smartly dressed people sitting at a smart table in a luxurious room. Two of the heads would be bald and their suit jackets would look expensive. A glamorous woman, let's call her Mrs Anderson, would be serving strands of pasta, slick and shiny with olive oil, onto the plates of her guests. The word RECONSTRUCTION would appear in the bottom left-hand corner of the screen. A disclaimer would say: 'Actors have been used to recreate this scene.'

One of the bald men, the one with the goatee, would take a mouthful of pasta, nod his head in approval, then put down his fork, pick up a pen, an expensive fountain pen made in Switzerland, and sign a contract worth £800,000 a year.

This is not a television documentary, of course, but that dramatised version of events gives you an impression of how the behind-the-scenes seduction played out. It is said that Vialli was convinced to join Watford after dining with Brian Anderson, one of the club's directors. Anderson's wife made pasta. And the rest is history. That was one costly tagliatelle.

* * *

Be honest now, what was your reaction when you first heard that Watford were linked with Vialli? Were you excited? Of course you were.

And why not? Vialli was a terrific footballer. He played for Sampdoria, Juventus and Chelsea. He won the Champions League with Juventus and represented Italy in the World Cup and European Championships. He usually played with towelling wristbands on, making them cool again. As Chelsea's player-manager he won the European Cup Winners' Cup and League Cup within months of taking over from Ruud Gullit, then went on to finish third in the Premiership before winning the FA Cup. He managed to last more than two-and-a-half years before being given the sack by Evil Father Christmas, which is presumably evidence of his patience and sense of humour. To lapse into Ray Wilkins speak, Vialli's Chelsea played wonderful football even if they were still Chelsea. But most of all, Vialli was famous, and respected, and admired by almost everyone in the game. And he would be coming to Watford. After years of ill-informed criticism of Watford's so-called long-ball football, weren't you keen to embrace the beautiful game? The press wouldn't be able to assign their glib, lazy epithets to any team managed by Vialli.

But something didn't feel quite right, did it?

The indecent haste with which Graham Taylor seemed to be hurried towards the door left a sour taste. Vialli was officially announced as Watford's new manager on May 2, the day after Taylor's team had won 3-0 at Gillingham and four days before his farewell at Burnley. The news had already leaked out but couldn't they have delayed the official announcement for a week or so and at least allowed Taylor to collect his hat and scarf, have a last look around and exit the building in his own time? After all he'd done, he deserved that, at the very least.

* * *

Before you could say: 'Don't throw baby out with the bath water' there was a screaming infant with its fingers jammed in the plug hole.

Luther Blissett, Kenny Jackett and Tom Walley, with their experience and coaching qualifications, were told they were no longer wanted. Vialli wrote down a list of the players who would be surplus to requirements – including Robert Page, Steve Palmer and Tommy Mooney – and left it to the chief executive to break the news.

Admittedly, there is no room for sentiment in football. Taylor could be just as ruthless when he decided to get rid of someone – although he would have done the firing himself.

Vialli's arrival and his determination to get on with the job, bringing in his own people – Ray Wilkins as assistant manager, fitness coaches and physios, a nutritionist and a chef, performance analysts, masseurs, masseurs for the masseurs – merely signalled that he meant business. Professional business. Vialli had played at the top, managed pretty close to it and was now going to power Watford there with an army of expert staff.

We didn't hear a great deal about his philosophy. Why did we need to? His philosophy was engraved on the back of his Champions League winner's medal.

All we needed to do was wait for the influx of brilliant new players and enjoy the ride.

Here, I must make a confession.

During that summer, I decided to engage in a bit of light mischief making – nothing that hadn't been done to good effect by others before – by planting a delicious rumour on an internet message board and waiting to see if it got picked up. Using a pseudonym, I wrote that one of Vialli's signings would be Roberto Baggio.

This was just about believable. Baggio, who was 34, was still playing for Brescia in Serie A and was on old team-mate of Vialli's. A few days later, the *Daily Express* suggested, in that breathless way the tabloids do when they're talking out of their hat, that *Il Divin Codino* – the Divine Ponytail – was on his way to Vicarage Road and even went as far to say that Baggio and Vialli had talked. To the best of my knowledge, there was absolutely no truth in it but it was interesting to see how far the seeds of excitement would blow.

* * *

In late June, rumours with more substance began to circulate and eventually Vialli began to recruit. We all wanted to be positive but as players began to arrive the doubts were too great to ignore. Did Vialli know anything about the demands of the English First Division?

At the risk of defaming the club's current sponsors, it was as if Vialli was engaged in a real-life game of Football Manager, pointing his mouse and clicking on everyone he'd heard of and increasing the weekly wage until they said 'yes'.

Ramon Vega, a Swiss central defender, joined from Celtic, turning down advances from Everton. Vega became the highest paid player in Watford's history, reportedly on £21,000 a week – a record that was not broken until the team reached the Premiership under Aidy Boothroyd in 2006.

Shortly after Vega signed, I passed a Tottenham supporter I

worked with in the corridor. He chuckled and said: 'Bad luck.'

'But... but... he'll be alright in the First Division, won't he?'
I stammered.

He laughed the hollow laugh of bitter experience.

So, I checked out a Celtic supporters' message board. The
title of the first thread read: 'Watford – thank-you very much for
signing Vega.' Extraordinary, considering they won the treble.

Patrick Blondeau, a 33-year-old French right-back who had
played for Monaco, Sheffield Wednesday and Marseille, came
in. There was Stephen Hughes, a show pony made of glass,
and Stephen Glass a winger who wasn't and who possessed a
left-foot with the accuracy of a professional golfer's pitching
wedge. David Noble, a young midfielder from Arsenal, joined
on loan. And then there was Filippo Galli, a veteran defender
who had been released by Brescia but who had an impressive
pedigree. It may have been uncharitable and it turned out to be
proved wrong but the first impression was that Watford was
being used as a retirement home for one of Vialli's mates.

The season was looming large, Vialli had three-quarters of
a new defence and two dozen new midfielders, it seemed, but
had not added a centre forward. Four days before the opening match, he spent £900,000 on Marcus Gayle, the former
Wimbledon player who had endured a few goalless months at
Glasgow Rangers.

On paper, it looked as if Vialli had been prudent, adding
significantly to the squad for less than a million pounds but the
free transfers masked a huge increase in the wage bill.

Still, what does the football supporter have but hope? We
cannot influence the decisions or the outcome and so we had
no option but to feel optimistic. Unfortunately every positive
could be countered by a worrying negative.

Vega had played for Switzerland in Euro '96. (He was at the
heart of their defence for a 1-0 defeat to Scotland.)

Blondeau was a French international. (Capped twice.)

Everton paid £3million for Stephen Hughes. (And let him go for nothing 16 months later.)

Marcus Gayle was excellent for Wimbledon. (True, but as a left winger, not a striker. He'd scored five goals in 18 months.)

Filippo Galli won five Serie A titles and the European Cup with Milan. (But he's 38 years old.)

* * *

So, let us pause for a moment and learn about Galli who, with his three European Cups, must surely rank as the highest achiever to pull on a Watford shirt. He was not, however, the first European Cup winner to play for Watford – that honour goes to Gary Williams, who was in the Aston Villa side that beat Bayern Munich in 1982. After 15 years at Milan, Galli's career was meandering downstream with Reggiana and Brescia before the opportunity to fulfil a lifetime's ambition came up.

What's this? It was Galli's ambition to play for Watford? Not quite, but he did want to play in England before retiring.

Galli was born in Monza in 1963. Monza is in northern Italy, not far from Milan, and is most famous for its motor racing circuit. As a boy, Galli would play in the street outside his home with his friends. The two passions were football and motor racing so sometimes he'd kick a ball pretending they were representing the *rossoneri*, other times they'd be on their hands and knees re-enacting the grand prix with their toy cars.

In Monza, where Ferrari's red car is an iconic symbol stronger even than Milan's red and black stripes (or Inter's blue and black), Galli was a McLaren fan. 'In Italy, that is not easy,' he says. When he was seven he was given a toy racing car – a McLaren – and that was it. 'I still remember the driver was Denny Hulme and ever since then McLaren is my team.'

Galli's love of English football came a little later. Before football, in fact, there was gymnastics, which, he says, was every young boy's introduction to sport where he lived. There was no stigma, no sniggering at the boys who liked gym. 'From age eight to 11, I did everything – the parallel bars, somersaults, climbing the rope,' he says. 'No one in Italy laughs at boys doing gym. It's great for your strength and flexibility. It's one of the reasons I was able to carry on playing football until I was 40. Throughout my career, I had injuries but they were impact injuries, broken bones. I didn't tear muscles, I had a strong core.'

As a young footballer, Galli's strengths were obvious. He was aggressive and had an innate sense of timing, a combination that lent itself to playing in defence. In England, the big lads go at the back, the skilful ones up front. In Italy, where defending is seen as an art, Galli was quickly identified as a talent. At 15 he was playing for a senior non-league club, shortly after that he was spotted by a scout from Milan's youth team.

His first taste of league football came while on loan at Pescara in Serie C1 (Italy's third division) in 1982. They won promotion to Serie B during Galli's year there. In his absence, Milan, who had been demoted after a match-fixing scandal, regained their position in Serie A.

When Galli returned to Milan, he was introduced to the team's new £1 million signing – Luther Blissett, from Watford. 'At that time, very few people in Italy spoke English,' says Galli. 'I liked English football and I learned a bit of English at school. When Luther arrived, I tried to help him settle. The club gave him an apartment outside Milan, in a small village between the training ground and the city. It probably wasn't the right place for him to learn Italian or settle in the right way but that is what the club thought was best at that time – stay out of the city, away from the supporters and the distractions.

'In training I tried to help him with the language. In the

games, he was unlucky. This was not the Milan team of President Berlusconi. We were not the strongest. We could have only one or two foreign players so there was a lot of pressure. Luther was so fast and strong and he worked really hard – much harder than a lot of others – but he didn't manage to score many goals. The style of the game was not for him. We were too patient, much more defensive than they were in England. We didn't play to his strengths, we expected him to change everything.'

Galli's love of English football began when Joe Jordan joined Milan in 1981. 'I know he was Scottish but he came from English football. Please don't say he was English!' says Galli. After Blissett, Milan signed Mark Hateley and Ray Wilkins. 'It's unbelievable. Wilkins was assistant coach at Watford. Maybe it was destiny. Wilkins was a great person and his play was ideal for Serie A at that time.'

But what was it that attracted Galli to the English game?

By way of an answer, he suddenly reels off the Liverpool team that defeated Roma on penalties in the 1984 European Cup final, rolling each name into the next until it is just one long word: 'Grobbelaar-Neal-Kennedy-Lawrenson-Whelan-'Ansen-Dalglish-Lee-Rush-Johnston-Souness.'

Later, when I check the Liverpool team, I am impressed to see that not only had Galli got it right but he listed them in 1-11 order too. The team clearly left an impression on him.

'I can't even list the Milan team I played in like that,' he says. 'I'd have to think about it.

'We didn't see much English football on television – Some goals, the cup final, or European matches – but I fell in love with it. The passion of the supporters.'

Galli won the Serie A title with Milan five times between 1988 and 1996, playing for Arrigo Sacchi and Fabio Capello. He was a substitute for Milan's European Cup wins in 1989 and 1990 but played alongside Paolo Maldini at the heart of the defence in arguably the most complete performance by a club side, when they demolished Barcelona 4-0 in Athens in the 1994 final. 'It was the golden age of Milan,' he says.

When he was 35, Galli joined Brescia, led them out of Serie B and helped them survive in Serie A playing behind Andrea Pirlo and Roberto Baggio.

'In 2001, Brescia told me they didn't want to sign me again,' says Galli. 'I didn't know what I was going to do but I knew I wanted to carry on playing for another couple of years.'

One day, Galli got a call from Nicola Caricola, a former player who was now working with Vialli, helping to identify targets for Watford. 'Nicola called me and asked about Igli Tare, the Albanian striker who had played with me at Brescia.

'Caricola wanted to know if I thought Tare would be good for English football. I said, oh yes, because Tare was good in the air, very strong, very good with his back to the goal. Then Nicola said: "We're also looking for a central defender because we've just signed Ramon Vega from Celtic." I joked to him: "I am available. I'll come over. It's my dream to play in England." Then the phone cut off, the line just went dead.'

Ten days later, while on holiday in America, Galli's phone rang again. 'This time it was Vialli. We agreed a contract in two minutes on the phone. There was no agent, nothing. It was a good contract – not as big as Brescia – but it was very good. But I wasn't thinking about money, I was thinking about the experience. I wanted to play in England, I wanted to improve my English. If it had been half as much I'd have come.'

As Galli was about to board the plane for England to meet Vialli and to sign the contract, his phone rang. It was Brescia, asking him to stay, but his mind was already made up.

Galli knew Vialli but they were not close friends. 'We played for Italy under-21s together. When I was doing my national service in Cremona, we played a friendly with Cremonese and I had to mark Vialli. I spent my time kicking him…'

Galli threw himself into the Watford experience. At the pre-season camp in Fiuggi, he had to go through the typical football club induction by standing in front of the rest of the squad and singing a song. What did he choose?

He breaks into song: 'It's a little bit funny…' *Your Song*, by Elton John, of course.

* * *

Galli joined up with his new team-mates at their pre-season training camp in Fiuggi, not far from Rome and played his first game against Queens Park Rangers at Loftus Road. During the training camp, the players were asked to vote for who they thought should be the captain. Galli won it, comfortably, which is perhaps not surprising although he was touched. 'It was a great honour to be captain of the club. They didn't know me well but they still wanted me to be their captain.'

Then came a couple of friendlies in Italy against Inter – with famous players we'd seen in World Cups and European Championships, Laurent Blanc, Sergio Conceicao and Christian Vieri – at their pre-season training base in Lecco and then against Vialli's old team Sampdoria in Genoa.

Watford had unveiled a new home shirt, plain yellow and beautifully minimalist, particularly in the early weeks before a sponsorship deal was confirmed. Seeing it brush against Inter's famous black and blue stripes in such an idyllic setting as Lecco's little stadium nestling in the mountains near Lake Como was very pleasing. Oakwell and Gresty Road felt a very, very long way away.

As the sun set over the rocky points on the horizon, it was possible to imagine a not too distant future when Watford versus Inter might be a European fixture. Not in the Champions

League, of course, let's not get too carried away, but perhaps in the UEFA Cup if Inter fell on slightly hard times.

* * *

Stop dreaming. Back to reality and Maine Road.

Watford's defence was under sustained pressure. It was hard to tell who was out of position and who was manfully sticking to their task as Wanchope and Goater stretched to breaking point the invisible elastic that is supposed to link a well-drilled back four. Eyal Berkovic kept running into the ample space, causing more problems. Oh for Steve Palmer to be there to disrupt the City flow.

There was a moment when Vega was beaten by Wanchope, or was it Goater, leaving Galli to cope. The Italian slid in, won the ball and put it out for a throw-in. Vega jogged back into position looking far too casual under fire for comfort. Galli hauled himself to his feet, bent double, his hands on his knees for a breather. His body language said it all. 'What have I let myself in for here?'

We talk about the Manchester City game and the moment Galli's romantic vision of the English game revealed itself to have very sharp edges.

'Wanchope, Goater...' he says, almost weary at the memory. 'They were too fast for me. And Berkovic too...' he exhales. 'Maine Road was an amazing experience. I was in the referee's room with Keegan and Pearce. They are English football to me. The stadium was so noisy. I've played in the San Siro all my career but the English atmosphere was so... so...' he searches for he word... 'intense.'

'That game, we hit the earth, eh? You know what I mean?'

Although Galli's English was good, he found that communicating on the pitch was not a simple matter of understanding the language. He took a couple of months to learn the football speak. 'There's a big difference between being in a restaurant, looking at a menu, having time to think about the words you want to say. In a game, you have to say it NOW.'

Although the early results were not too bad, away from home, Watford were too often a soft touch. Galli's assessment of the squad is frank. 'We were a good group but our mentality was too European. In the First Division at that time we needed more aggression. There were some very, very tough teams. Manchester City were quality but some of the others were so hard. Places like Bradford, Sheffield, Coventry, Nottingham Forest – the fans were so passionate and there was so much history. They didn't care that I had won the European Cup because it meant nothing, and that is the right attitude. The game was high-tempo and the rhythm was very fast. We tried to have a positive attitude, we tried to pass, build out the play from the back, which was good, but we were not ready. Maybe we weren't good enough to do that.'

I suggest that Vialli's problem was that he changed the team too often, altered the formation, presumably to cope with the opposition… 'I can't really say, but you are probably right,' says Galli. 'We never blended as a team.

'But let me say, Vialli was very professional and he worked very hard, it's just that it didn't work out for us. There were a lot of new players – maybe too many at once.'

* * *

Focusing on the positives became more difficult as the season went on. In September, Vialli signed another midfielder to pass the ball sideways. Pierre Issa, a South African who had been playing for Olympique Marseille had spent much of his career as a centre half but he pressed into action in the middle of the pitch. Suddenly, it all fell into place. This was Ray Wilkins' final revenge on Watford's long ball ways. His masterplan was to flood the squad with crab-like midfielders incapable of hurting the opposition.

Issa's greatest contribution in a Watford shirt came against Birmingham City, when he dislocated his shoulder and was dropped off the stretcher when one of the bearers slipped on the greasy pitch. As metaphors go, this was almost as powerful as ITV Digital's knitted monkey.

The most frustrating thing was that the passing game looked half decent when it clicked. In the League Cup matches against Bradford and Charlton, Watford played with a freedom they had struggled to find. Noble played particularly well in the 4-1 win over Bradford, although the crowd's eager chants of 'Sign him up, sign him up, sign him up,' hinted at the desperation that was already creeping in. Noble really wasn't that good, as his subsequent journey to Boston United, Exeter City and Rotherham proved.

Even when he was onto a good thing, Vialli managed to squander the opportunity to put his building blocks in place. Having reached the quarter-finals of the League Cup, Watford faced a long Wednesday night trip to Hillsborough the week before Christmas. Was Vialli trying to be too clever or was he concentrating on the league? Either way, he tinkered with the team – dropping Heidar Helguson and Tommy Smith to the bench – and they were cut to ribbons by Sheffield Wednesday.

There was so much that began to grate: Stephen Hughes prancing round like a dressage pony, superfluous to the play. (If someone had dipped his hooves in yellow paint before the match the footprints would barely have extended outside the centre circle.) Helguson, the most instinctive goalscorer on the books, being used as a wing back. Vialli calling Smith 'Smudger'.

Football fans can cope with failure. It's what we're brought up to accept. But knowing this was the most expensive failure in the club's history by quite some distance was hard to stomach. There were reports of the club paying a fortune to keep rooms at Sopwell House so the players could snooze in the afternoon before evening games. The backroom staff were so numerous it was impossible to keep track of them all.

There was a rumour that Vega, fed up at being hit with repeated fines for breaking Vialli's rules (wearing a baseball cap, wearing his own suit instead of the club-issued one, using his mobile phone), dumped a bag of cash on the manager's desk and said: 'I like wearing caps, I like to wear my own suit, and I use my phone when I want.'

Blondeau apparently flew back to his home in the south of France for his days off. It became unavoidably apparent that some of the players did not care about the club they were playing for anything like as much as the supporters. Nothing new in that, perhaps. It is for many, despite all the badge-kissing, a profession.

Galli was one of the exceptions. He embraced life in England, leaving his wife and two sons, who were 12 and 14, back in Italy. 'They came over three times and I went back home, when I was injured,' he says. 'It was hard to leave my boys but they were at an important stage at school. I only had a one-year contract at Watford, so it made sense that I came by myself.

'Vialli told me to rent a house in Hampstead, the posh village in London. The club paid the rent for me. It was very, very expensive. At that time Italy still had the Lira and it was on the floor so it seemed even more expensive.

'I wanted to get to know the people in my area, to improve my English. There was a café near by, called the Base Café, run by Mohammed and Mary and I was in there drinking coffee, talking to them. I had an English teacher too and I'd often eat at Villa Bianca, an Italian restaurant in the village.'

Although Galli was Italian and a similar age to the manager, he did not have a close relationship with him. 'We lived near each other in Hampstead but I never went for lunch or dinner with him, we never spoke about what was happening or what was going wrong. It wasn't for me to be close to him. I was the player, he was the manager.'

He socialised mostly with the older players. 'They were a good group. Glassy, Robinson, Cox, Alec Chamberlain, he's a ledge [legend] in Watford, no?'

One of the Christmas parties was that typically English pursuit, a pub crawl in London, or as Galli describes it 'We went pub by pub.' Galli is teetotal and asked for a lemonade. 'They got me this drink called Smirnoff,' he says. 'I had no idea it had vodka in it. I couldn't understand why I felt strange. On the tube on the way home I was quite drunk.'

Ahhh, those guys. Welcome to England, Filippo.

* * *

Whenever the team looked to have settled into some sort of rhythm, something upset the balance. Galli missed a couple of months of the season when he injured his calf and the team missed his leadership and calming influence.

As the anticipated promotion challenge faded and then fizzled out Vialli's two-year plan became three and the supporters had to find coping strategies, as they often do in times of bitter disappointment.

I remember a surreal post-match discussion in the pub that had us comparing the defenders to cheeses. Galli was Parmesan, of course. Immaculately aged but strong and an unmistakable classic. Paul Robinson was a robust Cheddar that could make your tastebuds sting. Blondeau was soft, a bland supermarket Brie or Camembert, that would melt into a congealed mess at the merest rise in temperature. And Vega was a rubbery lump of Emmental, full of holes.

After Christmas, Vialli looked like he was catching on and losing the plot all at the same time. After recruiting the expensive, foreign guns for hire he suddenly realised that he needed a defender in hobnail boots. In came Wayne Brown on loan from Ipswich and he was twice the player then than he later looked when he signed permanently.

Jermaine Pennant and Danny Webber, two young, exciting forwards from Arsenal and Manchester United, who would return to play for Ray Lewington and establish themselves as popular and effective operators, added something that most of the earlier arrivals did not. And, it should not be forgotten that Vialli gave Lloyd Doyley his debut.

But in January, Vialli signed Paul Okon from Middlesbrough, reportedly offering to pay the Australian's wages himself, which suggested that he hadn't learned a thing about the First Division. Hughes and Issa were injured, and would be out for the rest of the season, but nothing they had done suggested that what the team needed was someone to take the sting out of things with a beautifully weighted sideways pass. Watford were crying out for a bit more oomph in midfield.

By now, the national media were sniggering at the extravagance of Watford's punt on Vialli and it seemed others wanted in on the joke. At Rotherham, as he stood in the technical area issuing instructions, Vialli was hit by a pie, said to be meat and potato. The custom in that part of Yorkshire is to eat the pie lid first so after the pie was thrown, it stuck to Vialli's shoulder before sliding down and hitting the floor. He tried to laugh it off, picking up the pie and pretending to take a bite, but if there is a single moment that spelled the end, it was that.

Your reputation as a suave, eloquent, urbane professional simply cannot survive being hit by a pie at Millmoor.

The end was painful. Some fans wanted to give Vialli time. That old favourite phrase 'It'll take time for them to gel' was still being used, albeit with less conviction. Promotion was now out of the question and the board, knowing that the parachute payments were running out, knew that there was no longer the cash to back the manager's methods.

Vialli had offered Galli the chance to stay on as player-coach, which Galli would have accepted, but the drums were already beating. 'I didn't know officially but at least a month before the season ended I knew Vialli was going. There was something in the air.'

At Stockport County's Edgeley Park on, aptly enough, April Fool's Day, the reality could be avoided no longer. Stockport were rock bottom, already relegated and 21 points adrift of the next worst team.

Galli was injured in a collision with a Stockport player and broke his collarbone. It was as brutal a departure from the English game as his introduction at Maine Road had been.

Watford lost the game 2-1 and in the post-match press conference, Vialli's all-too-familiar reaction was beginning to sound very weary. 'There are no easy games in this division.' '…a struggling team is like a wounded animal…'

A veteran hack from one of the local papers said: 'You said in the summer you wanted to make Watford the Manchester United of the division. Losing at Stockport must be a disappointment.'

Vialli began to say: 'Stockport is a difficult place to win…'

The hack cut him short. 'That hasn't stopped 16 other teams doing it this season.'

The final game of the season, against Gillingham, ended in a 3-2 defeat. Watford finished 14th, 16 points adrift of the play-offs and only ten clear of the drop. As the players walked, disconsolately around the pitch after the match, applauding the supporters almost apologetically, it was obvious that Vialli would have to go.

'The greatest thing about English football, to me, was the supporters. We lost the game, we had a very disappointing season but they stayed after the finish and clapped us,' says Galli. 'We knew it was not going to be easy to get to the Premiership but I gave my heart to Watford, I always did my best.'

On June 14, Vialli was sacked. The wage bill had risen by £4m and the collapse of ITV Digital meant there was to be no television jam – only gruel. The bloated backroom team was dismantled. Vialli and the board had disagreed about the need to cut costs but there was no alternative. Watford spent the next three years counting the cost. Within six months, the club was on the brink of administration. The players were asked to take a wage cut, the fans shook the begging buckets at the turnstiles.

* * *

These days, Galli is back at Milan, as technical director of the youth department. He still looks out for Watford's results but has not been back. 'I would love to visit, but I don't know if they'd want to see me,' he says, with a modesty that is typical. 'I still watch English football. Whenever Bolton or WBA,' – he calls them 'Double You Bee Ay – 'were on television in Italy, I would watch to see Paul Robinson.'

And Watford's fortunes post-Vialli have swung wildly. Having avoided the jaws of financial ruin, the club returned briefly to the Premiership, only to flirt with financial ruin again. The team has flat-lined in recent seasons.

Then, in the summer of 2012, came another Italian revolution. The Pozzo family, led by Giampaolo, added Watford to a portfolio that already contained Udinese in Italy and Granada in Spain. Pozzo took over Udinese in 1986 and slowly, steadily, took them into the Champions League. In Spain they led Granada into La Liga for the first time since the mid-Seventies.

'I know the Godfather… Giampaolo,' says Galli, before realising his, possibly Freudian, slip. 'No, no, I mean, the father,' he laughs. 'He is a good man. They are working very well in Italy and in Spain and they are intelligent. They have a huge scouting network. They want to reach the Premier League but they won't spend silly money.'

It must be hoped that Gianfranco Zola, the Pozzos' choice to replace Sean Dyche, fares better than Vialli.

Perhaps those who remembered the heady excitement of Vialli's early days and the desperate disappointment that followed were right to be a little more circumspect when the Pozzos and Zola arrived.

The two regimes are very different and yet there are similarities which are a little too great for comfort. Zola, like Vialli, was a world-class player. He joined Chelsea in November 1996, just a few months after his fellow Italian, and illuminated the Premiership with his play.

Zola's time as manager at West Ham was reasonable and his sacking by David Gold and David Sullivan looked rash, particularly when they decided the downtrodden genius, Avram Grant, was the man to pilot their nose-dive into the Championship.

But as great a player as Zola was, the question of his suitability for a muck and nettles Championship job is as valid as it was for Vialli, although Galli says: 'Gianfranco knows the English league. To do well, you have to know the English league.'

Unlike the board that fell head-over-heels for Vialli and his celebrity status, the Pozzos do not appear to be the type to get star-struck. They have had a regular turnover of coaching staff at their other clubs and the fact that Nani and Scott Duxbury appeared to be in charge of player recruitment suggests that they want the head coach to know the boundaries of his role.

And, whether the influx of young foreigners from the Pozzos' other clubs excites or concerns you, at least Watford do not appear to be spending beyond their means. But there must be some caution. A desire to ask questions should not be interpreted as a lack of support. It is often amazing how willingly the supporters embrace new owners. Too often, the lyrics of The Who's song *Won't Get Fooled Again*, spring to mind.

'Meet the new boss, same as the old boss.'

Supporters have to be optimistic. We have to wait and see. What choice do we have, because fan power no longer exists? You either like it or lump it. If the new owners want to import a dozen players on loan from their other clubs there's no other response than to hope some of them are good enough for the job and that the team improves.

And if they're not, what do we do about it?

We had no choice 11 years ago, when Vialli signed Vega, Hughes and Blondeau, increasing the wage bill significantly in the process. The only people who could have applied the handbrake were the directors, and they were in the back seat of the open-topped sports car, enjoying the thrill of the breeze in their hair as Vialli took the wheel.

Did Watford pay the price for the excesses of that crazy summer? Yes, painfully. Were the lessons learned? It's hard to say because the majority of those who made the decisions moved on and did not have to face the consequences, allowing a new bunch to come in and make some of the same mistakes.

* * *

Back to the beginning of our tale, and the match between Manchester City and Watford on August 11 2001. City won the game 3-0 and got stronger as the season went on, finally winning the league comfortably by racking up 99 points.

They have remained in the Premier League ever since – their longest unbroken run in the top flight for more than 40 years.

They attracted one billionaire owner, the dubious Thai businessman and politician Thaksin Shinawatra, then another, the Abu Dhabi Group, headed by Sheikh Mansour.

City tried Stuart Pearce, Sven Goran Eriksson and Mark Hughes before Roberto Mancini delivered the Premier League title. They are now a player on the global stage.

Is this to suggest that, had Watford played their cards differently in 2001 they might have become a billionaire's plaything and a Champions League contender? No, of course not. Manchester City, for all their travails, have always been a big-city club with potential. Besides, would we even have wanted that? Probably not.

We can look back with the benefit of hindsight and see that English football stood at a fork in the road in the summer of 2001. There was the promise of riches, although it turned out to be false.

Watford had a choice and those charged with the responsibility of picking which direction to take opted to gamble. Everything that has happened to the club since can be traced back to the decisions taken in 2001.

The summer just gone placed Watford at another fork in the road. As ever, the club's fate rests with individuals whose decisions we cannot influence. All we can do is hope they make the right call and at least acknowledge the lessons of the past.

Because the Vialli experiment is a stark reminder of what can happen if you forget what you are in the rush towards what you want to be.

Lionel Birnie is the cycling correspondent for *The Sunday Times*. Every July he covers the Tour de France, which, he can assure you, is far more than an enjoyable three-week gastronomic jaunt. Despite his love of the Tour, there's only ever one *maillot jaune* that counts.

12

Stuart Hutchison is a producer for BBC Sport.

Not long after starting his job at the corporation, he discovered that Auntie's drawers contained a treasure trove of Watford memories.

After that followed dark nights in the edit suite, hunched over the desk with a furtive look of concentration on his face. Probably.

Until now, this was just his little secret.

HORNOGRAPHY

BY STUART HUTCHISON

I usually wait until my wife and children have left the house before I reach under the bed for the clutch of DVDs. Only once I've heard the soft, diminishing rumble of the pushchair's vulcanised rubber wheels over cobbles, can I be certain to be free of unwanted, surprise returns. Then I slide it gently in, and press play.

What shall be today's pleasure?

It wasn't always like this. The relationship was once a wholesome one. Of course it was... after all, it began when I was five years old. But over the last decade or more, I've taken my place on the margins, a twilight, covert world where shame and pride cast equally long shadows.

A place for me, and the entire history of Watford Football Club on film.

My Hornography.

* * *

It's the BBC's fault – as so many things are, it would seem. My life had a steady rhythm of Home-Away-Home-Away for many years until, some time between Alec Chamberlain saving a penalty in Birmingham and Nicky Wright scoring an overhead kick in London, I got a job in the Corporation's sport department as a researcher. Not the worst week-and-a-bit I've ever had, to be honest.

Anyhoo, Saturday was now a working day for me... and most midweek evenings were, also. My interest in Watford FC now needed a new outlet. And as is often the case when mere interests become obsessions, the tipping point came when alone in a darkened room.

As a researcher, I was in awe of the producers, who were a rung above me. Essentially, we told them stuff, and they'd go and make some telly out of it. They wore achingly-cool imported Japanese trainers, carried their stuff in record bags – *'Yeah Jules from uni gave me it, he's something big in A&R'* – and ate olives, because – and I shit you not – they actually liked them. And coming from Garston as I did, *that* was extraordinary. I wouldn't have been any more amazed, frankly, if one of them had ordered a dish of wasps cooked in their own business.

I may paint a picture of arrogance, but that would be entirely unfair. To a man and woman they were helpful and kind (BBC folk tend to be) and were only too keen to let you help out in order to learn how to make telly programmes.

And one day, quite early in my career, one of the Assistant Producers from *Grandstand* handed me a miscellaneous sports archive tape. They needed it 'spotted-up' at the point where Greville Starkey had won the 2,000 Guineas. Or something. Those details aren't important. What is important, is what I found.

As I scanned through the 90-minute tape trying to find a largely green picture with brightly-coloured dots each coupled with larger brown blobs, I saw a flash of yellow on the screen. I shuttled back at a more considered pace until I found the right spot, pressed play and there it was. Grainy, Betamax-quality footage of Sparta Prague versus Watford from 1983-84, with, naturally, Italian commentary. It looked as if it had come from their version of *Midweek Sports Special*. I could just about make out skilful, maroon-coloured figures effortlessly gliding around static yellow ones, on what appeared to be a snowy pitch. But that could have been interference.

And I thought, hang on... if this is here... what else?

Immediate enquiries unearthed the following pieces of information: The basement of Television Centre housed much of the BBC Sport archive, with the rest at an overspill site in nearby Perivale. And, there existed a database which, if you typed in a keyword – say 'Watford' – for instance, it would return results listing everything in the archive featuring that team, by date, tape number and time-code (the place on the tape where that particular item would be found).

A century before, another Englishman, George B Reynolds had stood before the Persian Gulf and wondered what untold riches lay beneath his feet. What he found changed the course of history. What would I find under my pair of newly-purchased-at-great-expense hand-stitched, limited-edition Onitsukas?

As I sat in front of the database, I felt like George. My search of 'Watford' from 1964 (the first year of regular football broadcasting in the UK) to 2001, returned a whopping 98 pages of entries. I asked myself: what would George do? I replied that George wouldn't be bothered messing around with this sort of nerdy rubbish and would instead be wallowing in his oil.

But, undeterred, I decided that I would find it all. And collect it all. The entire history of Watford FC on film. And it would be mine.

The good news was that, professionally, I was perfectly placed to undertake this mammoth project. The bad news, was that I also had a job to hold down, so I would have to spend my evenings, days off (Mondays, usually) and holidays on the project. But the good news was that I didn't have a girlfriend to get in the way. But the bad news was that I might die before completing it. But the good news was that around a third of those 98 pages referred to the recent 1999-2000 season, and

having just sat through that on *Match of the Day* each week, I
didn't want evidence of that wretched campaign in my house.
As far as I was concerned, the tapes from that season could be
collected by someone and burnt. Then he could collect the ashy
fragments and throw them in a bin. Then throw that bin into
another bin. Then blow up those bins. Then throw the shrapnel
against a wall. Then blow up the wall.

So, I decided that I would find (nearly) it all. And collect
(almost) it all. The (sort of) entire history of Watford FC on
film. And it would (nearly all) be mine.

It's hard to remain inconspicuous when you're tottering
through the office carrying a pile of 40 or more blue cassette
boxes, so it wasn't long before word got around, and came back
to me accompanied by its good friend, scorn.

Have you ever wondered what people must have made of
the man who discovered you can get milk from a cow? Genius?
Oddball? In my head, I was a pioneer – I genuinely couldn't
understand why, given this opportunity, all my colleagues weren't
doing the same with Ipswich, Barnsley and Chester footage. To
them, I was just a strange fellow with way, waaaay too much
time on my hands.

It took me three years to collect the entire archive of
Watford FC from the BBC Sport archives. But it's a fascinating
sporting and social document, that sheds new light on the
history of the club.

For example, the earliest recorded entry was from
summer 1965. A BBC *Sportsnight* camera crew had followed
Watford to the Lake District for their pre-season training camp
of fell running and campfire singing. Good wholesome fun,
you would have thought. A pioneering exercise in team bond-
ing, you might think, coming as it did decades before the trend
of sending groups of management accountants up Cadair Idris
in the vain hope they would come back down the mountain

crying salt tears and functioning as normal human beings.

Yet, right at the very end of the feature, the Watford squad are filmed having a sing-song round the campfire before bed. Two players have guitars and are leading their teammates in a version of The Weavers' *Ramblin Boy*. I know what you're thinking. Did the Watford squad really openly sing Communist music on national television? Music that had fallen foul of Senate hearings in the United States and led to its authors, Pete Seeger and his Weavers, being banished underground?

One could only imagine how this would have been viewed by the notoriously conservative stewardship of English football – elderly men who, lest we forget, for decades stamped upon such subversive ideas as 'playing competitive fixtures against foreigners' and 'allowing players to have a say over where they might be transferred'.

With this seething undercurrent of revolution – and with sentiments such as *'Fare ye well, my ramblin boy... may all your rambles, bring you joy'*, (I'm sure you'll agree the subversion is clear... overt, if you will. Ovversion. Is that a word? It is now) – bubbling under Vicarage Road, it's hard indeed to escape the conclusion that decades of non-achievement was caused, not as was previously thought by the inherent crapness of the players, but by an ideological faultline between Watford FC and the governing bodies of English football, which saw in the club a Red Peril, an insidious, creeping Marxist magma, and in turn conspired to halt their progress, like the McCarthyite witch-hunts that threatened to destroy Seeger and his fellow Greenwich Village beatniks.

Only with the arrival of Graham Taylor, with his love for the largely-apolitical Japanese prog-rock scene of the early 1970s, was this Trotskyite boil finally lanced.

Or maybe the players were singing about rambling cos they'd been, like, rambling an' shit. I dunno.

But it was these features that proved more interesting than the football. For every rare gem of match action unearthed – extended colour highlights of the FA Cup giantkilling of Liverpool from 1970, complete with a rare-as-rocking-horse-shit full-speed low angle of Barry Endean's winner from a camera behind the Rookery end goal – I took greater interest in the behind-the-scenes footage. A tour by the 1977-78 squad of the Rolls Royce factory in Leavesden (again for *Sportsnight*) was notable for two things – the genuine, humble interest of the players in the work of the ordinary man and, those being more innocent times an' all, at no point during the eight-minute feature was a professional footballer spotted trying to have sex with anything. And I mean ANYTHING. Not one cylinder, not a single exhaust pipe, was abused in the making of that feature. Extraordinary.

My favourite piece of film was some work John Motson did with Graham Taylor in 1979-80. He used Watford's League Cup tie against Stoke City as a hook for a series of features profiling 'two of the game's most progressive young manage-rial minds' in our Mr Taylor and Alan Durban of the Potters. And the access granted to the cameras on that night makes it something truly special.

Years later, in 2010, I was asked to make a montage of Watford's glory days for a live game we were showing, away at QPR. It's pretty much the only feature I've made on the Hornets since I started producing telly in 2002, and it was presumably commissioned as something to show at half-time in case the first half was a bit... shit (it wasn't, we killed 'em, but they still ran the piece, God love 'em).

I leant heavily on the access-all-areas footage from the Stoke game – Elton John arriving on Occupation Road in his limo, Graham sitting in his beige office explaining his team selection to the chairman. Elton striding into the dressing room to seek out his favourite player: *'Luther! Where's Luther?'* and then the cameraman hunkered down next to the Watford dug-out for the whole match, which gave us Elton leading the crowd chants from the bench, and Graham bellowing 'AY! AY! YOU DON'T GET CRAMP AT THIS CLUB!' at one of his charges, as the Hornets ran their more illustrious opponents into the ground *en route* to another giantkilling.

As for the football archive... well, it's great, obviously. These were golden years; the years of our lives. There's Sam Ellis leading Taylor's first championship side on a lap of honour in their bright yellow bomber jackets before playing Southend in 1978 (hard to believe that in those days *Match of the Day* habitually selected two highlights matches from the top flight each week and one from the lower divisions... and would show a 12-minute edit even it was 0-0, as they would've had nothing else to show), Cally trawling through the Meadow Lane mud to score his Goal of the Month, Kaiserslautern...

Yet I have to admit, I can kinda see what our critics were getting at, all those years. I feel guilty when this feeling stalks me as I watch the Hornets from my childhood. I remember sitting in Highbury's East Stand Lower watching Barnes, Luther and Cally take Arsenal, ARSENAL, to the cleaners, and it looked magnificent, imperious. Yet when I found the highlights, each of our goals was a scrabbly, messy affair. And this kept happening – games and goals I thought were great, in reality, weren't. I was disappointed, but also disappointed with myself for being disappointed – part of being a Watford fan was and is fronting up to our critics from that time. That defiance is what I love most about the club. That, and the danga-danga-danga-danga-danga-danga bit in Z-Cars. So I just tell myself: 'Don't knock it... it's the best we've ever been and it ain't ever coming back.'

It's been nigh on two decades since TV companies started sending cameras to every Football League game, so we've taken for granted the opportunity to see Watford's highlights each week. It seems incredible that for years we accepted that if we didn't go to a game, we would almost certainly forfeit the right to ever see the action.

Of course, Watford plugged the gap somewhat when they started filming their home games from the gantry on the roof of the Shrodells stand soon after Graham arrived at the club. He had been trying to persuade Elton that it was necessary for analytical purposes, and he got his way when the chairman, on cloud nine after the remarkable League Cup triumph at Manchester United in 1978, gave in. These highlights would make their way onto the market as end-of-season videos sold in the Hornets Shop. Although, perhaps the club's finest night of its finest era was never covered. It is said that the club's cameraman was ill when Southampton visited on the evening of September 2, 1980.

I think the word is 'bugger'.

If a goal isn't captured by television, does it really exist? I mean, *obviously* it exists – its ramifications are in the league table for all to see – but does it exist in its actual form? Only when it's recorded for posterity does it live on in any true sense. Of course, there's empirical evidence that exists in the memory of every person present, but each of those – fan, player, manager – will have an imperfect, subjective memory of the incident. Each of these accounts are, to varying degrees, untrue and, therefore, unsatisfactory. Here's an example.

I've long held the belief that the perfect grounding for a war correspondent would be a stint spent on the *Watford Observer* sports desk collecting the football reports from the West Herts Youth League. In terms of sifting fact from fiction and weighing up the veracity of violently-conflicting accounts of the same incident, anyone who's come through the sports desk would find reporting the Middle East an absolute doddle.

This is how it worked. As the cub reporter, each junior team's manager would have my phone number and be encouraged to leave a voicemail every Sunday with a brief report of their game that morning. And without the benefit of TV cameras to adjudicate, the following was often the raw material from which I would have to compile a report for Friday's paper.

Beep.

'Allo. Allo? Is this fing on? Ugh... I hate these fings. Allo? Anyway. Charlie Arseholes 'ere, manager of Parkside United under-10s. Today it was 'Emel Rovers free, Parkside one. 'Parkside were denied the win they deserved by free lucky goals, but at least we had the honour of scorin' the goal of the game when little Colin Arseholes beat six men before firin' into the top corner from 35 yards. That's it really."

Beep.

'Graham from 'Emel Rovers 'ere with our report from today's game. 'Emel eight, Parkside one. 'Emel dominated from start to finish, with five goals comin' from the prolific Danny Andrews and Matty Stone in good form at the uvver end. The only black spot was the goal he conceded, when his clearance hit their striker on the arse and rebounded into our net. Never mind eh? Speak next week.'

You see? Hopeless. Utterly without worth. So, despite all the ills that modern television has visited upon football (and there are many), the ability to watch and keep and treasure your team's goals and successes shouldn't be underestimated.

I know the counter argument – that past players, the Great Ghosts of the Game, live on in the minds of those who watched them play, and that these shared-yet-different memories cast those deeds in a golden glow that will never dim. Romantic, I know. And there is something in this... as I've said already, watching back my Watford archive, I'm occasionally crestfallen by the standard of play – at the time it seemed so polished – and viewing it through the unforgiving prism of a TV camera does take the shine off.

This, I accept. But photographs, sports-writing, the very best radio commentary, all are fine, some are wonderful, but without television pictures, these games are lost forever. Watford 7 Southampton 1 is lost forever if, like me, you have rubbish recall of even the best matches you've seen.

So, anyway, three years in... the entire BBC Sport archive of Watford FC committed to disc, I thought I had reached the end. Then a whole new horizon opened up before me. It turned out that BBC News had a huge tape archive in Television Centre also. This consists of thousand upon thousands of tapes containing every VT item that's ever been cut for the One, Six, Nine or Ten O'Clock News, plus associated programmes such as local news bulletins, or Newsnight. Before you could ask me when was the last time I had met a woman, I'd navigated my way around the news database and was ordering up tapes by the hundred.

What set this news footage apart was the fact that much of it was shot on film. Proper, expensive film. There is nothing, with the possible exception of an overripe Brie, that pleases the senses as much as football that's been shot on colour film. Everything seems slower, more balletic, the colours less saturated, it just feels so much more... intimate.

Take a look at the Pathé or Movietone footage of the 1966 World Cup Final if you get the chance. It's hard to explain the appeal, as my risible attempt just then demonstrates. So it was a genuine thrill to find for example, rare colour film footage of Watford's first-ever FA Cup semi-final in 1970. Like much film archive, it's mute. You can almost hear the rattle of the film canister inside as you watch.

Perhaps my favourite rarity of all was found in this news library. I can only presume it was in the hope of grabbing a quote with the new Watford chairman that BBC London News sent a film crew to the Fourth Division strugglers' FA Cup second round tie at Hillingdon Borough in the low winter sun of 1976. The four-minute report betrays a truly woeful football team (nicely shot, mind) struggling but somehow succeeding in overcoming their amateur opponents, on what appears to be some sort of farm.

The TV crew got what they went for. Doorstepping Elton as he leaves the stand, the chairman makes little or no attempt to disguise his disappointment at what he has just witnessed. Having witnessed it myself 30 years later, I went to our shelves of Rothmans Football Yearbooks and wasn't massively surprised to learn that Mike Keen's Hornets succumbed to the might of Northwich Victoria in round three. Keen was sacked soon afterwards. Hello, Mr Taylor.

News, as anyone who works in it never fails to remind anyone who works in 'the toy department' of sport, is serious business. So it's appropriate that their archive allowed me to clear-up some pretty grave business. Or to dig-up a decomposing corpse that's best left buried. Whatever.

It only seems right that this duty has fallen to me as the 'corpse' in question prompted this author to administer probably the only punch ever delivered on Vicarage Road's Family Terrace. I say punch... I lost my nerve halfway through the swing so the end result was more of a vigorous stroke, of the kind an uncomprehending toddler might give a cat.

I refer of course to the 1986 FA Cup quarter-final replay between Watford and Liverpool. I'd seen the club's footage before, but I'd never seen the highlights filmed by the BBC News crew that was there that night – taken from a slightly different angle and shot a bit tighter.

It's single camera coverage of course, so alas there were no shots of the incredible number of fans who were clinging five or six-high to the Vicarage Road end floodlights that night, nor did the camera pick out a kid in a red and grey Puma kagool on the far side, gently pawing the child standing next to him in impotent rage.

But what the coverage did suggest was that Ian Rush was indeed fouled by Tony Coton for the equalising penalty four minutes from time. Sacrilege, I know. I've stepped through this incident frame-by-frame, blown it up, sharpened the image – devoted more time to it than the Warren Commission did to the JFK assassination – and I must admit, it looks like a foul. Now don't shoot me (see what I did there?), I know feelings are still strong, but whereas before I always believed Rush tumbled over Coton to fool the referee, according to this BBC News angle, it looks a pen. Or at least, 'you see 'em given'. Rush appears to be still on his feet until Our Tone's arms disappear under the striker's legs.

Probably a good job I didn't properly lamp that Scouse kid in extra time, then.

It took me another three years to collect all the footage from the news library, and to be honest, to this day I'm still working my way through it, such was the wealth of material generated around the time of the Cup Final and, bizarrely, the Robert Maxwell takeover furore a few years later. And also, because I got married – to a Luton Town fan, and she doesn't appreciate me devoting so much time to this project. And also, because as soon as I'd finished transferring it all, another horizon opened up, what I call – and I think I'm the first writer ever to use this pithy bit of alliteration – The Final Frontier.

With the sort of insular disregard for other broadcasters that is IN NO WAY common at the BBC, I'd always assumed that collecting all the WFC archive from Auntie Beeb would equate to 'The Entire History of The Club On Film.' And, to be fair, you'd need a Bank Holiday weekend to watch it all without a break.

But No! It turns out there are other broadcasters (who

knew?!) While researching another piece of work, I was in desperate need of this or that goal from this or that game (it didn't involve WFC, it's not important), and our TV librarian, Swifty (an Albion-supporting Charles Hawtrey lookalike, but likewise, that's not important) said: 'I think that was an ITV game, I'll check on this website I've found and see if we can do a swap.'

'This website' turned out to be a full and entire record of every match (live or highlights) put out by every ITV region from 1968 to 1983, plus a comprehensive history of their flagship show, *The Big Match*. I know not who compiled it, so it would be unfair in the extreme for me to speculate on the effervescence or otherwise of their love-life, suffice to say that one passage reads a follows:

'The following lists detail all of the Saturday fixtures recorded by LWT for highlights on *The Big Match*. For full details of other regions' matches go here. Re-edits of regional games included on *The Big Match* are, where known, indicated by a letter (G = Granada, Y = Yorkshire, T = Tyne-Tees, H = HTV, M = ATV/Central (Midlands), E = East (Anglia), W = Westward, S = Southern/TVS, and X = Scottish).'

I love the use of the words 'where known', as if the guy doesn't have a complete record of how many hairs adorned Brian Moore's head on every edition of *The Big Match*. He's clearly thought: 'This whole thing makes me look a bit obsessive, let's chuck a few "where knowns" in so I look like I'm kinda across the subject, but don't really spend much time on it, cos I'm in Vegas mostly, you know.'

There's just a small part of me that thinks 'yes, I love my family, but I think I love Scary ITV Football History Internet Man a bit more'.

And there is upwards of 50 Watford games on there. I've got two of them – collected in the course of duty – our first-ever game in the top flight, 2-0 v Everton, and the 4-2 win at Highbury not long after. Sorry, we always won at Arsenal in those days – let me be more specific. It was 1982.

The trouble is, legitimate reasons to swap footage with ITV – particularly Watford games from the 1980s – are rare indeed, so I guess if this whole project is ever going to have an end, I'll just have to get a job there instead.

But the one from that list that I want, what I really, really want, is Watford 0 Swansea City 2 (Waddell, Moore) on the ninth day of the ninth month in the year of Our Lord, nineteen hundred and seventy eight. For that was the day that a Plymouth Argyle fan exiled a long way from his Devon home by the need to find work on the railways, took his five-year-old son to watch the local team, so as the pair of them had something to share in the few precious hours the dad spent at home.

Nearly three decades later, all the boy could remember about the day was standing on an upturned orange fruit crate on a crumbling concrete step, and the long-haired man in the denim jacket down at the fence, who kept shouting 'go on, Chalkie' to the Watford centre-forward, much to the amusement of almost all around, it's horrible to recall.

The boy thought the match was lost to him forever, apart from those two eminently forgettable recollections. And then, to his amazement, he saw the match listed among other televised matches on a website compiled by a man he will never know. And he vowed right then, to rediscover one of the most important days in his life.

And sitting here now, he realises he really must get round to that sometime soon.

Stuart Hutchison has been a producer at BBC Sport since 2002. If you recall seeing a brilliant montage or feature on the Beeb's coverage of football or the Olympics, there's every chance it was made by one of his more talented colleagues.

TALES FROM THE VICARAGE

VOLUME II WILL BE PUBLISHED IN AUTUMN 2013

If you would like to contribute to the next volume of
Tales from the Vicarage email the editor with
a short proposal – info@lionelbirnie.com

ALSO FROM PELOTON PUBLISHING

FOUR SEASONS
by Lionel Birnie & Alan Cozzi
Superb colour photography by Alan Cozzi and a deft commentary written by Lionel Birnie tell the story of Graham Taylor's second spell as Watford manager. Published in 2001

ENJOY THE GAME
by Lionel Birnie
The story of the 1980s, pieced together from exclusive interviews with the players and staff who steered the club from the Fourth Division to Europe and the FA Cup final. Packed with previously untold stories and insight this is the definitive account of a magical era. Published in 2010

THE 100 GREATEST WATFORD WINS
by Lionel Birnie
This is the perfect subject for a pub debate. Which is the greatest Watford win you have ever seen? This book counts down promotion clinchers, relegation nail-biters, cup thrillers and some good, old-fashioned hammerings. Published in 2011.

To buy these books visit:
www.lionelbirnie.com/books
www.pelotonpublishing.co.uk